GLOBAL RELIGIOUS MOVEMENTS
ACROSS BORDERS

From global missionizing among proselytic faiths to mass migration through religious diasporas, religion has traveled from one side of the world and back again. It continues to play a prominent role in shaping world politics and has been a vital force in the continued emergence, spread, and creation of a transnational civil society.

Exploring how religious roots are shaping organizations that seek to aid people across political and geographic boundaries—"service movements"—this book focuses on how religious movements establish structures to assist people with basic human needs such as food, clothing, shelter, education, and health. Examining a multitude of faith traditions with origins in different parts of the world, seven contributing chapters, with an introduction and conclusions by the senior author, offer a unique discussion of the intersections between religious transnationalism and social movements.

D1741291

Ashgate Inform Series on Minority Religions and Spiritual Movements

Series Editor: Eileen Barker,
London School of Economics, Chair and Honorary Director of Inform

Advisory Board:
Afe Adogame, University of Edinburgh, UK,
Madawi Al-Rasheed, King's College, London, UK,
François Bellanger, Université de Genève, Switzerland,
Irena Borowik, Jagiellonian University, Krakow, Poland,
Douglas E. Cowan, University of Waterloo, Ontario, Canada,
Adam Possamai, University of Western Sydney, Australia,
James T. Richardson, University of Nevada, Reno, USA,
Fenggang Yang, Purdue University, USA

Inform is an independent charity that collects and disseminates accurate, balanced and up-to-date information about minority religious and spiritual movements. The Ashgate Inform book series addresses themes related to new religions, many of which have been the topics of Inform seminars. Books in the series will attract both an academic and interested general readership, particularly in the areas of Religious Studies, and the Sociology of Religion and Theology.

Global Religious Movements Across Borders
Sacred Service

Edited by

STEPHEN M. CHERRY
University of Houston-Clear Lake, USA

HELEN ROSE EBAUGH
University of Houston, USA

ASHGATE

Published by

Ashgate Publishing Limited
Wey Court East
Union Road
Farnham
Surrey, GU9 7PT
England

Ashgate Publishing Company
110 Cherry Street
Suite 3-1
Burlington, VT 05401-3818
USA

www.ashgate.com

British Library Cataloguing in Publication Data
A catalogue record for this book is available from the British Library

The Library of Congress has cataloged the printed edition as follows:
Library of Congress data has been applied for

ISBN 9781409456872 (hbk)
ISBN 9781409456889 (pbk)
ISBN 9781409456896 (ebk – PDF)
ISBN 9781472407122 (ebk – ePUB)

MIX
Paper from
responsible sources
FSC
www.fsc.org   FSC® C013985

Printed in the United Kingdom by Henry Ling Limited,
at the Dorset Press, Dorchester, DT1 1HD

For our friends and family here at home and around the world

Contents

List of Figures and Tables

Figures

Tables

Notes on Contributors

Afe Adogame received his PhD in History of Religions from Bayreuth University, Germany. He is Associate Professor in Religious Studies and World Christianity at the University of Edinburgh, United Kingdom where he teaches courses in Indigenous Religions, Religions of Africa and the African Diaspora, Religion, Migration and Globalization, and Sociology of Religion. His most recent book publications include: *The African Christian Diaspora: New Currents and Emerging Trends in World Christianity* (2013); *Religion on the Move? New Dynamics of Religious Expansion in a Globalizing World* (co-edited with Shobana Shankar, 2012); and *Religion Crossing Boundaries: Transnational Religious and Social Dynamics in Africa and the new African Diaspora* (co-edited with James Spickard, 2010).

Arun Brahmbhatt holds a Master of Theological Studies from Harvard Divinity School and is currently a doctoral candidate in the Department for the Study of Religion and the Centre for South Asian Studies at the University of Toronto. His doctoral research, made possible in part by fellowships from the Fulbright Program and the American Academy of Religion, is focused on Sanskrit textual practices in the Swaminarayan Hindu tradition in late colonial Gujarat. He is broadly interested in intellectual history, print culture, hermeneutics, and historiography, and has taught undergraduate courses in South Asian religions and modern Hinduism.

Stephen M. Cherry received his PhD in Sociology from the University of Texas at Austin. He is currently an Assistant Professor of Sociology at the University of Houston-Clear Lake. His research interests include immigration, race, religion, Asian Americans, and civic life with a particular focus on Filipino-American Catholics post 1965. He is the author of *Faith, Family, and Filipino American Community Life* (forthcoming 2014 from Rutgers University Press) in addition to several journal articles including the article (coauthored with Michael P. Young) "The Secularization of Confessional Protests: The Role of Religious Processes of Rationalization and Differentiation," for which he received the Society for the Scientific Study of Religion Distinguished Article Award in 2006.

Helen Rose Ebaugh received her PhD in Sociology from Columbia University with specialties in Organizational Sociology and the Sociology of Religion. She is Professor of Sociology at the University of Houston, Central Campus, where she routinely teaches courses in world religions and immigration. With the support of several Pew Charitable Trust grants, she directed a study of the role of religion among new immigrants to the United States, a project that resulted in two books, *Religion and the New Immigrants* (2000) and *Religon Across Borders* (2002). Her recent work focuses on the Gulen Movement, a moderate Islamic movement from Turkey and, most recently, she is tracing the movement globally as it spreads around the world.

Karim H. Karim is a Professor at Carleton University in Ottawa, Canada. He has served as Director of Carleton's School of Journalism and Communication and the Institute of Ismaili Studies in London and has been a Fellow of Harvard's Center for the Study of World Religions. He holds degrees in Islamic Studies and Communication Studies from Columbia and McGill universities. Dr. Karim has been a distinguished lecturer at venues in North America, Europe, and Asia. He won the inaugural Robinson Book Prize in 2001 for *Islamic Peril: Media and Global Violence* and is currently working on a series of publications on Western-Muslim relations.

Mike McMullen is an Associate Professor of Sociology and Cross Cultural Studies at the University of Houston-Clear Lake in Houston, Texas. He received his doctorate from Emory University (Atlanta, Georgia). His first book, *The Bahá'i: The Religious Construction of a Global Identity*, came out in 2000 with Rutgers University Press. His areas of interest include Bahá'í studies, the sociology of religion, organizational development and change, and conflict resolution and mediation. He continues to do research in the American Bahá'í community and is working on a book on the history of conflict resolution in the United States. Most recently, Mike spent a year living in Cairo, Egypt as a Fulbright Scholar, teaching at American University in Cairo during the 2009-10 academic year.

Daniel A. Metraux received his PhD from the Department of East Asian Languages and Cultures at Columbia University in 1978. He is Professor of Asian Studies and International Relations at Mary Baldwin College in Staunton, Virginia and Adjunct Professor of History and Culture at Union Institute and University. He has written numerous books, book chapters and journal articles on Japanese history and religion and on contemporary Asian affairs. His works include: *The Soka Gakkai Revolution* (1994), *Burma's Modern Tragedy* (2004), *Problems Facing China Today* (2006), and *The Asian Writings of Jack London* (2010). He has received two Fulbright research grants for work in China and Taiwan.

Preface

This book originated at the meetings of the Society for the Scientific Study of Religion (SSSR) in Baltimore in 2010 as an outgrowth of a thematic panel on global religious movements. Professor Kay Meyer, then president of the society, selected the theme of Religion in Global Perspective for the meetings and asked me to organize a panel of scholars who are engaged in studying global movements rooted in religious traditions. Daniel Metraux gave a paper on Soka Gakkai, a Buddhist movement that began in Japan but now exists all over the world; Afe Adogame described his research on the Redeemed Christian Church of God, almost exclusively African in both origin and current membership, that has spread through the African diaspora to about 110 countries. Stephen Cherry reported his research findings on Gawad Kalinga, a Catholic Filipino movement that has maintained its Catholic and Filipino roots and has been transplanted to over 12 countries through Filipino migration. What emerged in all three of these papers is the development of large social service organizations on a global scale that serve the needs of the immigrants but also others in need within their own communities and, in many cases, throughout the world. My own research on the Gulen Movement in Turkey has expanded to a study of the global spread of the movement to over 180 countries, with the proliferation of social service programs wherever the movement exists.

Over coffee after the panel, Stephen Cherry and I mused about the role that social service agencies play within immigrant diasporas as well as ways that religious roots shape service movements that seek to aid people across political and geographic boundaries. In all three of the papers presented in the panel it was obvious that immigrants are creating NGOs (non-governmental organizations) rooted in their various religious traditions. While an increasing number of social science scholars are focusing on religion and immigration, there are very few studies that discuss the emergence of RNGOs (religious non-governmental organizations) as part of global migration. Yet, one way in which religious traditions and institutions gain a foothold and followers in regions in which they were previously little known is often through their service movements such as schools, tutoring programs, health clinics, development efforts, and so on. Oftentimes many of those who become supporters of the religion first come into contact with it through the services it provides to those in need in a society. Additionally, the increasing presence of religious NGO groups and organizations at the United Nations alone (now well over 110) is a reminder that religion is an important part of a global world and the avenue through which many people serve others transnationally. Moreover, many service movements rooted in religious traditions are among the largest non-profit providers of human services in the world.

Based on social movement literature, along with work on NGOs and transnational/global studies of the role of religious institutions in providing social services, Stephen and I mapped out ten questions/issues that we considered important in order to understand the similarities and differences among large service providers whose roots are in various religious traditions. The issues and how we arrived at them are described in the Introduction. We were interested in how these variables influence the global spread of the movement and the evolution of the services provided by each one. We decided to invite the panelists to be part of a book that we would edit on global service movements, rooted in various religious traditions and spread by immigrants as they relocate throughout the world. In order to include a variety of religious traditions from different parts of the world, we invited three additional scholars to contribute chapters: Arun Grahmbhatt who studies the Hindu Swaminarayan Community; Mike McMullen whose expertise is the Baha'is; and Karim H. Karim who focuses on Shia Ismailis and the Aga Khan Development Network. I agreed to write the chapter on the social service activities of the Gulen Movement. Obviously, these seven cases do not represent all religious traditions and geographical areas; however, we hope that they will suffice to demonstrate important similarities and differences among global service movements that arise within religious traditions.

In order to address the ten issues we posed, the authors relied on data that they had already collected in the course of their scholarly work on the movement. However, in a number of cases, they also collected additional data that were not required for their previous research questions. We gave each author as much leeway as possible to describe their case as they saw fit within our general guidelines of what issues to include. This resulted in chapters that are distinctive in both their approaches and style. We are grateful for the diligence with which each contributor addressed the questions we posed and for the fact that each chapter is unique to this book and not just a reprint of earlier published work.

Together Stephen and I framed the book, generated questions that we wanted each author to address, and wrote the prospectus for the book. I then took the lead in inviting the contributors, working with them throughout the process, and soliciting a publisher. Stephen, who researches and teaches in the area of social movements and NGOs, basically wrote the Introduction and Conclusions, after we discussed issues that we considered important to address. While C (Cherry) precedes E (Ebaugh) alphabetically, he is truly the senior author in conceptualizing and framing the book in terms of social movement theory and the NGO literature.

Helen Rose Ebaugh
University of Houston

List of Abbreviations

AKDN	Aga Khan Development Network
BAPS	Bochasanwasi Shri Akshar Purushottam Swaminarayan Sanstha
BIC	Bahá'í International Community
FBO	Faith-based organization
GK	Gawad Kalinga
MDG	Millennium development goals
NGO	Non-governmental organization
NRM	New religious movement
RCCG	Redeemed Christian Church of God
RNGO	Religious non-governmental organization
SGI	Soka Gakkai International
UN	United Nations
WCRP	World Conference of Religions for Peace
WFDD	World Faiths Development Dialogue
WTO	World Trade Organization

Chapter 1
Introduction to Religious and Global Transnational Service Movements

Stephen M. Cherry

Amidst revolutions in transportation and communication that have eased and accelerated flows of people, goods, and services across borders, the terms globalization and transnationalism have become the hallmarks of a new theoretical paradigm for the twenty-first century. The terms were hardly used in academic literature or everyday language prior to the late 1980s, but today they are commonplace (see Giddens 2002). Although there is a great deal of debate as to what these processes entail, most scholars across a host of fields readily accept that they are occurring on some level (Ebaugh and Chafetz 2002; Lechner and Boli 2000; Smart 1993; Waters 1995). Publically, the concepts have also gained considerable acceptance and have become almost cliché in their use to describe local and international trends or rationalize economic and environmental woes such as global stock market collapses or climate change (Lechner and Boli 2000). This does not mean, however, that these terms have become any easier to define or subject to less debate.

Globalization can be defined as a process whereby the historical constraints of geography on cultural, economic, and social interactions and relations recede, and people become increasingly aware that this is occurring (see Waters 1995; Wiarda 2008). It involves geographic spreads and exchanges to more than two continental regions, and it is a phenomenon people readily recognize or can feel in their everyday lives (see discussion in Hytrek and Zentgraf 2008; Maiba 2005). Transnationalism, on the other hand, can be defined as the flow of people, goods, information, and culture across two or more national boundaries (Ebaugh and Chafetz 2002; Menjívar 2000; Levitt 2001; Portes, Guarnizo, and Landolt 1999). It is not necessarily global, but like globalization, can be equally recognized or felt. In both cases, transnationalism and globalization are not things but processes that are subject to theorizing and considerable debate (Eitzen and Zinn 2006). In providing rudimentary definitions of these concepts, we understand that not everyone in the academic community will agree with our summation. In the public domain, people might also view the differences we highlight between the terms as purely semantic; however, whether we collectively agree on these definitions or not, any disagreement reminds us that these concepts can form the very core of some of our most intense public and academic debates (Giddens 2002). Oddly, these discussions often have not historically extended to the subject of global and transnational religion (see Meyer et al. 2011).

Over two decades ago, sociologist Roland Robertson stated that the social-scientific study of religion from a global perspective was in its infancy and hampered by a widely held notion that religion had lost its saliency in the world (Gane 2001; Hargrove 1988; Robertson 1985; 1990; 1994; Robertson and Lechtner 1985; Wuthnow 1980). Today, few people, academics or otherwise, can deny that theories of widespread secularization were largely overstated (Sherkat and Ellison 1999; Stark 1999). Religion has not died out in an age of scientific discovery nor has it completely lost its ability to shape people's lives or inform public policy. One needs to look no further than the recent history of nations, such as the United States or the Philippines, as an example of the saliency of religion in the lives of average citizens and/or the extent to which religion has shaped governmental debates and policies in these countries. Yet scholars are just now only beginning to discuss the impact of globalization and transnationalism on religion, as well as the impact religion has on globalization and transnationalism (Csordas 2009).

Religion, Globalization, and Transnational Migration

Religion has always been transnational and over time has become increasingly global. Historically, religious traditions and communities have fluidly transcended borders and, as such, are among the oldest of transnational entities (Csordas 2009). From global missionization among proselytic faiths to mass migration through religious diasporas, religion has traveled from one side of the world and back again (Jenkins 2002; Juergensmeyer 2006; Robertson 1992; Rudolph and Piscatori 1997; Wolfe 2002). While the fluidity of these flows is very old, advances in communication and transportation, as well as increases in migration, have all heightened the impact of these flows to unprecedented levels over the last several decades (Rudolph and Piscatori 1997). Exploring these flows in greater detail, it is useful, at least analytically, to distinguish between the global and transnational migration of religious people and flows of religious resources. At the same time, we must also acknowledge that both processes can obviously travel hand-in-hand.

As people move across the globe, for leisure travel, work, or in migration to new homes, they often bring their religions with them. Religious messages and practices can be portable and transposable and, hence, unbound geographically (Csordas 2009). Even in the short term, temporary residency can lead to an exchange of religious ideals or foster new religious ties and experiences. Whether this comes through a religious pilgrimage, visiting a congregation while on vacation, or a sharing of faith on a business trip, transnational and global religious exchanges do not necessarily need to be long-term to make a lasting impact both at the micro and macro levels (Cunfu and Tianhai 2004; Khan 2005; Kurien 2007; Wuthnow and Offutt 2008; Yamamori and Eldred 2003).

People may also be forced to leave their countries of origin due to natural disaster, economic collapse, war, or even religious persecution. When this occurs, migrants may turn to a common religious tradition and faith as a source of unity in diaspora. Even when this is not the situation, religion can be a source of comfort or a rallying point of identity in the face of uncertainty, confusion, and distress, both for people who are religiously active and those who do not consider themselves to be religious. Understanding this, we highlight the fact migration can be a *theologizing* experience (Ebaugh and Chafetz 2000; Smith 1978; Warner and Wittner 1998). If people were not religious before they migrated, they very well may be after they migrate, given the stressors inherent in the migration process and the extent to which religion is so vital to the reproduction and maintenance of ethnic and cultural identities (Ebaugh and Chafetz 2000; Hagan 2008; Wuthnow and Offutt 2008). Faced with new cultural, social, economic, and political situations in their destination countries, immigrants can often find a certain amount of security and comfort in their collective religious beliefs, practices, and material structures (Dolan 1985; Ebaugh and Chafetz 2000; Warner and Wittner 1998).

Historically, as nineteenth- and early twentieth-century immigrants settled in the United States, one of their first goals was to build a church in the architectural style of their home country churches (Dolan 1985; Holifield 1994; Stout and Brekas 1994). Church architecture, interior furnishings, and visual representations of the sacred became a part of the "localization of immigrant cultures" (Conzen 1991: 5) that reinforced identity and a sense of ethnic community; (see also Conzen et al. 1992). As such, immigrant communities frequently settled around a church and built a social life embedded in the customs, rituals, and festivals reminiscent of their home countries. Today, this still remains the case. With the arrival of large numbers of new immigrants to the United States after 1965, the appearance of temples, shrines, mosques, guadwaras, and other houses of worship have dotted the landscape of America, alongside new Christian churches. Ethnic festivals and celebrations of saints and gods once unfamiliar to most Americans have become regular spectacles in many ethnic neighborhoods and have also begun to gain a certain amount of wider public recognition (Cherry 2014; Levitt 2007; Tweed 1997; Williams 1988).

However, in the course of recreating these religious rituals and institutions, immigrants often introduce various kinds of changes in organization and practices, either by choice or necessity, to adapt to their new settings. Immigrant religious institutions in the United States, for example, tend to become more congregational in nature over time and often seek to increase more lay involvement in their congregations, in addition to establishing voluntary memberships and prescribed times of worship that fit the American work week (Yang and Ebaugh 2001). They also tend to establish community centers that stand side-by-side with their places of worship (Ebaugh and Chafetz 2000). Immigrant congregations are often composed of people who share the same faith (for example, Islam or Hinduism) but come from different regions of the world where that faith is practiced. As such, they tend to become aware of what is essential in their faith and what expressions are cultural, a process Yang and Ebaugh (2001) describe as *pristinization*. Given these processes, after a while, immigrant congregations often become more ethnically and religiously inclusive, as a critical mass of people and resources are required to not only establish a place of worship, but to also maintain it.

In the past two decades, scholarship on religion and immigrants has increasingly focused on the global impact that immigration is having on the globalization of religion (Appadurai 2004; Bowen 2004; Csordas 2009; Ebaugh and Chafetz 2002; Hannerz 1996; Marquardt 2005; Vertovec 2000; 2004). As scholars now recognize, many contemporary migrants maintain a variety of physical ties to their home communities while becoming incorporated into the countries where they settle (Basch, Glick-Schiller, and Blanc 1994; Cherry 2014; Ebaugh and Chafetz 2002; Faist 2000; Levitt 2001; 2007; Mahler 1998; Portes et al. 1999). However, a sense of community is often maintained more virtually through the media as well as international travel (Levitt 2007). As immigrants travel back and forth to their home countries and communicate via social media, they often transport their adaptive ways of "doing religion" back to family, kin, and friends there. Religion becomes one of many social remittances that immigrants share back home, thus influencing religious changes there and preparing future migrants for changes they might experience in migration. These social remittances ultimately influence their religious beliefs, practices, and institutions wherever these migrants go (Levitt 1998).

In many cases, these connections are established through religious congregations as a means for religious continuity (Ebaugh and Chafetz 2002; Levitt 2004). In other cases, the connections between these congregations can foster financial exchanges between national communities, lead to civic exchanges, or result in an exchange of clergy that collectively allow immigrants to actively participate in several nations simultaneously through their religious communities (Ebaugh and Chafetz 2002; Levitt 2004). Whether this comes through volunteering on a mission trip or sponsoring a monk or imam on pilgrimage, the link between nations through congregations and religious adherents is not only an important part of global and transnational trends but also one that can involve considerable resources. Take, for example, the exchange of monies between nations through migrants' remittances sent back home to their families each year. Remittances to developing countries totaled nearly $316 billion United States dollars in 2009. In a recent Gallup poll, 45 percent of foreign-born Latino immigrants who stated that religion is important to them sent remittances abroad compared to 35 percent who said that religion is not important to them (Torres, Pelham, and Crabtree 2009). Among United States born Latinos, 26 percent who stated that religion was important to them sent remittances abroad compared to only 7 percent who stated that religion was not important to them (Torres et al. 2009).

However, this money represents only a fraction of more private financial flows and other means of support such as volunteering that often go unnoticed (Ratha, Mohapatra, and Silwal 2010). For example, in 2010, over a million Americans volunteered overseas. Among these were an estimated 110,000 first-generation immigrants and 76,000 second-generation immigrants (Terrazas 2010). These volunteers represent only a small portion of their respective populations, but their volunteerism provides invaluable technical advice and specialized skills for their homelands. While religion may not always be outwardly seen as an important part of these exchanges, it can be crucial; and this aid is above and beyond the numerous churches, temples, and mosques that are built in the home communities of migrants who send specific remittances for the construction of these religious institutions (Hagan 2008; Menjivar 2000).

Those who are more religious are more likely to help physically through volunteering, send money home, or fund projects; however, this behavior does not only apply to Latinos in the United States but also migrants worldwide (Gonzalez 2009; Welliver and Northcutt 2004). While a number of scholars have described global religious communities around the world that have been created by immigrants who share national origins (Bowen 2004; Ebaugh and Chafetz 2002; Levitt 2007; Marquardt 2005; Yang 2002), almost no research has been done on the service movements these immigrants have established through their faith traditions. This is somewhat surprising given that many of these service movements are among the largest philanthropies in the world. Seeking to address this need for research, this book is one of the first attempts to describe these global service movements rooted in faith traditions. Acknowledging this, however, it is not simply goods and services that are flowing across global borders through these movements but ideas, values, and truths.

The age of mass missionary activity may commonly be thought to be over, but missionaries are still a vital part of the globalization of religion (Csordas 2009; McLeod 2004; Wuthnow and Offutt 2008). In the United States, for example, 74 percent of church members surveyed stated that their congregations supported missionary work in other countries (see Wuthnow and Offutt 2008). These missionaries are not simply spreading the good word of their faiths, as many of the contributions to this volume will highlight, but engaging in civic works through which both an exchange of goods and services and religious values and truths are seen as an extension of each other. Under some circumstances, the establishment of new religious institutions and the importation of foreign-born clergy can lead to the same civic ends. Once in their new countries, these foreign-born clergy often do not simply serve their co-ethnics or other foreign-born populations but also serve native-born congregants as well. In doing so, they not only facilitate changes in religious practices or institutional structures in their host countries but also encourage their parishioners, foreign-born or not, to join them in fundraising activities for projects in their homelands or to volunteer across several borders, in addition to encouraging them to join in protest against what they consider unjust (see Cherry 2014; Menjivar 1999). Although these events and projects often go unnoticed, they can have far-reaching political consequences nonetheless.

In 1996, when Al Gore attended a fundraising luncheon at Hsi Lai Chinese Buddhist temple in Hacienda Heights, California, the event drew criticism from many and became the focus of controversy over campaign financing. The fact that the event was at a Chinese Buddhist temple raised additional concerns over the role of foreign religions in American politics and led many to question if Clinton and Gore were secretly making policy concessions with the People's Republic of China in exchange for campaign support (Prebish 1999). Conversely, when Cardinal Robert Sarah, president of the Pontifical Council Cor Unum, delivered $1.2 million dollars of aid to Haiti to rebuild schools destroyed by earthquakes, it reminded us that religion not only continues to play prominent roles in shaping world politics but has been a vital force in the continued emergence, spread, and creation of a transnational civil society (Rudolph and Piscatori 1997). Today, well over a decade later, nothing has changed. If anything, these roles have only intensified in recent years as globalization continues to accelerate.

Religion has shaped and continues to shape globalization and transnationalism as much as these forces have shaped religion. Understanding this, in this book we ask how religious roots are shaping service movements and collective action that seeks to aid people across political and geographic boundaries. By movements, we refer to conscious, concerted, and sustained efforts by ordinary people to change society both inside and outside of normative institutional means (Goodwin and Jasper 2009). These movements typically come from the people for the people and involve some form of collective action. When this is not the case, whatever their origins, the movements must still be adopted and adapted to serve the people they seek to mobilize. Regardless of the circumstances, religion can be both a source of inspiration and provide the physical resources that sustain their collective action.

The movements discussed in this volume fit this description on a global and transnational scale. However, we acknowledge that not all scholars may agree. The field of social movements is, as Sidney Tarrow (1983) once remarked, an elusive endeavor because the movements themselves are so difficult to define. Social movements can be transformative, reformative, redemptive, revolutionary, political and/or non-political, norm-oriented or value-oriented, and they can also seek the full revitalization of society through religious means, just to name a few (Buechler 1995; DeFronzo 1991; Fitzgerald and Rodgers 2000; Gusfield 1963; Johnston, Larana, and Gusfield 1994; Melucci 1996; Neuman 2005; Schwartz and Paul 1992; Tilly 1978; Wallace 1956; Wilson 1973; Wood and Jackson 1982). Complicating matters, studying these wide-ranging phenomena can be hampered by temporal contexts. We recognize that we are catching the movements in this volume at various points in time in their history, and thus we do not have the luxury of looking at them in hindsight.

Social movement research has had a long history of looking at movements after they succeed or fail, but that is not necessarily the circumstance we find for the movements in this volume. In some cases, the people involved in these groups consider themselves to be a part of a movement, and many scholars might agree or disagree. In other cases, scholars might rightly see these groups as movements despite the fact that the members of these movements adamantly do not think of themselves in these terms. In yet still other cases, scholars might question whether some of these groups, which they would have recognized at one point as movements, have ceased to be so by working with the state or becoming non-governmental organizations (NGOs) or religious non-governmental organizations (RNGOs). Ultimately, much of this may be a matter of when and where our contributors have taken their snapshots of these groups and where individual scholars seek to situate them in the social movement literature. We do not attempt to stake claims in either direction for any of these movements but simply seek to situate these groups within the literatures that can best help us explore not only what they are but also understand where and how they are engaging religious migrants and diaspora peoples across borders on service projects that have spread around the globe. Turning to this task, in the following sections, we review several sets of literature that we believe help to further this cause.

Religion, Social Movements, and Collective Action

Over the last thirty years social movement scholars have increasingly explored the role of culture in constraining and mobilizing collective action (Pollenta 2008). During this cultural turn, however, the role of religion was curiously underexplored until scholars in the late 1970s began to take note of the rise of the Christian Right movement in the United States and revolutionary Islamic movements in the Middle East (Sherkat and Ellison 1999; Smith 1996a). Prior to this, several factors, including the predominance of secularization theories in the social sciences, the assumption of many social movement scholars that movements were essentially strategic and rational, and hence, religion was somehow too emotional or irrational, and a lack of movements in 1960s and early 1970s in which religion was not an obvious force to be studied, all led to religion being largely ignored by social movement scholars (Sherkat and Ellison 1999; Smith 1996a). Today, this view has dramatically changed.

Few scholars can in retrospection deny that religion played important roles in the Iranian Revolution in the late 1970s and early 1980s (see Munson 1988; Pipes 1983; Salehi 1988), the various revolutions in Latin American countries such as El Salvador in the 1980s and 1990s (Martin-Baro and Sloan 1990; McDonald 2006; Nepstad 1996; Smith 1991; Smith 1996b), the People Power Movement in the Philippines during the mid-1980s (Ackerman and Duvall 2000; Mercado 1987), the Solidarity Movement in Poland during the 1980s (Ackerman and Duvall 2000; Osa 1996), or even various movements across Africa today (Gilford 2003; Haynes 1995; Kane 1997; Laurent and Mary 2001; Selinger 2004), to name but a few. In studying these movements and trends, scholars have widely come to acknowledge the role that religious beliefs, commitments, and networks can play in framing, mobilizing, and sustaining collective action (see, for example, Rudolph and Piscatori 1997; Sherkat and Ellison 1997; Young 2006). While much of this renewed interest in the role of religion in social movements is a direct result of the more cultural turn in movement theorization, scholars, who suggest that a movement's ability to mobilize is often solely dependent on the availability of scarce resources, also now acknowledge that religion can be such a resource

(Harris 2001; Smith 1996a). Drawing attention to this, sociologist Christian Smith (1996a) suggests that religion can not only serve movements as a source of transcendent motivation, but they can also provide movements with a variety of organizational resources, facilitate network communication through a shared identity, and act as a physical buffer between a movement and the state.

As a source of motivation, religion can legitimize protest by aligning movement aspirations and goals with the divine or a higher power. Religion can also mobilize moral imperatives such as love, peace, and justice by citing sacred texts or drawing on powerful icons and symbols that compel people to take social action as an extension of their faith or a moral injunction to do what is right (Hart 1992; McAdam 1982; Smith 1996a). Likewise, religious clergy, such as Dr. Martin Luther King Jr. during the American Civil Rights Movement, can serve social movements as respected sources of organizational authority and become the voice of these movements (see Morris 1984). By speaking truth to power, these clergy can take on the role of a prophet or sage who is not only seen as speaking for the divine but who also provides the spiritual and emotional resources that can sustain movements over time (Oberschall and Kim 1996; Zald 1982). In doing this, clergy can also gain widespread public recognition as spiritual leaders whose voice on social or public matters is respected and given a measure of political legitimacy (Smith 1996a). When the Dalai Lama, for example, speaks out about human rights violations in China or when Pope Benedict XVI spoke out against abortion in Mexico, people around the world listen.

As an organization or institution, religion can provide a host of physical resources that can also be mobilized for collective action. Beyond being legitimized sources of authority or a source of transcendent inspiration, religious clergy are trained and experienced leaders who can mobilize their congregations by drawing on existing membership rolls and pre-existing networks of communication. This can lead to quick and decisive grassroots organization and can also become the source from which financial resources can be mobilized to a cause (Barkun 1994; Zald 1992; Aho 1990). Additionally, congregations can mobilize other enterprising tools such as computers with internet access and email, phones, fax machines, photocopying machines, office supplies, office space, trained or voluntary office staff, connections to in-house or networked legal advice, and newsletters and papers/magazines (Smith 1996a). These resources can be vital to both a movement's longevity and its ultimate successes.

As a publically defined sacred space, congregations are also often the only safe or neutral spaces where movements can meet without fear of state intervention or persecution from oppositional forces (Marullo and Meyer 1992; Smith 1991; Smith 1996a). For these reasons and others, several scholars have rightly suggested that religious congregations act as movement midwives who give birth to and help to sustain the early lives of social movements around the world (Beyer 1994; Billings and Scott 1994; Casanova 1994; Morris 1984; Smith 1996b). Acknowledging the impact religion has on social movements, we join other scholars who have challenged a passive view of the role of religion in society and rightly point to its potentially disruptive nature as a source for social change and collective action (Smith 1996a).

After the terroristic attacks of 9/11 few can deny that religion can be a disruptive force. However, the collective response of Muslims around the world that condemned the attacks and proclaimed that the terrorists were not good Muslims is more telling about the role of religion in collective action than the religious fanaticism of the terrorists themselves (see discussion in Ebaugh 2010). The mass condemnation of the attacks by a global Islamic faithful reminds us how religion can bind people with ease through a common identity that can transcend national and regional lines. It can be a unifier against an outside threat that cuts across gender, race, and class lines and one that links people transnationally (Smith 1996a; Wickham-Crowley 1990). In the post-9/11 situation, the outside threat to the global Islamic faithful was the distorted Islamophobic view that all Muslims were terrorists and that the terrorists somehow spoke for Islam. Their counter-mobilization to these views was swift and would not have been possible without the strategic mobilization of a shared sacred identity across borders.

Conversely, roughly two decades earlier, the collective mobilization of Christians against United States President Reagan's foreign policy to support the Contras in El Salvador and Nicaragua was made possible by a common religious bond between Christians in North and Central America (Smith 1996b). Without these bonds and the influence of a pre-existing religious identity that transcended borders, the opposition peace movement that halted Contra support would not have grown so large as it eventually did, nor would it have been nearly as successful (Smith 1996b). In either case, the opposition to Islamophobia or mobilizations against Reagan's support of the Contras highlights the importance of shared religious identities as a strategic source for collective action amongst globally dispersed people.

Movements remind us that religiously motivated people, including adherents of orthodox traditions, can lay claim to civil society as they seek to do the will of a higher power. Whatever their aim or mission may be, these movements can work to permeate all facets and arenas of civil society with religious institutions, symbols, and narratives. In doing so, some movements may by-pass the state or at the least partner with it as they build vast networks of organizations, associations, agencies, schools, businesses, hospitals, and places of worship to carry out their visions of a better society (Davis and Robinson 2012). This is a key observation of Davis and Robinson's (2012) most recent work on the Muslim Brotherhood in Egypt and the Salvation Army in the United States, among others. However, Davis and Robinson's work, insightful as it is, looks only at the localized effects of these processes and not the context of a more global civil society.

Collective action and social movements can be, and are increasingly becoming, transnational and global in scope (see contributions in della Porta and Tarrow 2005; Johnston and Almeida 2006; McDonald 2006). Transnational and global movements, unlike traditional collective action, cross national borders and often wide expanses of geography. They can involve new or innovative forms of communication and networks that allow for flows of resources, ideas, actions, and experiences across an increasingly borderless civil society (Giddens 2002; Habermas 1981; 1987; McDonald 2006; Maiba 2005; Rudolph and Piscatori 1997; Urry 2003). They can link the local with the global and vice versa but not always (Mednicoff 2003; Montagna 2010; Olesen 2005; Tarrow 2001; 2005; Tilly 2004). Some of these movements are truly global, crossing more than two continental regions (Tarrow 2001). Others are more transnational, limited in geographic scope by only crossing one border (Tarrow and McAdam 2004).

Beyond geographic scope, global and transnational movements can vary both in the target of their collective action and the causes that drive them. Some movements can fight against globalization from above through grassroots counter-global organization from below. The now infamous 1999 "Battle in Seattle" is a prime example. When a host of groups from around the world converged on Seattle in 1999 to oppose the promotion on neo-liberal policies in developing worlds through the World Trade Organization (WTO), the ensuing riots announced to G-77 countries that global collective action could not only be disruptive to unilateral talks but also signaled that anti-globalization mobilizations were not going away any time soon (Maiba 2005; Yuen, Burton-Rose, and Katsiaficas 2002). Conversely, movements, such as Greenpeace, the Anti-Nuclear movement, or protests against the United States' military involvement in Iraq, all highlight the diversity of causes that can mobilize people across borders and remind us that global problems do not necessarily lead to global or transnational collective action; they can be very localized (see contributions to della Porta and Tarrow 2005; Olesen 2005). In both cases, and in all points in between, religion can be just as important a resource for global and transnational collective action as more national or localized movements. While religion may not always be the central focus in these movements or clearly visible to outsiders around the world, it is there, particularly in mobilizations involving issues of global human rights or pandemic problems such as AIDS/HIV, child malnutrition, illiteracy, and poverty (Marshall and Van Saanen 2007; Mylek and Nel 2010; Petersen 2010).

Religion, Non-Governmental Organizations, and Development

A little over a decade ago, sociologist Kurt Alan Ver Beek (2000) suggested that the academic study of the role of religion and spirituality in global and transnational development was a taboo subject. After surveying three of the most prominent development studies journals in the field, Ver Beek found that relatively few if any of the articles published between the early 1980s and the late 1990s explored the role of religion and spirituality. Some ten years later, Leah Selinger (2004) updated and confirmed this with a larger survey of the field. Like the study of social movements prior to the late 1970s, religion was curiously absent from development studies, in large part because of a widespread belief that the modern world was increasingly secular and religion had lost its saliency in people's personal lives and in global affairs (Berger 2003; Berger 2009; Jones and Petersen 2011; de Kadt 2009; Marshall and Van Saanen 2007; Mylek and Nel 2010; Petersen 2010; Selinger 2004; Ver Beek 2000). At the same time, development studies had long been driven by models of economic progress and bureaucratic rationalism that considered religion to be a traditional force that could hinder development around the world as a result of cultural clashes or by legally breaching the separation of religion from state projects (Marshall 2001; Selinger 2004; Ver Beek 2000).

Today, as is the case with social movement studies and the social sciences more generally, the view of religion in development studies has dramatically changed. In fact, it has recently become somewhat fashionable to study (Jones and Petersen 2011; de Kadt 2009; Petersen 2010). There are several reasons for this academic shift including the growing and visible presence of religion in global affairs, the influence of political scientist Samuel Huntington's Clash of Civilizations thesis coupled with the terrorist events of 9/11, and the dramatic increase and visibility of faith-based organizations (FBOs) and religious non-governmental organizations (RNGOs) doing development work (Berger 2003; Clarke 2006; contributions in Clarke and Jennings 2008; Huntington 1996; Jones and Petersen 2011; de Kadt 2009; Mylek and Nel 2010; Norris and Inglehart 2004; Petersen 2010; Selinger 2004). Much of this renewed interest has also come from Christian FBOs and RNGOs that have called on the academic community to study them or are interested in studying themselves and their various projects.

While doing much the same work as their secular counterparts, FBOs and RNGOs are distinct in their mission and identity, both of which are shaped by religious roots (Davis and Robinson 2012; Mylek and Nel 2010; Petersen 2010). However, this does not mean that the sole goal of these organizations is missionization and proselytization. In many circumstances, these groups do neither but draw on religion simply as a source of inspiration or a resource for mobilizing people, money, and other various materials to a given project or cause. At a comparative level, many academics and others have been increasingly interested in evaluating whether FBOs and RNGOs are more or less effective in development work because of their religious roots compared to more secular organizations. They have also questioned the degree to which these religiously based groups are different in their approaches. One thing that is clear is that religion is taking an increasing role in development but not without controversy. After 9/11, religion was thrust into debates over foreign affairs and issues of global security (Lombardi and Wellman 2011; Wellman and Lombardi 2011). Many questioned the mission of Islamic RGNOs, for example, and raised suspicions over their fundraising. At the same time, others, particularly in the West, increasingly partnered with moderate Islamic RGNOs as a means to promote peaceful cooperation on shared development concerns (Alterman and Von Hippel 2007; Howell and Lind 2009; Jones and Petersen 2011; Kroessin 2007a; 2007b; 2009). Despite these trends and the questions they raise, it is somewhat surprising that academics have not taken quicker notice of the role of religion in development.

As early as the twentieth century, social scientists such as Max Weber (1904—*Protestant Ethic and the Spirit of Capitalism*) and Emile Durkheim (1912—*Elementary Forms of Religious Life*) argued that religion could bring about social change and shape economic development. Religion's role in development is not new, nor has it gone completely unrecognized. Historically, Buddhist monasteries, Catholic hospitals, Islamic foundations, and other various Christian relief agencies, to name a few, have all provided aid to the poor, often doing so across borders. These efforts have certainly been well recognized by their recipients but have also earned them international accolades. For example, in 1947, the Nobel Peace Prize was jointly awarded to two Quaker organizations for their international humanitarian service. In 1979, Mother Theresa, founder of Missionaries of Charity, was awarded the Nobel Peace Prize for her charity work in India. In 1988, Dr. Inamullah Khan, the long-time president of the World Muslim Congress and promoter of peace initiatives between nations, was awarded the Templeton Prize for Progress in Religion some fifteen years after Mother Theresa had won the same prize. And these are but a few examples.

It is true that global increases in the number of FBOs and RNGOs has brought greater attention to these individuals and groups, but several other high profile individuals such James D. Wolfensohn, former president of the World Bank, have also played major roles in the renewed interest in religion and development (Jones and Petersen 2011; Marshall and Van Saanen 2007). From its inception, the World Bank's approach to all aspects of development was grounded by a focus on economic theory (Petersen 2010). Although many Bank officials acknowledged that faith communities were involved in various aspects of global development or were religious themselves and, hence, interested in the link between faith and development, they were concerned that if the Bank were to focus on faith, it would breach its Articles of Agreement. As a result of these concerns, an informal group known as the Friday Morning Group began to meet outside of the Bank in the early 1980s to discuss the place of faith in their lives and in development work. In 1998, after seventeen years of informal meetings, James D. Wolfensohn co-chaired a gathering of world religious leaders with George Carey, the Archbishop of Canterbury, to not only discuss a common interest in faith and development but to explore ways to bridge the gaps in communication between secular and faith organizations doing development work.

In 1999, the group met again and eventually formed the World Faiths Development Dialogue (WFDD). Although controversy arose over the relationship that should exist between the WFDD and the World Bank, the two eventually agreed that the WFDD would remain an informal group and report any insights from its meetings to the Development Dialogue on Values and Ethics, a subcommittee of the World Bank (Jones and Petersen 2011; Marshall and Van Saanen 2007; Petersen 2010). It is in these exchanges where religion and faith has become a major focus in the Bank's ongoing development dialogues with nations and leaders around the world (Marshall 2001; Marshall and Keough 2005; Marshall and Marsh 2003; Tyndale 2006). One of the largest collaborative initiatives to emerge from these dialogues is the AIDS Campaign Team for Africa (ACT*africa*) started in 1999 to stop the spread of HIV/AIDS in the continent (Belshaw, Calderisi, and Sugden 2001; Green 2003; Keough and Van Saanen 2007; Marshall and Van Saanen 2007; Ter Haare and Ellis 2006).

In the years following this initiative from the World Bank and the WFDD, other FBOs and RNGOs around the world launched similar initiatives (Jones and Petersen 2011). Although these subsequent initiatives may seem to be reactionary, they are historically part of a larger trend that precedes the WFDD. Since the end of the Cold War and on through the 1990s, the number of transnational advocacy networks (TANS), such as the controversial Jubilee 2000 Movement that called for the end of Third World debt by the year 2000, has dramatically increased and drawn together a number of groups over common global concerns (Rudolph and Piscatori 1997; Shawki 2010). Not all that surprising, many of the people in these groups or the groups themselves have been religious and, hence, frame their understanding of these concerns from religious roots. Global poverty, as an example, has been unilaterally denounced by these groups as a moral outrage (Marshall and Van Saanen 2007). As a result, at the United Nations Millennium Summit in 2000, world leaders writing the Millennium Development Goals (MDG) declared the fight against poverty a moral imperative that binds all nations of all creeds (Marshall 2001). The ensuing meetings of the World Conference of Religions for Peace (WCRP) furthered these goals among other FBOs and RGNOs and in subsequent years ultimately led to the United Nation calling upon the WCRP to help market the MDG campaign goals amongst its partnering religious organizations.

As these calls were made, the number of FBOs and RNGOs around the world has steadily increased in part because the boundaries that have prevented their historical partnership with the World Bank or governmental states around the world have been relaxed. From 2001 to 2005, in the United States alone, the number of religious-based groups has doubled (Neusner and Chilton 2005). Roughly 10 percent, or 320, of the 3,183 NGOs with current consulting status with the Economic and Social Council (ECOSOC) at the United Nations are religious and, therefore, can be classified as FBOs or RNGOs (Petersen 2010). Likewise, some of the largest development organizations, such as the Salvation Army, World Vision, the Aga Khan Foundation, Christian Aid, Caritas, Cenro Magis, the Micah Network, and Catholic Relief services, to name a few, are all faith-based (Jones and Petersen 2011). More than simply being rooted in religious traditions, these groups have raised a tremendous amount of money and have aided countless people. In 2001, for example, the Salvation Army, World Vision, and Catholic Relief Services raised in excess of $1.6 billion dollars (United States) and claimed an outreach of nearly 150 million people (see discussion in Berger 2003). Although secular NGOs have raised as much, if not more money for global causes, and have been equally successful at aiding people around the globe, studies have increasingly demonstrated that the recipients of this aid trust FBOs and RNGOs more than secular NGOs even when the organizations are from different religious traditions than themselves (Chambers, Narayan, Shah, and Petesch 2001; Clarke and Jennings 2008; McGregor 2008; Ver Beek 2000).

This is not to say by any stretch of the imagination that the role of religion in development is without its negatives or is somehow better than secular NGOs and networks (McLennan 2007). Historically, religion has had an undeniably controversial relationship with development projects around the world (see discussion in de Kadt 2009; Gaskill 1997). From the offering of aid in exchange for religious conversion to groups who give aid solely to aggressively proselytize their religious beliefs, both the motives and methods of FBOs and RNGOs have been questioned in the past (de Kadt 2009; Hovland 2005; Mylek and Nel 2010). Today, while these questions persist, we simply do not know enough about the inner workings of these groups nor have they been systematically studied as a field well enough to answer the questions (Berger 2003; Mylek and Nel 2010; Petersen 2010).

What we do know has largely been drawn from studies of Christian FBOs and NGOs from the global north, essentially the West, and have been rather positive in their assessment of the role of religion in development (Butler 2000; Jones and Petersen 2011; Richter 2001). It is true that Christian organizations make up the largest number of FBOs and NGOs in the field, but Muslim organizations are the second largest and have been virtually ignored despite their size and the scope of their reach (Kroessin 2009; Petersen 2010). Likewise, Hindu, and Buddhist organizations, while considerably smaller in size compared to the latter, have also been sorely understudied (Jaffrelot 2011; Petersen 2010). We are beginning to have a better understanding of the goals and fields of work for these organizations, but we do not know where religious promotion falls into their work and projects (see Petersen 2010 on RGNOs at the United Nations). The overwhelming majority of these groups, as we currently understand them, focus on education, health, environment, and other types of social services. However, they also state or make explicit in their literature that religious promotion is their secondary focus or is equally important as a larger part of their development goals.

To this point, the study of global and transnational religion and development has taken a rather instrumental approach to religion (Jones and Petersen 2011). It has focused on whether religion makes a difference in development work versus what religion actually does or what it means to both those conducting these projects and their beneficiaries. Understanding this, we approach the intersection of religion and development in this book from a more social movement perspective. We acknowledge that people in religious groups and institutions experience many of the same constraints and opportunities as those in nonreligious associations (Lichterman 2005). It is not so much whether religion is good or bad for development as it is a matter of understanding its impact on individuals and groups. This requires a grounded exploration of what it means to be religious and one that is open to questioning the fundamental differences that previous studies have assumed existed between secular and faith-based organizations (Ebaugh, Chafetz, and Pipes 2006; Jones and Petersen 2011). Development organizations and projects can have just as great an impact on global and transnational religion as they can have on development. The exchange is not unidirectional.

Several studies of religion and development have called for a more open-ended and reflexive approach to the field (de Kadt 2009; Hovland 2005; Jones and Petersen 2011; Petersen 2010; Mylek and Nel 2010). They suggest that while there is perhaps no alternative to a nuanced case-by-case approach to studying development, these cases must be historically rooted with a firm understanding of the local to transnational or global context in mind and vice versa. These studies also understand that religion may not always be the variable of analysis but one of several that must be systematically analyzed and compared across cases (Alkire 2006; Berger 2009; Holenstein 2005). Understanding this approach, this volume builds on burgeoning research on global and transnational religion and takes it into new directions. Whereas previous scholars have focused on the global spread of religious traditions or the relationship of local faith communities to the process of globalization (see, for example, discussion and contributions in Csordas 2009; Ebaugh and Chafetz 2002; Levitt 2004), we highlight transnational service movements within these traditions and forces. Like Wolfe (2002), we understand the importance of studying religion from both a regional and a global perspective. However, the emphasis of this study is not on the globalization of local religious contexts but service movements around the world that are rooted in religion and are transnational in nature.

Studying Global Transnational Service Movements Rooted in Religious Traditions

We use the phrase "global religious movements across borders" to categorize and describe an emergent phenomenon that is under-theorized but vital to our understanding of the influence of religion on global movements that are impacting civil society transnationally. We characterize these movements as global transnational service movements rooted in religious traditions. While at first "global transnationalism" may appear to be somewhat redundant or even oxymoronic, it specifies a variety of transnationalism that originates from multiple global locales and is not necessarily uniform across them. Each of the groups presented in this volume is collectively organized, sustained, and, for the most part, advancing non-institutional challenges to authorities, power-holders, or cultural beliefs and practices across borders (Goodwin and Jasper 2009). They bridge local and global divides to impact transnational civil society through new and emerging forms of communication, networks, and experiences (see McDonald 2006; Melucci 1996). As such, they not only meet the most rudimentary criteria for what most scholars define as social movements but also meet the criteria to be considered truly global or transnational movements.

In many ways, the movements in this study are akin to what Melucci (1996) and others have defined as new social movements. Although they can and do share qualities with so-called old or traditional movements, the movements in this volume are often driven by protest or collective actions in the name of moral authority rather than the direct interest of any particular social group (Calhoun 1995; Crook, Pakulski, and Waters 1992; Scott 1990). They are more oriented toward a global understanding of civil society rather than any one state. They also tend to be suspicious of centralized bureaucratic structures and are often organized in loose or more flexible ways with very fluid hierarchies and loose authority structures. They translate their actions into symbolic challenges to the dominant codes of society (Melucci 1996) and are not necessarily concerned with political conflicts, as is or was the case with traditional social movements. Public action is only part of their experience, and in many cases, the majority of their efforts are carried out through a multiplicity of groups and individuals that are dispersed, fragmented, and submerged into the fabric of everyday life (Melucci 1996). These submerged networks, while often visible, are not always essentially public and directed toward the state but act as cultural laboratories that seek to rethink or reimagine the normative social and cultural codes that dominate their societies or the entire globe (Melucci 1996). This requires networks that are held together by shared beliefs and a sense of solidary through which essential resources for action, as well as specific world-views and lifestyles, can be elaborated and articulated to further facilitate the movement's aims and goals. In the movements we present, these orienting views are rooted in religious traditions and are linked and transmitted through a vast series of religious networks and religious adherents.

Many of the global service movements in this volume are rooted in older established religious traditions such as Christianity and Islam. Others are rooted in traditions, such as the Bahá'í Faith or Nichiren Buddhism, that can either be classified as new religious movements or may be less familiar to people outside of certain geographic locales (see Dawson 1998; Robbins 2000). Regardless of these factors, all the religious groups and movements in this study mobilize a particular variety of religiosity that not only transcends nation states or at least bypasses them, but also crosses multiple borders in the process. These movements can be carried out by religion from below—that is, popular or indigenous religiosity rooted in the experiences of those who are both the originators and targets of the movement—or carried out by religious roots that are distinctly foreign and introduced and extend from above by those who seek to aid others through these movements.

The studies included in this book are, by no means, exhaustive of the overabundance of social movement organizations that are established and/or maintained by transnational immigrant groups around the world. Rather, we attempted to include organizations from a variety of faith traditions that originated and are headquartered in various geographical locales and ones that differ not only in organizational structure and goals, but also for whom we could identify social scientists who have conducted research and published on these group. Hence, we include Soka Gakkai, a Buddhist movement that originated in Japan; the Aga Khan Foundation, rooted in the Ismaili tradition of Islam, with roots in Iran and India; the Gulen Movement, inspired by Sunni Islam with origins in Turkey; the

Swaminarayan (BAPS), a Hindu social service group begun in Gujarat, India; the Baha'is, self-defined as a "universalistic" religion that incorporates the one common faith of all religions, with its beginnings traced to Persia; Gawad Kalinga, a Catholic movement from the Philippines; and The Redeemed Church of God, an indigenous African Pentecostal church that emerged in Lagos, Nigeria.

None of the studies included in this volume are found elsewhere but were written specifically for this project with the issues and debates outlined in the previous pages in mind. Providing a means by which we could compare and contrast what we have learned from each of these unique movements, the contributing authors were asked to address the same subset of topics and issues. Following the lead of social movement scholars such as Jeff Goodwin and James Jasper (2009), we have grouped these wide-ranging topics and issues into ten central themes. In the following section, we describe the basis upon which we chose these specific issues and where certain subsets of questions fall within the literature on social movements. In some cases, given the nature of the groups in this volume, we were forced to chart new areas of study. Where possible, however, we developed lines of exploration that allow us to comparatively situate these unique movements both within specific literatures and in comparison with each other.

Guiding Issues and Questions

1. The Origins and History of the Respective Movement within a Specific Country and Religious Tradition

Many of the movements that we include in this volume, for example, Aga Khan Foundation, Soka Gakkai, Redeemed Christian Church of God, and Gawad Kalinga, may be unfamiliar to many readers. It is important, therefore, to understand when and where the movement began, the vision of the founder(s), and the original goals of the group. Since the 1980s, social movement theory has come to appreciate the cultural side of movements, along with their political and economic history. Cultural variables such as symbols, rituals, beliefs, and practices help frame issues in movements and create a collective identity for those who adhere to the goals and vision of the movements' founder(s) and leaders (Goodwin and Jasper 2009). Understanding the original roots of a movement is important when tracing its global spread, both from the perspective of continuity of ideas and the ability to analyze changes that occur when a movement crosses national borders and adapts to new cultural and political situations.

2. Goals of the Service Movement and the Religious Roots of These Aims within Specific Traditions and Denominations

Each of the movements discussed in this volume is rooted in a specific religious tradition such as Christianity, Hinduism, and Islam. To understand the goals and services provided by the movement, it must be placed within its broader religious tradition unpacking both the motivations and ethos inherent in its particular brand of religious thought and practice. Such understanding will provide insight into both differences and similarities among the groups in the expression and institutions that are developed to provide humanitarian services both in their home countries and in those areas to which the movement spreads in the course of its globalization. Soka Gakkai, for example, is deeply rooted in Japanese Nichiren Buddhism, while Gawad Kalinga is a Filipino movement, rooted in the deep and historical charismatic Catholicism of the Philippines. Likewise, the Gulen Movement and the Aga Khan Foundation are expressions of Islam that originated in different countries. These religious roots are essential to the formation of these movements, their goals, and ways in which leaders motivate members.

3. Specific Types of Civic Engagement and Social Outreach

The types of involvement that each movement has in its respective societies and the kinds of social outreach programs each establishes vary across the groups, dependent in part on their goals and mission. Soka Gakkai, for example, provides a sense of identity, community and sense of belonging to those in the movement, both for the Japanese diaspora and, increasingly, for other ethnic groups drawn by the call to practice lay Buddhism. The Aga Khan Foundation and the Gulen Movement are both centrally involved in developing institutions to provide education, health, and civil society in as many countries as possible. Gawad Kalinga is focusing on development by establishing villages worldwide that provide an array of services for its inhabitants and neighbors. We asked that each author outline, in as detailed a fashion as possible, the range and the depth of the types of humanitarian aid that each of the groups provide internationally.

4. Organizational Structure of the Movement

Since the 1960s, social movement theorists have realized that social movements are not the disorganized collective behavior that was once assumed but are rather highly organized, both formally and informally (Goodwin and Jasper 2009). Informal social networks are the means by which members are recruited, trained and motivated to be active participants in the goals and projects of the movement (McCarthy 1996). Some movements, such as the Gulen Movement, have little formal structure but are constituted as a "network society" consisting of individuals who organize informally through interpersonal relationships that link the participants of local communities to each other. These relationships are embedded in friendships, neighborhoods, professions, past educational experiences, and family ties that provide networks, whereby participants in the movement interact and exchange skills, goods, and ideas (Cetin 2009; Yavuz 2013). Other movements, such as the Aga Khan Foundation and the Redeemed Christian Church of God have highly formalized structures that coordinate outreach activities around the world. These formal transnational organizations tend to have structures for regular communication and cooperation that are clearly established and around which actors can operate with shared expectations and commitments. These formal ties have explicit guidelines for resolving disputes within the organization and mechanisms to incorporate input and participation from members. Conversely, Gawad Kalinga, while having a fairly top-down organization in the Philippines, has in other countries turned over its management to local partners and governmental agencies.

5. Financial Structure of the Movement

As McCarthy and Zald (1977) argued, every social movement faces the challenges of resource mobilization, and its success depends on the degree to which it can mobilize needed resources to its cause. This may include money and the physical or professional capacities it can buy, as well as telephones, FAX machines, computers, direct-mail fundraising services, lobbyists, photocopiers and postage. Thirty years later, we might also add to this list cellphones, i-pads, listserves and access to social media. All of the movements in this volume depend on these resources on some level. However, the movements described in this volume differ in the degree to which finances are centralized (for example, Aga Khan Foundation and Soka Gakkai) or localized to regional projects (for example, The Gulen Movement). As a movement becomes increasingly global, it both demands additional resources and has a broader base of contributors; the degree to which globalization impacts the financial structure of these movements is also explored in each of the chapters.

6. Spread of the Movement across Borders Highlighting the Carriers of the Movement, Who It Attracts and Why, and the Scope of Its Transnational Service

Most analyses of social movements still assume a national movement interacting with a single nation state (Goodwin and Jasper 2009). However, with the development of more sophisticated communication technology and increased international migration, global social movements are rapidly increasing (Wolfe 2002), raising a set of interesting issues regarding continuities and adaptations as they migrate across social, cultural, religious, and political contexts. Who "carries" the movement into a new locale in terms of entrepreneurs/leaders, members of a diaspora from a home country, or formal representatives from a central headquarters greatly affects how the movement is received, whom the movement attracts, what services are provided, and how the movement activities are funded. We have asked each contributor to trace these developments in careful detail so that we can view similarities and differences among the groups in terms of international services as well as the vitality of the movement in various countries.

7. Adaptation of the Movement to Local Cultures and Political Systems

Social movements are shaped in important ways by the political and economic institutions that exist in a society. Daniel Metraux argues that one reason that Soka Gakkai has been very successful in its global outreach is that it has succeeded in assimilating into local cultures through practices that are universal in their application. The Gulen Movement has had to take into account the political arrangements in each country regarding the establishment and financing of schools. For instance, in Turkey, Gulen-inspired schools are universally private and financed by tuition and local supporters, while in the United States the schools are public charter schools financed by taxpayers. In Australia, Denmark, and Germany the schools are a mix of private and government funding. These varying adaptations to the local political environments have significant consequences for the growth of service activities and responses of the public to the outreach of the movement. In North America and the United Kingdom, for example, Swaminarayan (BAPS) Charities emphasizes collaborating with other charities in its social service projects because it has fewer specifically BAPS institutions and supporting members than in other locales, such as is in India. In another instance, the Redeemed Christian Church of God adapted its requirement of having local churches built within five minutes' walking distance in developing countries and within five minutes' driving distance in developed nations to thirty minutes' driving distance in North America because of the vast and geographically dispersed neighborhoods that exist there.

8. Systems and Degrees of Communication among Members Transnationally or Globally

The extent to which movement followers communicate with one another transnationally, as well as the mechanisms whereby they do so, varies among the movements described in this volume. This relates, in part, to variations in the organizational structure of the movement, as well as to the history of members in the movement. The Aga Khan Foundation and the Redeemed Christian Church of God have elaborate websites, media outlets, and international gatherings that promote interaction among members worldwide. Less hierarchically organized movements, such as the Gulen Movement, rely more on personal networks that were created by members who were students together at Turkish universities or involved in the movement while in Turkey. As the movement ages and more young people become involved, these home country ties become less intense and cross national communication. This raises the question whether reliance on informal ties can sustain a global movement as members age and increasingly become native-born in countries other than the country of origin of the movement.

9. Response of the Media to the Movement as well as the Response of the Group Itself to the Media

Social movements, by their very nature, challenge aspects of the status quo and introduce novel ways of framing the world and responding to it. Inevitably, some aspect of the taken-for-granted, busy-as-usual world will be challenged as a movement gains visibility and begins to effect change. How the media frames movement activities often affects how it is viewed in a society and responses of significant others to those who support a movement. As Ryan and Gamson (2006:168) argue, "facts take on their meaning by being embedded in frames, which render them relevant and significant or irrelevant and trivial." Hence, the contest is lost from the beginning if movement members allow adversaries to define what facts are relevant. Therefore, most movements have media liaisons whose job is to respond to "attacks" by the media. For instance, the Gulen Movement, has recently established an entire office in New York to deal with issues in the media. Soka Gakkai, along with a number of other movements, also has divisions whose responsibility is to monitor and respond to media reports.

10. Change in the Movement over Time Highlighting Its Growth and/or Decline in Terms of Membership or Relative Scope, Its Aims and Goals, and the Impact of Its Transnational or Global Service

The final issue that is addressed in each of the chapters focuses on how the global spread of the movement has effected changes in the original movement in terms of the numbers of members, goals of the movement, and its service outreach. For some movements (for example, the Redeemed Christian Church of God, the Bahá'ís and, to some extent, the Gulen Movement), major headquarters or worship centers in the movement have shifted to a country different from where it originated. While movement supporters in some cases remain members of the original national origin group (for example, Soka Gakkai Japanese and Turkish Gulen supporters), in other cases, ethnic and racial diversity is increasing as the movement garners followers in each country to which it migrates.

Book Overview

The first case study in this book, Chapter 2 by Afe Adogame, describes the Redeemed Christian Church of God (RCCG), the fastest growing and one of the most popular indigenous African Pentecostal Churches in Nigeria. The church now exists in 110 countries with over 5 million members in Africa, America, Europe, Asia, Australia and the Middle East. Carried primarily by African immigrants, the church maintains its African roots while negotiating local identities. Strong network ties exist between the church in Nigeria and the new immigrant contexts in which African immigrants find themselves. These ties are both formal and informal. The organizational structure of the church is complex with many levels of hierarchy and administrative units. This organizational structure maintains unity within the church while encouraging some local adaptations. RCCG in diaspora remains largely an African church that provides identity, community, and security for new African immigrants. Increasingly, the RCCG is taking up extra-religious functions such as social welfare, schools, orphanages, health initiatives, and outreach to drug addicts, prostitutes, and HIV/AIDS victims. African Missions, initiated by the wife of the RCCG director, has as its focus HIV and AIDS in Africa and the African diaspora. It has assumed the task of breaking the silence on these diseases, as well as providing help for those devastated by the illness.

Chapter 3 by Helen Rose Ebaugh examines the international spread of the Gulen Movement, a Muslim-inspired cultural and educational movement that began in Turkey in the 1970s. The chapter highlights the movement's dedication to providing quality educational opportunities to youth in over 1,000 Gulen-inspired schools in 180 countries, including a growing number in all the African countries and in Asia as well. The movement also focuses upon intercultural and interfaith dialog with hundreds of dialog centers and activities located in every country where there are movement supporters. After describing the origins of the movement, the chapter focuses on similarities and differences in these projects in various countries, depending upon how the movement was introduced into a specific region, patterns of Turkish migration into the country, adaptations to local culture, the political contexts, and responses of the media to the movement. The chapter ends with changes in the movement as it moves from Turkey and becomes a global movement.

In Chapter 4, Daniel Metraux analyzes Soka Gakkai International (SGI), a Japanese lay Buddhist organization that claims 10 million members in Japan and 2 million followers in nearly 200 foreign nations and territories. Founded in 1930 as an association for educational reform, it later developed into a broader-based Buddhist movement for social and political reform. Its leaders were imprisoned during World War II for their opposition to Japan's war efforts, but after the war Soka Gakkai experienced explosive growth under the guidance of its current leader, Daisaku Ikeda, who began to internationalize the movement. Soka Gakkai is now a highly heterogeneous organization whose membership in each foreign chapter reflects the ethnic demography of the local population. A key factor for its growth worldwide is its emphasis on community and its ability to assimilate into local cultures while maintaining doctrines and practices that are universal in their appeal. Members all over the world report that the movement gives them a sense of confidence and self-empowerment, while providing a community to sustain these values. Today, Soka Gakkai exists in South Korea, Hong Kong, Southeast Asia, North and South America, Europe, India, Africa, Australia and New Zealand.

Chapter 5 by Arun Brahmbhatt focuses on Swaminarayan (BAPS), a Hindu religious community that saw rapid growth in Gujarat, India in the early nineteenth century. Its founder, Sahajanand Swami, stressed social development from the onset of the movement. He exhorted his followers to engage in charitable works and education. The chapter charts how various Swaminarayan movements spread, following Gujarati migration out of India to various parts of Africa, North America, the United Kingdom, and by the 1970s to North America. The chapter highlights how service to the community, specifically understood as a devotional practice, was encouraged and institutionalized through two prominent transnational organizations—BAPS Care International (the service wing of the Bochasanwasi Shri Aksharpurushottam Swaminarayan Sanstha, or BAPS) and ISSO Seva (under the International Swaminarayan Satsang Organization, or ISSO). The chapter examines their social service activities worldwide, especially in the United States and Canada, emphasizing the distinctive adaptations of the movement in the diaspora compared to social service provision in Gujarat. Despite the variations, however, basic similarities in charitable activities exist all over the world where the movement operates, achieved through the spiritual and administrative organizational structure which the chapter describes in detail.

In Chapter 6, Stephen M. Cherry explores the rise of the Gawad Kalinga (GK) movement in the Philippines from a grassroots outreach to the poor in the slums of Metro Manila to a rapidly expanding transnational movement in Cambodia, Indonesia, Papua New Guinea and Singapore. The chapter highlights how charismatic Catholic roots compelled the early movement into service projects for the poor across the Philippines, including building communities for Muslims in Mindanao. The movement focuses on a developmental model of "villages," which are built around clustered housing, neighborhood associations in each community, guidelines for community living decided upon by the members themselves, and the provision of social services such as youth programs, food sufficiency, healthcare, the environment, and social innovation. Through word of mouth from Filipinos living abroad and through increasing media coverage, in the past decade the development model spread to neighboring countries and then globally. The chapter examines how GK has remained a very Catholic enterprise despite a controversial split over the role of religion in projects that serve people around the world.

Chapter 7 by Karim H. Karim explores the role of Islam in the Aga Khan Development Network (AKDN), which is the charitable arm of the Shia Ismailis. The stated objective of AKDN is to raise the quality of life of the transnational Ismaili community and "those amongst whom it lives." Its operations on various continents enable members of this relatively small but ethnically diverse and geographically scattered religious group to interact with each other and to facilitate the transfer of resources from prosperous parts of the transnational community to disadvantaged ones. The Aga Khan Foundation, a central part of the network with the highest public awareness, has been successful in mobilizing volunteer and financial support from the community, as well as from external aid agencies, foundations, and other non-Ismaili sources. The chapter examines the outreach activities of the foundation with a focus on health, education, rural development, the environment, and strengthening civil society in 19 different countries. After describing the history and motivations of the Aga Khan in founding the organization, the chapter traces its growth into one of the largest and most effective charitable organizations in the world today.

Chapter 8, by Mike McMullen, draws attention to the Bahá'í Faith, one of the newest independent world religions that has translated its ethic of "unity in diversity" and the "oneness of religion and humanity" into a network of global services coordinated through its Bahá'í Administrative Order. The chapter charts how a religious movement forbidden from having clergy has been able to grow from a persecuted religious minority in Iran to a worldwide religious movement with millions of followers. Likewise, it examines how an institutional and theological focus on unity in diversity has led to the construction of schools, the development of curricula for teaching conflict resolution and anti-prejudice adopted by governments from India to Samoa, and thousands of social and economic service projects that promote Bahá'í messages around the world to "think globally but act locally." Their global service focuses on two areas of human development: education and equality in terms of racial unity, equality of women and men and human rights; and direct social services such as programs for literacy, agricultural improvement, and medical clinics. Bahá'ís consider their ecclesiastical organization to be unique in the world, in part because it was designed by the founder himself. Rather than clergy, who the Bahá'ís contend are subject to the enticements of power, the organization is structured around two pillars, the elected assemblies and the appointed boards that operate at the local, national, and international levels of society. The Bahá'í Faith has established communities in more countries and territories than any other independent religion, with the exception of Christianity. It experienced its greatest growth in the 1950s with the worldwide increase in transnational institutions and today is a global movement, expanding beyond a bi-polar concentration in the Middle East and the West and existing in most countries in the world.

The concluding chapter brings analytic light to these movements. It compares and contrasts the ten issues addressed in each of the case studies to focus on the ways that variations in these issues impact the growth, vitality, and decline of global movements. It closes by laying out the issues and debates that are critical to the analysis of global transnational service movements rooted in various religious traditions and outlining critical themes for the future study of these movements.

References

Ackerman, Peter and Jack Duvall. 2000. *A Force More Powerful: A Century of Nonviolent Conflict.* New York: Palgrave.

Aho, James Alfred. 1990. *The Politics of Righteousness: Idaho Christian Patriotism.* Seattle: University of Washington Press.

Alkire, Sabina. 2006. "Religion and Development." Pp. 502-10 in *The Elgar Companion to Development Studies,* edited by David Alexander Clark, Cheltenham, UK: Edward Elgar.

Alterman, Jon B. and Karin von Hippel, eds. 2007. *Understanding Islamic Charities*. Washington DC: Center for Strategic and International Studies.

Appadurai, Arjun. 1996. *Modernity at Large: Dimensions of Globalization*. Minneapolis: University of Minnesota Press.

Barkun, Michael. 1994. *Religion and the Racist Right*. Chapel Hill: University of North Carolina Press.

Basch, Linda, Nina Glick-Schiller, and Cristina Szanton Blanc. 1994. *Nations Unbound: Transnational Projects, Postcolonial Predicaments, and Deterritorialized Nation-States*. London: Gordon and Breach.

Belshaw, Deryke, Robert Calderisi, and Chris Sugden, eds. 2001. *Faith in Development: Partnership between World Bank and the Churches of Africa*. Oxford, UK: Regum Books/The World Bank.

Berger, Julia. 2003. "Religious Non-Governmental Organizations: An Exploratory Analysis." *International Society for Third-Sector Research* 14: 1-23.

Berger, Peter. 2009. "Faith and Development." *Global Society* 46: 69-75.

Beyer, Peter. 1994. *Religion and Globalization*. London: Sage.

Billings, Dwight and Shaunna Scott. 1994. "Religion and Political Legitimation." *Annual Review of Sociology* 20: 173-202.

Bowen, John. 2004. "Beyond Migration: Islam as a Transnational Public Space." *Journal of Ethnic Migration Studies* 30: 870-94.

Buechler, Steven M. 1995. "Social Movement Theories." *Sociological Quarterly* 35: 441-64.

Butler, Jennifer. 2000. "For Faith and Family: Christian Right Advocacy at the United Nations." *The Public Eye* 9: 1-17.

Calhoun, Craig. 1995. "'New Social Movements' of the Early Twentieth Century." Pp. 173-215 in *Repertoires and Cycles of Collective Action.*, edited by M. Traugott. Durham, NC: Duke University Press.

Casanova, Jose. 1994. *Public Religions in the Modern World*. Chicago, IL: University of Chicago Press.

Cetin, Muhammed. 2009. *The Gulen Movement: Civic Service Without Borders*. New York: Blue Dome Press.

Chambers, Robert, Deepa Narayan, Meera Shah, and Patt Petesch. 2001. *Crying Out for Change: Voices of the Poor*. Washington DC: The World Bank.

Cherry, Stephen M. 2014. *Faith, Family, and Filipino American Community Life*. New Brunswick, NJ: Rutgers University Press.

Clarke, Gerard. 2006. "Faith Matters. Faith-Based Organizations, Civil Society and International Development." *Journal of International Development* 18(6): 835-48.

Clarke, Gerard and Michael Jennings, eds. 2008. *Development, Civil Society, and Faith-Based Organizations*. Basingstoke: Palgrave Macmillan.

Conzen, Kathleen Neils. 1991. "Mainstreams and Side Channels: The Localization of Immigrant Cultures. *Journal of American Ethnic History* 11: 5-20.

Conzen, Kathleen Neils, David A. Gerber, Ewa Morawska, George E. Pozetta, and Rudolph J. Vecoli. 1992. "The Invention of Ethnicity: A Perspective from the U.S.A. *Journal of American Ethnic History* Fall: 3-41.

Crook, Stephen, Jan Pakulski, and Malcolm Waters. 1992. *Postmodernization: Change in Advanced Society.* London: Sage.

Csordas, Thomas J. 2009. *Transnational Transcendence: Essays on Religion and Globalization.* Berkeley: University of California Press.

Cunfu, Chen and Huang Tianhai. 2004. "The Emergence of a New Type Christian in China Today." *Review of Religious Research* 46: 183-200.

Davis, Nancy J. and Robert V. Robinson. 2012. *Claiming Society for God: Religious Movements and Social Welfare.* Bloomington: Indiana University Press.

Dawson, Lome. 1998. "Anti-Modernism, Modernism, and Post Modernism: Struggling with the Cultural Significance of New Religious Movements." *Sociology of Religion* 59(2): 131-56.

DeFronzo, James. 1991. *Revolutions and Revolutionary Movements.* Boulder, CO: Westview.

 De Kadt, Emanuel. 2009. "Should God Play a Role in Development?" *Journal of International Development* 21: 781-86.

Della Porta, Donatello and Sidney Tarrow. 2005. *Transnational Protest and Global Activism.* Lanham, MD: Rowan and Littlefield.

Dolan, Timothy. 1985. *The American Catholic Experience: A History from Colonial Times to the Present.* Garden City, NY: Doubleday.

Ebaugh, Helen Rose. 2010. *The Gulen Movement: A Sociological Analysis of a Civic Movement Rooted in Moderate Islam.* New York and London: Springer.

Ebaugh, Helen Rose and Janet Saltzman Chafetz. 2000. *Religion and the New Immigrants: Continuities and Adaptations in Immigrant Congregations.* Walnut Creek, CA: AltaMira Press.

Ebaugh, Helen Rose and Janet Saltzman Chafetz. 2002. *Religion across Borders: Transnational Immigrant Networks.* Walnut Creek, CA: AltaMira Press

Ebaugh, Helen Rose, Janet S. Chafetz, and Paula Pipes. 2006. "Where's the Faith in Faith-Based Organizations? Measures and Correlates of Religiosity in Faith-Based Social Coalitons." *Social Forces* 84(4): 2259-72.

Eitzen, D. Stanley and Maxine Baca Zinn, eds. 2006. *Globalization: The Transformation of Social Worlds.* Belmont, CA: Thomson-Wadsworth.

Faist, Thomas. 2000. *The Volume and Dynamics of International Migration and Transnational Social Spaces.* Oxford: Oxford University Press.

Fitzgerald, Kathleen and Dianne Rodgers. 2000. "Radical Social Movement Organizations: A Theoretical Model." *Sociological Quarterly* 41: 573-93.

Gane, Nichloas. 2001. "Chasing the 'Runaway World': The Politics of Recent Globalization Theory." *Acta Sociologica* 44(1): 81-89.

Gaskill, Newton. 1997. "Rethinking Protestantism and Democratic Consolidation in Latin America." *Sociology of Religion* 58(1): 69-91.

Giddens, Anthony. 2002. *Runaway World.* New York: Routledge.

Gilford, Paul. 2003. "Development and Today's African Christianity." Unpublished paper. School of Oriental and African Studies, London.

Goodwin, Jeff and James Jasper, eds. 2009. *The Social Movement Reader: Cases and Concepts*. Oxford: Wiley-Blackwell.

Gonzalez, Joaquin, III. 2009. *Filipino American Faith in Action: Immigration, Religion, and Civic Engagement*. New York: New York University Press.

Green, Edward. 2003. *Rethinking AIDS Prevention: Learning from Successes in Developing Countries*. Westport, CT: Praeger.

Gusfield, Joseph. 1963. *Symbolic Crusade: Status Political and the American Temperance Movement*. Urbana: University of Illinois Press.

Habermas, Jurgen. 1981. "New Social Movements." *Telos* 49: 33-37.

Habermas, Jurgen. 1987. *Theory of Communicative Action* Vol. 2. Cambridge, UK: Polity.

Hagan, Jacqueline. 2008. *Migration Miracle: Faith, Hope and Meaning on the Undocumented Journey*. Cambridge, MA: Harvard University Press.

Hannerz, Ulf. 1996. *Transnational Connections: Culture, People, Places*. New York: Routledge.

Hargrove, Barbara. 1988. "Religion, Development, and Changing Paradigms." *Sociological Analysis* 49(S): 33-48.

Harris, Fredrick. 2001. *Something Within: Religion in African American Political Activism*. New York: The Free Press.

Hart, Stephen. 1992. *What Does the Lord Require?* New York: Oxford University Press.

Haynes, Jeff. 1995 "The Revenge of Society? Religious Responses to Political Disequilibrium in Africa." *Third World Quarterly* 16(4): 728-36.

Holenstein, Ann-Marie. 2005. *Role and Significance of Religion and Spirituality in Development Co-operation*. SDC, Geneva. Retrieved June 15, 2012: www.deza.admin.ch

Holifield, Brooks E. 1994. "Toward a History of American Congregations." Pp. 23-53 in *American Congregations*, Vol. 2, edited by James P. Wind and James W. Lewis. Chicago, IL: University of Chicago Press.

Hovland, Ingie. 2005. "Who's Afraid of Religion? The Question of God in Development." Paper presented at the Annual Conference of the Development Studies Association 2005.

Howell, Jude and Jeremy Lind. 2009. *Counter-Terrorism, Aid and Civil Society: Before and After the War on Terror*. Basingstoke: Palgrave Macmillan.

Huntington, Samuel. 1996. *Clash of Civilizations*. New York: Simon & Schuster.

Hytrek, Gary and Kristine M. Zentgraf. 2008. *America Transformed: Globalization, Inequality, and Power*. New York: Oxford University Press.

Jaffrelot, Christophe. 2011. *Religion, Caste, and Politics in India*. New York: Columbia University Press.

Jenkins, Philip. 2002. *The Next Christiandom: The Coming of Global Christianity*. New York: Oxford University Press.

Johnston, Hank and Paul Almeida, eds. 2006. *Latin American Social Movements: Globalization, Democratization, and Transnational Networks*. Lanham, MD: Rowman and Littlefeild.

Johnston, Hank, Enrique Larana, and Joseph Gusfield. 1994. "Identities, Grievances, and New Social Movements." Pp. 3-35 in *Social Movements from Ideology to Identity*, edited by Enrique Larana, Hank Johnston, and Joseph Gusfield, Philadelphia, PA: Temple University Press.

Jones, Ben and Marie Juul Petersen. 2011. "Instrumental, Narrow, Normative? Reviewing Recent Work on Religion and Development." *Third World Quarterly* 22(7): 1291-306.

Juergensmeyer, Mark, ed. 2006. *The Oxford Handbook of Global Religions*. New York: Oxford University Press.

Kane, Ousmane. 1997. "Muslim Missionaries and African States." Pp. 47-62 in *Transnational Religion and Fading States,* edited by Susanne Hoeber Rudolph and James Piscatori. Boulder, CO: Westview Press.

Keough, Lucy and Marisa Van Saanen. 2007. "Faith Leaders and Institutions in Mozambique's HIV/AIDS Strategy." Washington DC: The World Bank.

Khan, Afzal. 2005. "American Muslims Perform Hajj, Celebrate Eid-ul Adha." *Washington File* January 21. Retrieved 11 June 2005 (http://usinfo.org/wf-archive/2005/050121/epf512.htm).

Kroessin, Mohammed. 2007a. "Islamic Charities and the 'War on Terror': Dispelling the Myths." *Humanitarian Exchange Magazine* 28: 27-29.

Kroessin, Mohammed. 2007b. Worlds Apart? Muslim Donors and International Humanitarianism. *Forced Migration Review* (29): 36.

Kroessin, Mohammed. 2009. "Mapping UK Muslim Development NGO's." Religions and Development Research Programme Working Paper 30. Birmingham: Birmingham University.

Kurien, Prema. 2007. A Place at the Multicultural Table: The Development of an American Hinduism. New Brunswick, NJ: Rutgers University Press.

Laurent, Pierre-Joseph and André Mary. 2001. "Visionaries and Healers of Contemporary Sub-Saharan Africa." *Social Compass* 48(3): 307-13.

Lechner, Frank J. and John Boli, eds. 2000. *The Globalization Reader*. Malden, MA: Blackwell Publishing.

Levitt, Peggy. 1998. "Local-Level Global Religion: The Case of U.S.-Dominican Migration." *Journal for the Scientific Study of Religion* 3:74-89.

Levitt, Peggy. 2001. *Transnational Villagers*. Berkeley: University of California Press.

Levitt, Peggy. 2004. "Redefining the Boundaries of Belonging: The Institutional Character of Transnational Religious Life." *Sociology of Religion* 65: 1-18.

Levitt, Peggy. 2007. *God Needs No Passport: Immigrants and the Changing American Religious Landscape*. New York: The New Press.

Lichterman, Paul. 2005. *Elusive Togetherness: Church Groups Trying to Bridge America's Divisions*. Princeton, NJ: Princeton University Press.

Lombardi, Clark and James K. Wellman, Jr. 2011. "Introduction: Religion and Human Security: An Understudied Relationship." Pp. 1-6 in *Religion and Human Security*, edited by James K. Wellman, Jr. and Clark Lombardi. New York: Oxford University Press.

McAdam, Doug. 1982. *Political Process and the Generation of Black Insurgency.* Chicago, IL: University of Chicago Press.

McCarthy, John D. 1996. "Making Robots Conscious of Their Mental States." Pp. 3-17 in *Machine Intelligence.* Vol. 15, edited by K. Furukawa, D. Michie, and S. Muggleton. New York: Oxford University Press.

McCarthy, John D. and Mayer N. Zald. 1977. "Resource Mobilization and Social Movements: A Partial Theory." *American Journal of Sociology* 82(6): 1212-41.

McDonald, Kevin. 2006. *Global Movements: Action and Culture.* Oxford: Blackwell.

McGregor, Andrew. 2008. "Religious NGOs: opportunities for post-development?" Pp. 165-83 in *Southern Perspectives on Development: Dialogue or Division?*, edited by Alec Thorton, and Andrew McGregor. Proceedings from the 5th Biennial Conference of the Aotearoa/New Zealand International Development Studies Network (DEVNET). Dunedin, NZ. Poverty, Inequality and Development Cluster: University of Otago.

McLennan, Gregor. 2007. "Towards Postsecular Sociology? *Sociology* 41(5): 857-70.

McLeod, Alex. 2004. "A New Reformation is Happening in Global Christianity." *Presbyterian Record* 128: 44-45.

Mahler, Sarah J. 1998. "Theoretical and Empirical Contributions Toward a Research Agenda for Transnationalism. Pp. 64-102 in *Transnationalism from Below*, edited by Michael P. Smith and Luis E. Guarnizo. New Brunswick, NJ: Transaction Books.

Maiba, Hermann. 2005. "Grassroots Transnational Social Movement Activism: The Case of Peoples' Global Action." *Sociological Focus* 38(1): 41-63.

Marquardt, Marie Friedmann. 2005. "From Shame to Confidence: Gender, Religious Conversion and Civic Engagement of Mexicans in the U.S. South." *Latin American Perspective* 32: 27-56.

Marshall, Katherine. 2001. "Religion and Development: A Different Lens on Development Debates." *Peabody Journal of Education* 76(3,4): 339-75.

Marshall, Katherine and Lucy Keough. 2004. *Mind, Heart, Soul in Fight against Poverty.* Washington DC: The World Bank.

Marshall, Katherine and Lucy Keough. 2005. *Finding Global Balance.* Washington DC: The World Bank.

Marshall, Katherine and Richard Marsh. 2003. *Millennium Challenge for Faith and Development Leaders.* Washington DC: The World Bank.

Marshall, Katherine and Marisa Van Saanen. 2007. *Development and Faith: Where Mind, Heart, and Soul Work Together.* Washington DC: The World Bank.

Martin-Baro, Ignacio and Tod Sloan. 1990. "Religion as an Instrument of Psychological Warfare." *The Journal of Social Issues* 46(3): 93-107.

Marullo, Sam and David Meyer. 1992. "Grassroots Mobilization and International Politics: Peace and the End of the Cold War." *Research in Social Movements, Conflict, and Change* 14: 99-147.

Mednicoff, David. 2003. "Thinking Locally—Act Globally? Cultural Framing and Human Rights Movements in Tunisia and Morocco." *International Journal of Human Rights* 7(3): 72-102.

Melucci, Alberto. 1996. *Challenging Codes: Collective Action in the Information Age.* Cambridge, MA: University of Cambridge Press.

Menjivar, Cecilia. 1999. "Religious Institutions and Transnationalism: A Case Study of Catholic and Evangelical Salvadoran Immigrants." *International Journal of Politics, Culture and Society* 12(4): 589-612.

Menjivar, Cecilia. 2000. *Fragmented Ties: Salvadoran Immigrant Networks in America.* Berkeley: University of California Press.

Mercado, Monina Allarye. 1987. *People Power, An Eye Witness History: The Philippine Revolution of 1986.* New York: Writers and Readers Publishing.

Meyer, Katherine, Helen Rose Ebaugh, Eileen Barker, and Mark Juergensmeyer. 2011. "Religion in Global Perspective: Presidential Panel." *Journal for the Scientific Study of Religion* 50(2): 240-51.

Montagna, Nicola. 2010. "The Making of Global Movement: Cycles of Protest and Scales of Action." *The Sociological Review* 58(4): 638-55.

Morris, Aldon. 1984. *The Origins of the Civil Rights Movement: Black Communities Organized for Change.* New York: The Free Press.

Munson, Henry. 1988. *Islam and Revolution in the Middle East.* New Haven, CT: Yale University Press.

Mylek, Iona and Philip Nel. 2010. "Religion and Relief: the Role of Religion in Mobilizing Civil Society Against Global Poverty." *Kotuitui: New Zealand Journal of Social Sciences Online* 5(2): 81-97.

Nepstad, Sharon Erickson. 1996. "Popular Religion, Protest, and Revolt: The Emergence of Political Insurgency in the Nicaraguan and Salvadoran Churches of the 1960s-80s." Pp. 105-24 in *Disruptive Religion: The Force of Faith in Social Movement Activism*, edited by Christian Smith. New York: Routledge.

Neuman, W. Lawrence. 2005. *Power, State, and Society: An Introduction to Political Sociology.* Long Grove, IL: Waveland Press.

Neusner, Jacob and Bruce Chilton. 2005. *Altruism in the World Religions.* Washington DC: Georgetown University Press.

Norris, Pippa and Ronald Inglehart. 2004. *Sacred and Secular: Religion and Politics Worldwide.* Cambridge, MA: Cambridge University Press.

Oberschall, Anthony and Hyojoung Kim. 1996. "Identity and Action." *Mobilization* 1: 63-86.

Olesen, Thomas. 2005. "The Use and Misuses of Globalization in the Study of Social Movements." *Social Movement Studies* 4(1): 49-63.

Osa, Maryjane. 1996. "Pastoral Mobilization and Contention: The Religious Foundations of the Solidarity Movement." Pp. 67-86 in *Disruptive Religion:*

The Force of Faith in Social Movement Activism, edited by Christian Smith. New York: Routledge.

Petersen, Marie Juul. 2010. "International Religious NGOs at the United Nations: A Study of a Group of Religious Organizations." *The Journal of Humanitarian Assistance* November 17. Retrieved May 2012 (http://sites.tufts.edu/jha/archives/847).

Pipes, Daniel. 1983. *In the Path of God: Islam and Political Power*. New York: Basic Books.

Pollenta, Francesca. 2008. "Culture and Movements." *Annuals of American Academy of Political and Social Science* 619: 78-96.

Portes, Alejandro, Luis Guarnizo, and Patricia Landolt. 1999. "Introduction: Pitfalls and Promise of an Emergent Field." *Ethnic and Racial Studies* 22(2): 217-38.

Prebish, Charles. 1999. *Luminous Passages: The Practice and Study of Buddhism in America*. Berkeley: University of California Press.

Ratha, Dilip, Sanket Mohapatra and Ani Silwal. 2010. *Outlook for Remittance Flows 2010-11*. Washington DC: World Bank.

Richter, Gerhard. 2001. "Christian Organizations at the UN as Representations of the Church: Study and Theological Reflection on the Work of One Governmental Organization and Five Non-Governmental Organizations at the UN." Unpublished Master's thesis. Union Theological Seminary, New York.

Robbins, Thomas. 2000. "Quo Vadis, the Scientific Study of New Religious Movements?" *Journal for the Scientific Study of Religion* 39(4): 515-23.

Robertson, Roland. 1985. "The Sacred and the World System." Pp. 347-58 in *The Sacred in a Secular Age*, edited by Phillip Hammond. Berkeley: University of California Press.

Robertson, Roland. 1990. "Mapping the Global Condition: Globalization as the Central Concept." *Theory, Culture, and Society* 7: 15-30.

Robertson, Roland. 1992. Globalization: Social Theory and Global Culture. London: Sage.

Robertson, Roland. 1994. "Religion in the Global Field." *Social Compass* 41(1): 1211-35.

Robertson, Roland and Frank Lechner. 1985. "Modernization, Globalization, and the Problem of Culture in World-Systems Theory." *Theory, Culture, and Society* 2(3): 103-17.

Rudolph, Susanne Hoeber and James Piscatori. 1997. *Transnational Religion and Fading States*. Boulder, CO: Westview Press.

Ryan, Charlotte and William A Gamson. 2006. "Are Frames Enough?" Pp. 167-74 in *The Social Movements Reader: Cases and Concepts*, edited by Jeff Goodwin and James M. Jasper. UK: Wiley-Blackwell.

Salehi, M. M. 1988. *Insurgency through Culture and Religion: The Islamic Revolution.* Santa Barbara, CA: Praeger Publishers.

Schwartz, Michael and Shuva Paul. 1992. "Resource Mobilization Versus Mobilization of the People." Pp. 205-23 in *Frontiers in Social Movement*

Theory, edited by Aldon D. Morris and Carol M. Mueller. New Haven, CT: Yale University Press.

Scott, Alan. 1990. *Ideology and New Social Movements*. London: Unwin University Books.

Selinger, Lea. 2004. "The Forgotten Factor: The Uneasy Relationship Between Religion and Development." *Social Compass* 51(4): 523-43.

Shawki, Noha. 2010. "Issue Frames and the Political Outcomes of Transnational Campaigns: A Comparison of the Jubilee 2000 Movement and the Currency Transaction Tax Campaign." *Global Society* 24(2): 203-30.

Sherkat, Darren E. and Christopher G. Ellison. 1997. "The Cognitive Structure of a Moral Crusade: Conservative Protestantism and Opposition to Pornography." *Social Forces* 75: 957-82.

Sherkat, Darren E. and Christopher Ellison. 1999. "Recent Developments and Current Controversies in the Sociology of Religion." *Annual Review of Sociology* 25: 363-94.

Smart, Barry. 1993. *Postmodernity*. London: Routledge.

Smith, Christian. 1991. *The Emergence of Liberation Theology: Radical Religion and Social Movement Theory*. Chicago, IL: University of Chicago Press.

Smith, Christian. 1996a. *Disruptive Religion: The Force of Faith in Social Movement Activism*. New York: Routledge.

Smith, Christian. 1996b. *Resisting Reagan: The U.S. Central American Peace Movement*. Chicago, IL: University of Chicago Press.

Smith, Timothy L. 1978. "Religion and Ethnicity in America." *American Historical Review* 83: 1155-85.

Stark, Rodney. 1999. "Secularization R.I.P." *Sociology of Religion* 60(3): 247-73.

Stout Harry S. and Catherine Brekas. 1994. "A New England Congregation: Center Church, New Haven 1638-1989." Pp. 14-102 in *American Congregations*, Vol. 1, edited by James P. Wind and James W. Lewis. Chicago, IL: University of Chicago Press.

Tarrow, Sidney. 1983. "Struggling to Reform: Social Movements and Policy Change during Cycles of Protest." *Western Society Paper 15*. Ithaca, NY: Cornell University.

Tarrow, Sidney. 2001. "Transnational Politics: Contention and Institutions in International Politics." *Annual Review of Political Science* 4: 1-20.

Tarrow, Sidney. 2005. The *New Transnational Activism*. Cambridge, MA: Cambridge University Press.

Tarrow, Sydney and Doug McAdam. 2004. "Scale Shift in Transnational Contention." Pp. 121-50 in *Transnational Movements and Global Activism,* edited by Donatello della Porta and Sydney Tarrow. Lanham, MD: Rowman and Littlefield.

Ter Haare, Gerrie and Stephen Ellis. 2006. "The Role of Religion in Development: Towards a New Relationship between the European Union and Africa." *European Journal of Development Research* 18(3): 351-67.

Terrazas, Aaron. 2010. *Connected Through Service: Diaspora Volunteers and Global Development.* Migration Policy Institute and U.S. Agency for International Development, Washington DC.

Tilly, Charles. 1978. *From Mobilization to Revolution.* Reading, MA: Addison-Wesley.

Tilly, Charles. 2004. *Social Movements, 1768-2004.* Boulder, CO: Paradigm.

Torres, Gerver, Brett Pelham, and Steve Crabtree. 2009. "Half of New Latino Immigrants to U.S. Send Money Abroad." Gallup Poll September 22. Retrieved June 11, 2012 (http://www.gallup.com/poll/123140/half-new-latino-immigrants-send-money-abroad.aspx).

Tweed, Thomas A. 1997. *Our Lady of the Exile: Diasporic Religion at a Cuban Catholic Shrine in Miami.* New York: Oxford University Press.

Tyndale, Wendy, ed. 2006. *Visions of Development: Faith-based Initiatives.* Aldershot, UK: Ashgate.

Urry, John. 2003. *Global Complexity.* Malden, MA: Polity.

Ver Beek, Kurt Allen. 2000. "'Spirituality' A Development Taboo." *Development in Practice* 10(1): 31-43.

Vertovec, Steven. 2000. "Cheap Calls: The Social Glue of Migrant Transnationalism." *Global News* 4: 219-24.

Vertovec, Steven. 2004. "Migrant Transnationalism and Modes of Transformation," *International Migration Review* 38(3): 970-1001.

Wallace, Anthony F. C. 1956. "Revitalization Movements." *American Anthropology* 58: 264-81.

Warner, R. Stephen and Judith G. Wittner. 1998. *Gatherings in Diaspora: Religious Communities and the New Immigration.* Philadelphia, PA: Temple University Press.

Waters, Malcolm. 1995. *Globalization.* New York: Routledge.

Welliver, Dotsy and Minnette Northcutt. 2004. *Missions Handbook, 2004-2006: U.S. and Canadian Protestant Ministries Overseas.* Wheaton, IL: Billy Graham Center.

Wellman, James K., Jr. and Clark Lombardi, eds. 2011. *Religion and Human Security.* New York: Oxford University Press.

Wiarda, Howard J. 2008. *Globalization: Universal Trends, Regional Implications.* Northeastern Series on Democratization and Political Development. Lebanon, NH: Northeastern University Press.

Wickham-Crowley, Timothy. 1990. "Winners, Losers, and Also-Rans: Toward a Comparative Sociology of Latin America Guerrilla Movements." Pp. 132-81 in *Power and Popular Protest*, edited by Susan Eckstein. Berkeley, CA: University of California Press.

Wilson, John. 1973. *Introduction to Social Movements.* New York: Basic Books.

Williams, Raymond. 1988. *Religions of Immigrants from India and Palestine: New Threads in the American Tapestry.* New York: Cambridge University Press.

Wolfe, John. 2002. *Global Religious Movements in Regional Context.* Aldershot, UK: Ashgate.

Wood, James and Maurice Jackson. 1982. *Social Movements: Development, Participation, and Dynamics*. Belmont, CA: Wadsworth.

Wuthnow, Robert. 1980. "World Order and Religious Movements." Pp. 57-75 in *Studies of the Modern World-System*, edited by Albert Bergesen. New York: Academic Press. Reprinted in Eileen Barker, ed., *The New Religious Movements: An Approach to Understanding Society*. Pp. 47-68, New York: Edwin Mellin Press, 1982.

Wuthnow, Robert. 1983. "Cultural Crisis." Pp. 57-71 in *Crisis in the World System*, edited by Albert Bergesen. Beverly Hills, CA: Sage.

Wuthnow, Robert and Stephen Offutt. 2008. "Transnational Religious Connections." *Sociology of Religion* 68(2): 209-32.

Yamamori, Tetsunao and Kenneth A. Eldred. eds. 2003. *On Kingdom Business: Transforming Missions Through Entrepreneurial Strategies*. Wheaton, IL: Crossway.

Yang, Fenggang. 2002. "Chinese Christian Transnationalism: Diverse Networks of a Houston Church." Pp. 175-204 in *Religion Across Borders*, edited by Helen Rose Ebaugh and Janet Saltzman Chafetz. Walnut Creek, CA: AltaMira.

Yang, Fenggang and Helen Rose Ebaugh. 2001. "Transformations in New Immigrant Religions and Their Global Implications." *American Sociological Review* 66: 269-88.

Yavuz, M. Hakan. 2013. *Toward an Islamic Enlightment: The Gulen Movement*. New York: Oxford University Press.

Young, Michael P. 2006. *Bearing Witness Against Sin: The Evangelical Birth of the American Social Movement*. Chicago, IL: University of Chicago Press.

Yuen, Eddie, Daniel Burton-Rose, and George Katsiaficas. 2002. *The Battle of Seattle: The New Challenge to Capitalist Globalization*. New York: Soft Skull Press.

Zald, Meyer. 1982. "Theological Crucibles: Social Movements in and of Religion." *Review of Religious Research* 23: 317-36.

Zald, Meyer. 1992. "Looking Backwards to Look Forward: Reflection on the Past and Future of the Resource Mobilization Research Program." Pp. 326-48 in *Frontiers in Social Movement Theory*, edited by Aldon Morris and Carol McClurg Mueller. New Haven, CT: Yale University Press.

Chapter 2

The Redeemed Christian Church of God: African Pentecostalism

Afe Adogame

The *Newsweek Magazine* issue of Monday, December 22, 2008 featured an interesting piece on the "50 Most Powerful People in the World." This lengthy article paraded names of the *Who's Who* in the world, including the United States President Barack Obama and other global political players, economic juggernauts, and religious entrepreneurs. One perhaps less-known global religious player listed among the most powerful people in the world was Enoch Adeboye. As Lisa Miller hinted in this highly insightful article:

> You may never have heard of E. A. Adeboye, but the pastor of The Redeemed Christian Church of God is one of the most successful preachers in the world. He boasts that his church has outposts in 110 countries. He has 14,000 branches—claiming 5 million members—in his home country of Nigeria alone. There are 360 RCCG churches in Britain, and about the same number in U.S. cities like Chicago, Dallas, and Tallahassee, Fla. Adeboye says he has sent missionaries to China and such Islamic countries as Pakistan and Malaysia. His aspirations are outsize. He wants to save souls, and he wants to do so by planting churches the way Starbucks used to build coffee shops: everywhere. (Miller 2008)

The above is one indication of how several African religions have been producing religious leaders of various hues, different "folks and strokes." In fact, the history of religious independency in Africa is replete with charismatic founders, prophets, and leaders, who are sometimes perceived as charlatans. New religious movements in Africa are integral to on-going processes of globalization, just as these movements are shaped by these processes. These new movements are engaging and negotiating the public sphere in diverse ways. At the same time, Africans who migrated to North America, Europe, and elsewhere have largely carried their religio-cultural identities with them. Most often, living in a new context has encouraged these immigrants to reconstruct, organize, and identify their religion both for themselves and for the non-Africans around them. A multitude of African religions has appeared in North America and Europe, especially in the last two decades (Adogame 2004). The most visible varieties in the contemporary geo-religious landscape are the African-led Charismatic/Pentecostal churches.

In *The Next Christendom* (2000), Philip Jenkins quite appropriately calls attention to the shifting contours of Christianity from the Northern to the Southern hemispheres. Also important is how these religious developments in Africa shape and are shaped by new African immigrant communities in North America and Europe and even the host Western societies generally. As if to echo some of Jenkins' observations, *The New York Times* of October 13 and 14, 2003, featured two stories: "The Changing Church: Faith Fades Where It Once Burned Strong," by Frank Bruni, and "Where Faith Grows, Fired by Pentecostalism," by Somini Sengupta and Larry Rohter (Bruni 2003; Sengupta and Rohter 2003). Bruni's article focuses on the decline of Christianity in Europe during the last quarter-century and the shift in its center of gravity to the Southern hemisphere. As Bruni notes, "Christianity has boomed in the developing world, competing successfully with Islam, deepening its influence and possibly finding its future there. But Europe already seems more and more like a series of tourist-trod monuments to Christianity's past ..." (Bruni 2003: A1). Although the focus on church-oriented religiosity in these stories was on Europe, the situation in the United States is only a little different. In the midst of this decline, the article refers to the appearance of African churches in the religious landscape. As Bruni further remarks, "Christianity's greatest hope in Europe may in fact be immigrants from the developing world, who in many cases learned the religion from European missionaries, adapted it to their own needs and tastes, then toted it back to the Continent" (Bruni 2003: A1).

Similar to these new religious developments in Europe, the United States is also currently witnessing a rapid proliferation of African religious influences within and beyond Christian, Islamic, and Indigenous communities. In a *Chicago Tribune* front-page report, for example, Julia Lieblich and Tom McCann (2002) wrote about the Redeemed Christian Church of God. The story describes the Nigerian-based Pentecostal church's efforts to spread its evangelistic form of Christianity to America. Lieblich and McCann note, "For years American missionaries brought Christianity to Africa. Now African Christians say they want to export their own brand of ecstatic worship and moral discipline to the United States, a country they believe has lost its fervor" (Lieblich and McCann 2002: 1). As Jenkins aptly remarks:

> Many African immigrants ... come from nations in which Christianity is enjoying an upsurge of passionate enthusiasm scarcely precedented in the whole history of the religion. Independent and prophetic African churches are now firmly rooted in American cities, from which they plan ambitious evangelistic expansion. To take one critical example that has attracted next to no media attention, consider the thriving Nigerian churches based in Houston, many of which stem from the prophetic healing tradition known as Aladura. Conceivably, these African-derived churches could soon represent a significant new phase in the history of American urban revivalism. (Jenkins 2002: 25)

The significance of African new religious movements, such as Pentecostal/ Charismatic brands of Christianity, within the framework of globalization is not merely with reference to a unique expression of African Christianity they exhibit. They constitute international ministries and groups that have implications on a global scale. As part of an increasing phenomenon of what they term, "reverse mission to a dead West," these African churches are systematically setting out to "evangelize the world." The impact and import of "exporting" their religious messages and ideologies, driven by a vision of winning converts and enlarging their clientele, is that it offers a unique opportunity to analyze their impact at a local level. The importance of global networks among these churches in Africa and the diaspora cannot be overemphasized. One way of comprehending this process is to see how transnational networks between these religious groups, in the original "home" (African) and the new "host" contexts, are assuming increasing significance for African immigrants.

The implications of the globalization process, prevailing political and socio-economic conditions of home countries, transformations in the technology of communication and transportation, increasing immigrants' development of networks, and activities has been largely responsible for this development. Next to the intentional expansion of religion (mission), migration is the most important factor determining the spread of religion. Although not altogether new, migration has been a substantial agent in processes of religious identity formation, on the one hand, and of religious diversification by launching religious exchanges and interaction between immigrant groups and host societies, thereby contributing to the emergence of variety and plurality in religious traditions, on the other. This new migratory dimension and trends in Africa and beyond demand an approach that recognizes both the complex dynamics of global migration and the impact of religion on immigrants and the migration process.

Drawing upon over a decade of religious ethnography (2000-2012), this chapter explores the nascence, demographic expansion, and mobility of the Redeemed Christian Church of God (RCCG), showing how it translates into local-global environments by assimilating notions of the global, while, at the same time, negotiating local identities. The movement has become global with participants and social service projects in several countries across the globe. The chapter also explores RCCG's authority structure, cultural adaptations in its spread, and carriers and finances of the movement as it becomes global. Other relevant questions will include: Who were the carriers of the movement as it spread beyond its country of origin to other countries? What types of adaptations/changes occurred in the movement in the process of settling in a different social and religious context? Who finances the activities and sustainability of the movement in its various locations? Has the movement experienced criticism or hostility from people/groups, either in its country of origin or in new locales to which it migrated? The research on which this chapter is based has depended largely on extensive field work— participant observation at church programs, house cells, and semi-structured oral interviewing methods at RCCG parishes (branches) in Africa, Europe, and North

America. Simple questionnaires were employed in some local parishes (branches) that focused on the demographic features of its membership and on some aspects of church life. Content analysis of church literature and audio and video cassettes produced by the church was also employed.

Origins, Demographic Expansion, and Mobility

The RCCG is a typical example of an indigenous African Pentecostal/Charismatic church, which has spread globally from Nigeria to about 110 countries with over five million members, scattered within Africa, America, Europe, Asia, Australia, the Middle East and other parts of the world. The RCCG was founded in Lagos (Nigeria) in 1952 by Pa Josiah Akindayomi following a claim to a divine call for a special mission. Pa Akindayomi became popular for his charismatic qualities and healing activities, although the church he founded did not witness much large-scale spread under his tutelage. Most parishes (branches) were limited to western Nigeria with only a few in eastern and northern Nigeria. Enoch Adejare Adeboye, a former University of Lagos Professor of Applied Mathematics and Hydrodynamics, succeeded as the General Overseer in 1980, and with his charisma, healing successes and modernizing focus transformed the stature of the RCCG into a global religious and social institution. Subsequently, the church has experienced considerable growth within Nigeria and beyond its borders, with a conservative estimate as at 2003 of 5,000 parishes worldwide (see RCCG 2002/2003).[1]

The RCCG is believed to be the fastest growing and one of the most popular Pentecostal churches in Nigeria today (Adogame 2004; 2007). Its official website states:

> Since 1981, an open explosion began with the number of parishes growing in leaps and bounds. At the last count, there are at least about 2000 parishes of the Redeemed Christian Church of God in Nigeria. On the International scene, the church is present in other African nations including Côte D'Ivoire, Ghana, Zambia, Malawi, Zaire, Tanzania, Kenya, Uganda, Gambia, Cameroon, and South Africa. In Europe, the church is fully established in the following countries: United Kingdom, Netherlands, Spain, Italy, Germany, Greece, France, Switzerland, Austria, Denmark, Sweden and Norway. In North America there are about 600 parishes (July 2011) spread in various cities and states of

---

[1] A conservative list of parishes worldwide is available at the RCCG Internet Outreach: http://main.rccg.org/parish_directory/parish_directory_main.htm. This list is far from complete. New parishes are updated frequently at: http://www.rccgnet.org/dir/ RCCG_World_Wide/ (accessed on April 10, 2012). A parish may comprise from several scores to a few thousand members.

the US and Canada. Also there are parishes in the Caribbean states of Haiti and Jamaica. There are parishes in South America, the Middle East, Australia, etc.[2]

The parish directory suggests even greater demographic spread. Although not an exhaustive list of parishes worldwide, it nevertheless shows that the RCCG has a relatively large membership across the globe.

The first RCCG parish in the United States was founded in 1992 in Detroit, Michigan. From 1994 onwards, new parishes sprang up in Florida, Texas, Massachusetts and other states in the United States. From my recent web-search of parishes in the RCCGNA, 617 parishes were listed (533 in the United States and 84 in Canada).[3] In Dallas, the initiative to establish a parish was raised by Nigerian employees and trainees on internship programs and special projects with Mobil Oil, as well as some other oil industries whose headquarters were located in Dallas. From this pioneer parish the Dallas metroplex played host to fourteen full-fledged RCCG parishes in 2003. There were twelve existing parishes (now fifteen) in the city of Houston and others located in different parts of Texas (Adogame 2004: 31-32).[4] Just as new parishes continue to spring up across the United States cities, so are local parishes acquiring real estate that are developed into local religious empires characterized by magnificent state-of-the-art edifices. Several parishes in many United States cities have acquired land where they have erected their church buildings and other facilities; others have leased or rented school halls, abandoned warehouses, defunct church buildings, hotel rooms, cinema halls, and shop-front rooms as alternative, temporary spaces of worship.

Hierarchical and Organizational Structure

RCCG's authority structure is rather complex. The overall head and leader of the RCCG is called the General Overseer (GO). The current RCCG hierarchy structure follows the following order: The General Overseer, The Governing Council, Deputy General Overseer, Mother-in-Israel, Assistant General Overseers, Elders, Assistant Elders, Secretaries, Provincial Coordinators, Directors, Assistant Secretaries, Provincial Pastors, Assistant Provincial Pastors, Zonal Pastors, Area Pastors, Parish Pastors, Assistant Parish Pastors, Deacons/Deaconesses, Ministers, Workers, the Faithful (Congregation), and Seekers/Visitors.

---

[2]   The RCCG North America area comprises the US, Canada and the Caribbean Islands. For more details on RCCGNA administrative structure, see Adogame (2004: 31-32). See RCCGNA network, available at: http://www.rccgna.org/zones.asp and http://www.rccgna.org/TheChurch/Origin.aspx (last accessed on April 10, 2012).

[3]   See the RCCGNA website available at: http://www.rccgna.org/Provinces/Search.aspx (accessed on June 15, 20/12).

[4]   The RCCGNA website search engine listed 99 current parishes in the US State of Texas (accessed on June 15, 2012).

The church maintains two headquarters, one national and the other international, with the GO's office overseeing both. Under the Office of the GO are six administrative blocs attached to the national headquarters: Fellowships; Parishes; Areas; Zones; Provinces; and Regions. The national headquarters oversees all branches in Nigeria presently numbering over 5,000. These branches are grouped into five administrative sections called "regions." Below the unit of regions are "Provinces," with each region comprising a number of provinces. The Lagos region, for example, has eleven provinces. This regional structure of administration illustrates the geographical spread of the RCCG. The next administrative unit is the "zones." A province is a collection of "zones." A zone, in turn, consists of "areas," each of which comprises a number of parishes. A parish is made up of "home fellowships," while the smallest unit is the church.

In summary, the RCCG is organizationally structured in the following order: Office of the General Overseer, International Headquarters, National Headquarters, Regions, Directorates, Provinces, African RCCG Zones, Europe Regions, RCCG Areas North America, Parishes, Home Fellowships. The structure at the international headquarters of the RCCG is much simpler than at the national headquarters. Through the International Office, the GO coordinates all activities involving foreign missions outside of Africa. Other RCCG branches in Africa are grouped into regions, each headed by a regional coordinator. In Africa, there are the West Coast, Cameroon, Ethiopia, East Africa, and South Africa. RCCG parishes worldwide are organizationally structured into "areas," with each "area" subdivided into "zones" for administrative purposes. Each zone is assigned a coordinator. Each country is divided into zones; states and provinces are grouped together to form a zone. In 2008, there were a total of 22 zones in RCCG North America, 19 in the United States and the Caribbean and 3 in Canada. At the RCCGNA Annual Convention held in Dallas (Texas) in 2003, over 120 parishes were listed (RCCG 2003b). In September 2008, 334 parishes were listed on the RCCGNA official website.[5] RCCG's religious cartographical maps of North America quite consciously illuminate the physical, demographic spread of parishes but also the extent to which the North American terrain has been mapped and partitioned for missionary, evangelistic ends.

Central Beliefs

The RCCG emphasizes biblical inerrancy, the power of the Holy Spirit, and divine healing and prophecy. The RCCG tenet of faith includes the belief in the divine inspiration of the Bible as the infallible word of God, the divine Trinity, and the Deity of Jesus Christ. RRCCG adherents also believe in the baptism of the Holy

---

[5]   See Parish Directory for a current list of parishes (branches) in North America listed according to parish/city, state/zone. Available at: http://www.rccgna.org/login/pdirectory. asp?offset=0 and http://www.rccgna.org/bocus.asp (accessed on September 5, 2008).

Ghost for "all believers who are living sanctified lives and that it is evidenced by the speaking in tongues as the Spirit gives utterances." Central to the RCCG world-view is the belief that divine healing of sickness for all believers is provided through atonement. Eschatological features concerning the second coming of Jesus and the rapture of the Church, the great white throne judgment, the new heaven and new earth, and eternal heaven and eternal hell as literal places of final destiny also dominate their belief system. The practice of restitution is rife in the church just as the "gospel of prosperity" is central. Adeboye (2003) asserts RCCG's perspective towards prosperity:

> The Lord has established a covenant of prosperity with the Redeemed Christian Church of God. So if you are linked up with it, your breakthrough becomes automatic. However, the first and greatest breakthrough you can ever have is the salvation of your soul. This is the foundation of all other blessings and breakthrough you desire to have.

In a new cultural context, the RCCG is in constant negotiation between old and new world-views, tradition and modernity, and maintaining and constructing old and new identities. As members declare:

> There is no alternative to maintaining the esteemed standard of "old-time religion." We must be totally obedient to follow Christ implicitly without reservations. This starts from Pastors as relates to integrity in ministry, manners of conduct, maturity, marriage, money, morality, being well informed. These attributes have to be assimilated first by the leaders then imparted on the followers .... We face the challenge of integrating our African inclination into the acceptable American values with a view of not limiting fellowship to Africans. The African Christian attributes we hold strongly are holiness, prayerfulness, strong faith, deepness of worship and hand of fellowship, while American virtues include effective time management, community service and strategic planning ... ("Addendum—Our Poise" n.d.)

Mission, Vision, and Goals

The desire and enthusiasm towards establishing parishes in Africa, North America, Europe, and other parts of the world is not unconnected with vision and goals of members as expressed in RCCG's Mission Statement:

> It is our goal to make heaven. It is our goal to take as many people as possible with us. In order to accomplish our goals, holiness will be our lifestyle. In order to take as many people with us as possible, we will plant churches within five minutes walking distance in every city and town of developing countries; and within five minutes driving distance in every city and town of developed

countries. We will pursue these objectives until every nation in the world is reached for Jesus Christ our Lord.[6]

In the case of RCCGNA, the goal of proximity between churches had to be qualified in view of the demographic peculiarities of the North American region. This statement took on a qualifying addendum. It also exemplifies how and to what extent contextual factors can shape the growth of a religious movement and serve as a dynamic of change in a new context. For planting new parishes in North America and Caribbean countries, the proximity to any existing parish must be at least 30 minutes' driving distance. The addendum states, "We believe in positioning our worship centers close to the people hence in North America we are challenged to establish parishes in every state, county, city and in fact within 30 minutes driving distance" ("Addendum—Our Poise" n.d.). Samuel Shorimade expressed the significance of evangelism in the RCCGNA: "The United States was often described in some circles as God's own country, but this country has become very slack morally and spiritually. So God is making us [RCCG] bring worship and praise to them [U.S.] as well as in rediscovering God."[7]

Although individual RCCG parishes have the initiative and leverage to sponsor and establish new parishes locally and internationally, the RCCG leadership plays an institutional role in international mission. While the opening of new RCCG parishes by individual local branches is not centrally controlled from the international headquarters in Lagos, the strategy towards foreign mission was, however, institutionalized with the appointment of the Assistant General Overseer to take charge of mission overseas. The General Overseer's wife, Folu Adeboye, led African Missions, that is, mission work within the continent. The International headquarters plays a supervisory, moderating role and intervenes where there are local problems, disputes and conflicts between different parishes. The provincial headquarters inaugurates a new parish, and the General Overseer, where possible, conducts the dedication ritual of the parish. According to RCCG Provincial Pastor, Brown Oyitso:

> The church was given a micro and macro vision, with the micro driving the macro vision. God gave the micro vision to the Founder that the church will go around the world, the General Overseer (Enoch Adeboye) came in and got the macro vision. We were recruited and charged to move abroad. God gives a mission with a provision, so the first RCCG parish in London was started by Leke Sanusi. There was contemplation on several options, and the next initiative was for the US. (Oyitso 2004)

---

[6] See RCCG official website: http://www.rccg.org created and maintained by the RCCG Internet Project, Houston Texas, USA (accessed on March 25, 2011).

[7] Personal Interview with Pastor Dr. Samuel Shorimade at the RCCG Cornerstone Worship Centre for All Nations parish, Cambridge, Massachusetts on November 23, 2003. Pastor Shorimade is the founder and current pastor of the parish.

Pastor Samuel Shorimade was officially commissioned by the RCCG leadership to return from Nigeria to the U.S. on missionary service, having studied and completed a Ph.D. in the United States earlier. He relocated with his family to the United States and opened a parish in Boston. As Oyitso remarks:

> The General Overseer commissioned the histrionics of church development in the US. New England was a prime target, as a gateway to aristocrats and to America. Harvard University and the Massachusetts Institute of Technology became potential targets. The Shorimades were forerunners ... It was inaugurated, funds were generated, initial take-off grants were provided — hall rents, musical instruments and PA system. Initial support for the RCCG Boston parish was essentially from the Pen Cinema parish in Agege, Lagos (Nigeria). (Oyitso 2004)

Occasionally, financial and material support was provided for the Boston and London parishes until they both became self-sufficient, and started to fend for themselves. Money was also sent from Nigeria to support new branches established in India, Pakistan, South Africa, and elsewhere. In 2004, when I interviewed Oyitso, he disclosed that the RCCG Victory House Parish in Festac Town (Lagos) had already established six branches in Italy. The parish committed financial and material resources to support the new parishes in Italy. Training materials and Sunday school manuals were sent from the RCCG headquarters to support mission work in all these new contexts. Besides, trainers were sent from Nigeria to conduct Ministers' training workshops and conferences.

In the case of international mission, pastors and church personnel were sent to head new branches. For instance, in 2002, the RCCG International missions department sent Bosun Ajayi to Bonn to co-ordinate RCCG branches in Germany (Ajayi 2002). In November 1994, Pastor Dr. Ajibike Akinkoye moved with his family to Dallas to oversee the first parish. From this pioneer parish, the Dallas metroplex played host to fourteen full-fledged RCCG parishes. Akinyoye confirmed receiving financial support from the RCCG International headquarters (Lagos) towards the physical development of the over 600 hectares of land acquired for building the RCCGNA headquarters. In the case of RCCG, the reverse mission process has gone beyond rhetoric in that the church consciously provides institutional support for new parishes, particularly in the diaspora. Pastor Oyitso (2004) summarized the rationale for reverse mission (overseas) when he said:

> In those days, missionaries came and were supported from the UK and the USA. They sow seeds and are now reaping the harvest. The harvest is churches in Africa that are now being sent money now being ploughed back. God has turned the table. Churches are founded now to bring back the faith to revive the European and US countries.

Oyitso asserts that financial and material support given to new parishes abroad has been, "a one-way thing … It is one way and deliberate. We do not want host governments to think that we are here (Europe, USA) to siphon money from their countries." Nonetheless, the RCCG financial organization is structured in such a way that all parishes are required to funnel a percentage of the total tithes and offerings, through their provincial and regional offices, to the international headquarters of the church in Lagos, Nigeria. RCCG missionary pastors are sent from this headquarters to Germany, the United States, and other parts of the globe, with responsibility for their financial support such as salaries or honorarium borne by the International headquarters in Lagos. While a specified proportion of income, dues, and remittances are transferred from all worldwide RCCG parishes to the international headquarters, the coordinating Pastors (missionaries) sent on mission abroad are, at the same time, remunerated directly from the international headquarters or some local parishes in Nigeria.

Financial Structure and Economic Base

One central discourse prevalent in the RCCG worldview is "health and wealth." The emphasis on prosperity teaching, the epistemologies of health/wealth, and the ritual attitudes they invoke in members are integrally linked to how the economic base of the church is shaped, reconfigured, and sustained. Health, for these religious communities, encompasses physical, spiritual, mental, material, psychological, and social well-being. It also includes belief in the right to gainful employment, fair wages, residence permits, and a safe environment that nurtures a life of dignity and decency. The networked culture of RCCG means that indigenous epistemologies of health and wealth—in other words, the quest for "the good things in life" as local iterations of prosperity—blend seamlessly with external discourses on prosperity.

Tithes and offerings represent one of RCCG's fundamental belief codes, the giving of which forms an essential part of worship and constitutes a potent way of invoking the blessings of God. As the church claims:

> Regular payment of tithe and offering is obligatory because it is God's command. It is God's way of providing for the Ministers in the Church. The ministers and other church employees are paid their food, allowance through tithe. The offering is used to cater for the needy in the Church. Tithe and Offering must be paid on every income e.g. salary, profit from business transaction, gifts, etc. Tithe is exclusively for the minister's welfare. ("RCCG Fundamental Beliefs" n.d.)

The practice of tithes and offerings is linked to Hebrew scriptures in which God enjoined the Israelites at different periods of their religious history to pay tithes and offerings (Malachi 3: 8-12; II Corinthians 9: 6-7). In the RCCG, tithes have continued to represent one-tenth of a member's total or gross income. While a tithe means 10 percent of all benefits that come a member's way, such as salary, inheritance, gifts, and even the interest earned on bank accounts, the offering is essentially different. Offering goes beyond the 10 percent in tithes and could be in cash or property. The giver takes the initiative on what to give towards needs of the church or an individual, mostly during worship services. RCCG worship services and programs include thanksgiving rituals for childbirth, naming, marriage, job promotion, recovery from sickness, procurement of visas, passing examinations, New Year and Christmas celebrations, safe journeys, buying a new car, or building a new house, as well as other rites of passage.

While the RCCG strongly encourages its members to engage in tithing, members are not compelled to do so. Still, the liturgical structure makes ample space for the collection of tithes, and within the sermons, the oft-cited biblical references are recited as a way of calling members to wake up to their responsibility. The failure to pay tithes is believed to automatically bring a curse on a member and his or her business. In one of his writings, Adeboye enjoined members to attach utmost priority to payment of tithes:

> What you have stolen from God, I appeal to you, restore and He will surprise you …God says when you begin to pay your tithes, all the devourers that have been eating up your money and all the abortive efforts that you have been making, He will silence. (Adeboye 1989: 16-17)

In one of his sermons, he outlines the intricate correlation between the acquisition of wealth and giving offerings to God:

> If you want a double portion of wealth, you have to do something greater than what Solomon did. You have to give an offering the kind that you have never given before. God is a God of principles: Do what nobody had done before; He will respond by giving you something that nobody had ever got before. (Adeboye 2002)

The importance of tithes and offerings is evident in members' adherence to these imperatives both in their giving as well as in their testimonies about tithing. The enormous financial resources generated through tithing are primarily geared towards the welfare of ministers and church employees, as well as for the poor and the needy within the church. In spite of this, only a very small percentage of RCCG parish pastors earn their pay from the church. Several of the local pastors operate as honorary pastors, while others are supported materially by local parishes.

Every RCCG parish is somewhat autonomous, yet there is a reasonable degree of cohesion without uniformity. Each individual parish is linked to the international headquarters in Lagos through an evolving hierarchical administrative structure (RCCGNA 2003a: 15 and 30). At the central organizational level, local parishes are required to make monthly financial remittances through administrative zonal headquarters to the international office. This includes 10 percent of total tithes and offerings of all RCCG fellowships and 10 percent of tithes and offerings of all parishes dedicated by the General Overseer. In addition, each local parish is expected to submit a comprehensive financial report. In the case of RCCG North America, each parish is required to send a portion of its monthly income to the Finance Coordinating Center in Houston. The funds accumulating there are used to assist new, young, or weak parishes that need financial help for a time and also for international missions (Ojo 2001). Thus, while the RCCG's primary source of internal revenue is tithes and offerings, other sources include Sunday worship offertory, thanksgiving offerings, special program offerings, donations, vows, pledges, and special levies for projects such as building constructions. The huge monies generated from these diverse sources and events form the economic bedrock of the church.

Socio-ethnic Configuration of RCCG in Diaspora

Most RCCG branches, which came to be established in Europe and North America during the 1970s and 1980s, were the initiative of individual students or people on business and official assignments who had no intention of residing permanently abroad. These groups, made up of just a few members, would meet and worship together in "house cells or fellowships," later transforming into full-fledged branches with acquired or leased properties as religious buildings. In some cases, a new branch sought official recognition or affiliation with headquarters in Africa. The demographic change of the migrant communities has slightly altered this original composition in the last two decades. The arrival of migrant families and the birth of children (first- and second-generation) has led to a major shift to long-term migrants or settlers. This no doubt has far-reaching implications on the status and growth of the RCCG, particularly in the diaspora.

The RCCG has demonstrated determination to make global links and to target non-Africans in their membership drives. Most branches lack a cross-cultural appeal, thus leaving their membership predominantly African. Generally, new African-led churches in the West such as the RCCG are yet to make significant incursions into white populations. This lack of a cross-cultural appeal and wherewithal, coupled with a myriad of contextual factors such as accommodation problems, language barriers, hostility of neighbors, poor economic base, fluid membership, and status of churches in host contexts and immigration regulations are largely responsible for this trend. However, there are a few exceptions where some RCCG branches have transcended racial-ethnic precincts to include sizeable non-Africans in their membership. There are even instances of essentially Spanish- and German-speaking branches. The existing non-African element is largely owing to bi-racial couples, friendship, and sometimes as a dividend of personal/ impersonal evangelism. This membership structure is likely to be transformed and altered in the future if the churches continue to gain inroads into the new religious landscapes. The social anatomy of parish members is complex and variegated. The majority of these members are not illiterates; rather they are elites of their countries or those who have ventured out in search of the "golden fleece." In most recent times, the membership has been characterized by skilled and unskilled factory workers, the unemployed, asylum seekers, and refugees. With such a socio-ethnic structure, RCCG in diaspora largely remains the locus of identity, community, and security for new African immigrants.

Communities of the African religious diaspora such as the RCCG organize themselves in such a way as to reinforce and revalidate their sense of ethnic and religious identities, ensure and maintain security, and seek solidarity, as well as develop "survival strategies," that is, ways of negotiating a way through the hazards of the new host societies. Typically, the RCCG develops structures and practices designed, simultaneously, to help members maintain and reproduce religio-cultural identities, on the one hand, and to assist immigrants in adaptive processes to new, host contexts, on the other. The RCCG represents a pivot of attraction, particularly to their African membership, owing to the fact that the church replicates the cultural and religious sensibilities of their home context in a way that creates a "comfort zone" for many African immigrants.

Appropriating New Media

African-led churches in diaspora, such as the RCCG, are increasingly appropriating new communication technologies in the transmission of their religious messages. Media texts now serve as one significant map through which African immigrant churches see themselves on local-global religious landscapes. Thus, another tendency of the RCCG towards globalization is evident in its appropriation of the new media, the deliberate effort towards making their presence known on the World Wide Web, and the use of the Internet for religious communication and public repositioning. RCCG's appropriation of media communication technologies, such as the Internet, electronic mail services, Facebook, Twitter, RCCG TV, webmail, chat rooms, blogging, and other social media as an impersonal means to communication and recruitment strategy is gaining prominence in a context where personal media with which members are very familiar in their homeland have largely failed in the new contexts. The RCCG appropriates the new media, the Internet, as conduits for disseminating religious ideologies, means of sustaining old/new communities, and as public-representation within global religious maps of the universe. While the church websites act as a new and relatively effective means of outreach to the larger community, most parishes that appropriate social media also do so to attract potential clientele. Such intentions are clearly portrayed in their introductory mission statements.

In the RCCG Internet Outreach, the introductory statement on the Parish directory states, *inter alia*:

Over the years The Redeemed Christian Church of God has experienced an explosive growth with branches being planted all over the world. It has become pertinent to create a directory and online data base for all The Redeemed Christian Church of God parishes worldwide ... This will enable us do a complete, relational online database that will be useful for the Body of Christ. Furthermore online database will help us in our evangelism, fellowship and interaction among member parishes. It will also serve to assist travellers in their efforts to find a place of worship wherever they find themselves.[8]

The members' visions and goals are expressed in the RCCG Mission Statement. Although these goals may appear somewhat ambitious and utopian to attain, one point of significance is the fact that RCCG has demonstrated optimism and enthusiasm towards the realization of its global vision. The church is not only concerned with the local setting but what transpires beyond it, within so-called "developing" and "developed" countries. The recourse by the RCCG in diaspora to new, alternative evangelistic strategies is intricately tied to new, global socio-cultural realities. The somewhat individualistic nature of Western societies, for instance, has largely rendered some of the known conventional modes inept and far less productive. Thus, the personal modes of communication—for example, door-to-door, street-to-street, marketplace and bus evangelism—are giving way systematically to more impersonal or neutral modes of communication, such as computer websites, electronic mail, and faxing.

Negotiating the Public Sphere

RCCG's vertical and horizontal growth is best captured not simply by its demographic spread but also by the extent to which it has carved out a niche for itself in terms of its public role, social relevance, and local/global impact in Africa and beyond. The RCCG contributes enormous bridging, bonding, and linking social capital but also confronts barriers to development and civic engagement. Its spaces of worship are not simply religious places; they are also spaces of socialization where business, politics, education, music, home country and food cultures, and even gossip are engaged and negotiated. Such spaces often transcend socio-ethnic, race, class, gender, and intergenerational boundaries. People meet others from different backgrounds as they share activities and build trust in one another, albeit temporarily. They facilitate bridge-building and links-building with others, thus generating local-global networking trends, new forms of association, and engendering trust in shared community initiatives. While their landscapes of worship can be sources of cohesion or conflict amongst members, as well as

---

[8]   See the official website of the RCCG in http://www.rccg.org created and maintained by the RCCG Internet Project, Houston Texas, USA. See also UK parish websites http://www.jesus-house.org.uk/ and http://www.rccgarea4.org.uk/

between the leadership and the followers, these landscapes can also be sources of cohesion or conflict between these religious communities and their neighborhoods.

In Europe and the United States, churches and faith-based organizations register under government corporate affairs departments, but in the United Kingdom the RCCG and most African-led churches register with the Charity Commission as charitable, non-profit organizations. They take up charitable initiatives and actively promote civic engagement through micro finance programs, supporting thrift shops, providing soup kitchens, warm clothing and blankets to the vulnerable during winter season, language classes, and tutoring for children and youth. They also provide training geared towards self-employment and poverty alleviation, youth and women empowerment, and making contributions to the welfare of their constituency through a multiplicity of spiritual and social resources. Initiatives to lift members out of poverty involve savings and credit schemes, where well-trusted principles of reciprocity assist people to establish small businesses. Through services such as loans, savings, insurance, and remittances, many women involved have become self-reliant and have built their own economic base to complement that of their husbands. Some have started small-scale businesses and even buy and sell within the church precincts.

The RCCG is increasingly taking up extra-religious functions such as social welfare programs within African and the diaspora context. Thus, its focus is not only on the spiritual wealth of members but also on their social, material, and psychological well-being as well. Beyond their church vicinity, they have taken up functions such as the regeneration and rehabilitation of drug-ridden youth in the society, the socially displaced, under-privileged refugees, and asylum seekers. RCCG members display a significant model of African Christianity in the way they organize themselves, with features emanating from both their new contexts as well as their African heritage.

On January 15, 2010, the *Nigerian Compass Magazine* reported how the RCCG blazed the trail as one of the first religious institutions to contribute aid and relief efforts following the terrible earthquake that left most of Haiti in ruins. The news reported that RCCG North America, with the approval of the General Overseer, donated $50,000 to Haiti at a time when many African and Western governments were still contemplating whether and in what way to respond to the emergency situation. To examine its social impact further, I shall focus on only three examples owing to space constraints: the reconfiguring of the Redemption City, a Christian Disneyland; structures established by the RCCG to combat HIV and AIDS; and mechanisms of recovery from dependent drug use. In terms of public involvement, the RCCG is largely interested in social work—schools, orphanages, health institutions, outreaches to drug addicts, "area boys" (street urchins), prostitutes, and HIV/AIDS victims. To these three features I shall now briefly turn.

Redemption City—Reconfiguring a Christian Disneyland

RCCG's character and maturity are evident as it has grown to acquire immense properties and real estate in Nigeria and the diaspora. The Redemption Camp,[9] also known as Redemption City, in Nigeria doubles as RCCG's International headquarters and its most important sacred space. The Congress Arena, a huge space measuring about three square kilometers, hosts religious programs such as the massively popular Holy Ghost Congress[10] and the monthly Holy Ghost Service. The first plots of land for the Camp were procured in the early 1980s along the Lagos-Ibadan motorway in Nigeria. The Camp now stands on an extensive property estimated at over fourteen square kilometers.

The geography of the camp is diversified including such physical structures as a massive auditorium called the Congress Arena, a conference center, guesthouses and chalets, and a presidential villa that is reserved for dignitaries who visit the Camp. The Christ Redeemer's Ministry (CRM), an organ of the RCCG, operates hospitality departments at the Redemption Camp, including the Resort Center, the White House, and the International Guest House,[11] with executive chalets that are open to the general public, tourists, visitors, and members alike. Also situated on the sacred site are the Redeemer's Clinic, a maternity center, an orphanage, a post office, security post, a gas station, bookstores, supermarkets, a public market, a bakery, and a canteen. Other facilities include five banks (Intercontinental Bank, Oceanic Bank, Haggai Community Bank, United Bank for Africa, and New Life Community Bank), the Redeemed Christian Bible College, Redeemer's Junior and High Schools, and its own university, the Redeemer's University.[12] An estate consisting of residential buildings have come to characterize its topography. The Haggai Community Bank, owned by RCCG, developed a sprawling Estate, now called Haggai Estates, adjacent to the Congress Arena, comprising semi-detached duplexes, three and four bedroom apartments, and bungalows.[13]

The significance of the Redemption Camp, described by members as RCCG's "New Jerusalem—a peaceful and beautiful place on earth," lies not only in the religious functions it serves for members and non-members alike, but also as a crossroads: a place where social, economic, cultural, ecological, and political concerns intersect and interact. In fact, the nexus between this singular sacred space and its complex functionality exemplifies the Redemption City as a microcosm of a global social movement.

---

[9]   For details about the RCCG Redemption City, see http://city.rccgnet.org/about_redemption.html

[10]   The Holy Ghost Congress attracts over two million participants, thus leading some observers to describe the religious festival as the largest Christian gathering on earth. See Grady (2002).

[11]   See CRM available at: http://city.rccgnet.org/crm.html

[12]   For details, see: http://city.rccgnet.org/facilities.html

[13]   For details, see: http://city.rccgnet.org/Haggai_estates.html

One way in which the RCCG is gradually imprinting itself on the American geo-cultural landscape is through the reproduction of the "Redemption Camp" (Adogame 2004). By 2003, the RCCGNA had acquired a multimillion-dollar property of over 400 hectares of land in Floyd (Hunt County), near Dallas, Texas. The property is being developed along the lines of the Redemption Camp international headquarters in Nigeria (Akinyoye 2004; cf. Akande 2003). This new Redemption Camp serves as RCCGNA headquarters; it includes such structures as the Holy Ghost Ground, chapels, a Bible College, a baptismal pool, a recreational center, an administrative building, a library, banquet and seminar halls, a shopping mall, restaurants, a community center, guesthouses, residential accommodations and an impressive driveway. The duplication of the original camp is important for a number of reasons. For one, it represents the decentralization of church programs that were previously concentrated at the international headquarters across the sea.

The RCCG has invested huge financial and material resources in establishing, maintaining, and sustaining the facilities, infrastructures, and manpower that these projects and institutions engender. Beyond a consideration of the religious impact in the national educational and health sectors, the RCCG is increasingly becoming a visible stakeholder in the banking, insurance and other sectors of the Nigerian and global economy. These religious-owned business outfits provide employment as well as being profit-oriented. In vital ways, they contribute to local/global economies as both economic players and stakeholders. The (re)production and negotiation of ritual spaces evident in the sacralizing of the Lagos-Ibadan motorway and Floyd County in Dallas are emplacements that evince ecological, spatial, demographic, aesthetic, social, cultural, and economic impact on local/global religious landscapes. The value of property, infrastructure, and other endowments in these invented religious spaces is quite enormous and monumental.

On July 17, 2005, Scott Farwell of the *Dallas Morning News* reported with an interesting news headline "African Church Plans Christian Disneyland," where he disclosed, *inter alia*, that "the Redeemed Christian Church of God—Africa's largest and most ambitious evangelical church—plans to build a 10,000-seat sanctuary, two elementary school-size lecture centers, a dormitory, several cottages, a lake and a Christian-themed water park in Floyd, Texas" (Farwell 2005). One senior Pastor of the church described the gigantic development project, then in its very early stages, as a "Christian Disneyland," evoking ambivalence as to what was really meant. Two interpretations may be canvassed here. First, the idea of a Christian Disneyland was not totally new. It may perhaps refer to Billy Sunday who started the trend toward Christian Disneyland (ChristianEbooks.com. n.d.). The concept of a Christian Disneyland is also reminiscent of the original Disneyland, an American theme park in Anaheim, California, built and marketed as "the happiest place on Earth."[14]

---

[14] See full details in Disneyland Resort Homepage available at: http://www.disneyland.com/

Incidentally, July 17, which has been currently acknowledged as the official opening day of the Disneyland in Anaheim, California, was also the date when Farwell reported on an African church's plan to build a Christian Disneyland. Ostensibly, there is a striking similarity beyond the date, in that both projects—the Disneyland in Anaheim and the "Christian Disneyland," RCCG's North American Redemption Camp in Floyd, Texas—boast of extensive acres of domesticated landscapes and localities that are now home to myriads of facilities. Such wide-ranging facilities are important for leisure and tourism on the one hand, but they also partly carry religious, spiritual, ecological and social import, on the other. Beneath the facade of aesthetics of these facilities lie crucial negotiations that are enacted via layers of economics, culture, religion, and identity.

RCCG's African Mission and HIV and AIDS

In 1996, African Missions was initiated as a body by the wife of the RCCG General Overseer, also known as Mummy G.O., following visits to the mission's field of operations in the West African sub-region. She expressed dismay with prevailing life situations and thus concluded that the missions urgently required assistance such as in the provision of basic infrastructure. The scope of this assistance widened to include the rest of Africa, leading to a name change from "West African Missions Committee" to "African Missions."[15] Its main task was:

> recruiting brethren that can reach out to missions in various ways; to identify the needs of the missions and prioritize them, thereby making these missions self-supporting; to train pastors and missionaries to satisfy the large manpower need in Africa; to assist with the establishment of more mission schools and bible colleges throughout Africa; to eradicate poverty by providing self-enrichment courses and community development programs; to educate on and reduce the spread of the AIDS epidemic in many African countries.[16]

African Missions has expanded both its scope and its seat of operation beyond Africa to Europe and the United States. The South African Region 2 (comprising Namibia, Botswana, Zimbabwe, South Africa, Swaziland, and Lesotho) and parts of East and Central Africa were assigned to African Missions North America (AMNA).[17]

During the RCCG's 7th Annual Convention, "The Latter Rain" held in Dallas, Texas in June 2003, the RCCG General Overseer Enoch Adeboye and his

---

[15]   For details on African Missions as an RCCG ministry, see: http://jfccenter.org/africa_missions.html

[16]   See African Missions at: http://jfccenter.org/africa_missions.html (accessed on March 24, 2005).

[17]   For some of the AMNA projects, see: http://jfccenter.org/AMprojects.html

wife, Folu Adeboye, led the "Walk for Africa," an organized procession around downtown Dallas to raise awareness and financial assistance for HIV and AIDS victims in Africa. On June 19, 2003, the AMNA organized "a walk for Africa to improve the quality of life of children, youth and families, help the needy, feed the poor, educate a child, help stop the spread of AIDS and make disciples of all nations" Subsequently, on July 11, 2003, AMNA, in collaboration with CitiHope International, a United States faith-based humanitarian aid organization, donated HIV and AIDS drugs (Pentam 300—Pentamidine) valued at $1.5 million to Nigeria for use in treating HIV and AIDS-related complications (Adogame 2007: 480). They claimed this was a move to support former President Bush's faith-based initiative to fight HIV and AIDS in Africa. This medication was distributed in five identified target areas: Abuja, the federal capital territory; Benue; Plateau; Ogun; and Oyo states.

The RCCG has assumed a leading role in breaking the silence on HIV/AIDS. They engage theotherapy (spiritual healing), providing spiritual succor, moral advocacy activities, and medical help with the provision of drugs, facilities, and funds to the infected and the affected. RCCG operates an office, the Redeemed AIDS Program Action Committee (RAPAC), to deal with HIV and AIDS from the spiritual and medical angles. RAPAC is a religious NGO that defines itself as "a non-profit, non-governmental, faith based organization with primary focus on creating awareness, educating on prevention, provision of spiritual support and counseling for People Living with HIV/AIDS (PLWH/A), People Affected by AIDS (PABA)." Pastor Olaide Adenuga summarized the work of the faith-based organization as "prevention, care and support for PLWH/A (People Living with HIV/AIDS) and PABA (People Affected by AIDS)" (Adenuga 2004).[18] RAPAC's vision is to "reduce the spread and transmission of HIV/STIs [sexually transmitted infections] using innovative spiritual intervention skills amongst the church membership and the society," complemented by practical medical care. RAPAC also promotes sexual and reproductive health with an educational program for youths/adults to improve the quality of life within the church by the provision of spiritual support and counseling for PABA.

AMNA receives assistance from the RAPAC office at the RCCG Redemption Camp in the dispensing, monitoring and reporting of the drugs in Nigeria. RAPAC collaborates with other health institutions and NGOs for treatment and clinical management of cases of HIV and AIDS. With some funding from the US Agency for International Development through Family Health International's IMPACT Project, RAPAC developed a dynamic HIV and AIDS prevention program that focused on changing risky behavior and campaigning for those affected by the disease. The project empowers individuals and families to prevent HIV by using peer education, interpersonal communication and counseling, spiritual counseling, drama and HIV and AIDS education modules in the church's Bible college

[18] For an extensive outline of RAPAC history, objectives and activities, see http://www.rccgrapac.org/main.htm

curriculum. For individuals, the church offers peer education and counseling to promote risk-reduction behaviors. For families, the church emphasizes parent-child communication and conducts seminars to empower parents to discuss frankly sexuality issues in the context of their faith and the growing epidemic. To further this process, the RCCG recruited counselors to incorporate HIV and AIDS into church-based counseling. Over 300 peer educators facilitate education sessions in various parishes of the church in Lagos alone. Adenuga notes that regular reference to HIV and AIDS in sermons and publications by the General Overseer, Enoch Adeboye, created an enabling environment for programming. Musical concerts, dramas, and sensitization seminars have also served as useful mediums of education. Church publications and drama productions reinforce HIV and AIDS advocacy messages targeted at decision-makers.

Thus, the RCCG's social role in civic life is further evident in the mutual relationship and enhancement between the RAPAC and NGOs such as the Family Health International (FHI)/IMPACT. The RAPAC takes an active role in receiving and making HIV and AIDS referrals. For instance, FHI/IMPACT refers persons living with HIV and AIDS, transport workers, and youth to faith-based projects such as the RAPAC for spiritual counseling. In turn, the church refers its members to HIV and AIDS care and support groups and other services provided through FHI/IMPACT programs.

RCCG multiple strategies have been both precautionary and therapeutic through spiritual and medical means. On the spiritual level, HIV and AIDS become personified as one of the several demonic spirits which populate the cosmos, and is dealt with theotherapically. On a more pragmatic level, RCCG has launched other programs to combat AIDS. Funds have been generated locally/internationally for procuring AIDS-related drugs. They evolve programs, which involve youth in AIDS prevention and encourage creative activities diverting youth from a way of life that would lead to its acquisition. In this way, RCCG's social role becomes visible and its extra-religious functions complementary in socio-contexts where efforts by local or international agencies have proved insufficient to combat the spread and impact of HIV and AIDS. Although RAPAC's contribution to prevention may be considered more in terms of broader development issues such as education and social services with the emphasis on abstinence and faithfulness as exclusive strategies for HIV prevention, they have nevertheless demonstrated commitment to contributing to HIV prevention and impact mitigation. In this way, the RCCG performs important religious, social, and other extra-religious functions in the global society.

Combating Drug Use and Abuse

The United Nations Office on Drugs and Crime Nigeria (2004) reported that there were 72 drug treatment and rehabilitation facilities in Nigeria. These facilities included government-owned specialized units for the treatment and rehabilitation of drug-dependent persons in psychiatric and general hospitals, non-governmental organizations, and traditional healing centers. In the last section of this chapter I shall examine some of the strategies undertaken by RCCG faith-based organizations and treatment agencies, such as the Wellspring Rehabilitation Centre in Ojodu and the Christ Against Drug Abuse Ministry (CADAM) in Ikeja. Other related faith-based treatment agencies are the House of Joy, Surulere and the New Life Drug Addicts Rehabilitation Centre, Lekki. All these agencies owned by the RCCG are situated in different locations in Lagos, Nigeria.

The Wellspring Rehabilitation Centre is a (RCCG) Christian faith-based residential center with programs of treatment for drug dependency. It is a registered non-governmental organization established in 2003 in Nigeria. The agency is an arm of the welfare ministry of the RCCG (Apapa family, an umbrella term for a collection of parishes within the RCCG). The agency is devoted to meeting the spiritual, recovery, vocational, and resettlement needs of dependent drug-using individuals, in particular, those living on the streets, popularly known as "area boys". The Centre provides a system of care which incorporates a Pentecostal Christian faith-based model of drug treatment of drug dependency, vocational training, social reintegration, and aftercare. The Wellspring's Centre's program for Recovery and Social Re-integration is organized in two phases. The first is a five-month treatment program in two stages: two weeks of detoxification from drugs and four and half months of training and counseling interventions. The second phase offers a six-month to two-year vocational training program focusing on skills acquisition, preparing service users for a new, drug-free life, and for playing a full part in society (Wellspring Rehabilitation Centre 2003).

Comfort Jinadu's recent in-depth investigation and qualitative study (Jinadu 2011) contributes to the understanding of recovery from dependent drug use by exploring the experiences of service users in Wellspring Rehabilitation Centre, owned by the RCCG in Lagos, Nigeria. The study explored the ways in which dependent drug users recover from drug dependency. Three stages of the recovery process were explored: motivation for recovery, disengagement from drugs, and maintenance of recovery. In each of these stages, psychological, socio-environmental, and spiritual elements were identified as significant factors in the recovery process. The offer of treatment from a Christian faith-based agency seemed to be the most important factor in motivating informants to engage in treatment in the first place. At the disengagement stage, psychological and socio-environmental issues come to the fore, with a personal commitment to change and support from significant others, including peers, becoming important. However, spiritual factors, including teaching, Bible study, and prayers, play a significant part during this time. Maintenance of recovery was found to be facilitated by psychological strategies such as positive self-talk and avoidance of triggers of drug dependency; by socio-environmental factors including supportive relationships; and by spiritual elements, which center on the adoption of a Christian lifestyle. The findings conclude that, although recovery from drug dependence is achieved through various routes, the most significant factor for the informants in this study was the spiritual intervention received. This study illuminates the significant role of faith and spirituality in recovery from drug use, a spiritual dimension to drug dependency, and recovery, which should not be ignored by policy-makers and practitioners. The study has demonstrated that Pentecostal Christian interventions such as salvation, prayer, and training in biblical principles contributed immensely to recovery from dependent drug use.

CADAM (an acronym for Christ Against Drug Abuse Ministry) is a fully registered faith-based NGO in Drug Demand Reduction (DDR) activities founded in the 1980s in Nigeria.[19] The menace of drug abuse and its associated problems in Nigeria provides ample opportunity for CADAM, which is the social arm of RCCG responsible for rehabilitation of drug addicts. CADAM recognizes the holistic care delivery to drug addicts and ex-addicts. The understanding is reflective of their integrative approach to delivery of health and spiritual care to drug addicts. CADAM ministry is led by Dr. Dokun Ayodeji, a medical practitioner. The corporate headquarters is currently at the RCCG Dominion Sanctuary, Ogba-Ikeja. CADAM currently runs three residential houses as the rehabilitation centers, located in Araga, Poka, and Eredo, all within the Epe axis of the Lagos State. The process of rehabilitation starts with personal care and medical treatment for residents of Jubilee House hostel for addicts. The integrative nature of CADAM activities entails post-traumatic assistance to residents of Jubilee House. Those who have demonstrated significant behavioral changes, with positive physiological assessments indicating they are ready to be integrated into the community, are transferred to another home in Akute, Lagos to undergo vocational training.

CADAM is recognized by both local and international agencies and organizations, including the National Drug Law Enforcement Agency, the Vienna NGO Committee, and the United Nations Office on Drugs and Crime. CADAM has enjoyed tremendous referrals throughout Nigeria. Adeboye (2007: 37) quotes one RCCG publication as follows:

> People who have attended the rehabilitation programs are many and diverse, including an American-based professor, who is also a medical practitioner, but became a drug addict, went through the program, and he is completely "washed" [drug free]. He is back in America and he is doing very well. A pastor now based in Norway and a pilot are some of those that have been saved [converted to the Christian faith] through the program.

The impact of CADAM is not restricted within the borders of Nigeria, validating the fact that the transnational status of RCCG provides ample leverage to contribute

---

[19]   For further details on CADAM's history and mission, see: http://cadamonline.org/history.php and http://cadamonline.org/index.php. See also: http://www.rccgonline.org/rccgnew/index.php?option=com_content&view=article&id=96&Itemid=76

significantly to human development through the CADAM initiative globally, as well as among Nigerians.

The "House of Joy," one of the social responsibility arms of the RCCG, Lagos Province 34 (Apapa Family), was established in June 2009 with a mission to reform and reintegrate drug-dependent persons into society through proper approach to treatment and rehabilitation.[20] The initiative started in October 2006 following a visit by Shola Balogun (pastor-in-charge of Province 34) to Akala, Mushin, a suburb of Lagos known for a high percentage of drug users, where she saw over 20 girls and boys below the age of 17 smoking marijuana mixed with heroin powder. House of Joy thus became involved in creating public awareness and enlightenment on drugs and drug abuse. The hospitals, clinics, maternities, faith-based agencies, and rehabilitation centers built and owned by RCCG evince their roles and stamina in ways that the social services they offer supplement and challenge the inadequacies of local government health-care schemes besides providing employment opportunities for members and non-members alike.

Conclusion

One crucial challenge for RCCG as a global service movement generally poised for demographic expansion in the West is to forge new expansion strategies, demonstrate public (social) relevance, and repackage rhetoric and narratives of evangelism in such a way as to appeal to the sensibilities of potential clientele within the new host society. This is more so the case against the backdrop of perceived secularizing tendencies that has characterized Western societies and churches in Europe. While the charisma of the current leader has endeared him to a huge followership and shot the RCCG into the global religious landscape, the church is probably not dealing with the reality of the problem of succession to leadership, the routinization of charisma, and the bureaucratization processes that will follow his demise. The lacunae created by the silence of such legal provisions in constitutions, edicts, by-laws, memorandum, and articles of association establishing the RCCG may result in legal imbroglios and succession crises likely to challenge the post-charismatic future and perhaps even the corporate existence of the church.

References

Adeboye, Enoch Adejare. 1989. *How to Turn Your Austerity to Prosperity.* Lagos, Nigeria: The CRM.

---

[20] For House of Joy Mission/Vision, see: http://houseofjoyng.org/theNGO.htm (accessed January 19, 2012).

Adeboye, Enoch A. 2002. "God of Double Portion." Sermon at the Holy Ghost Service, RCCG Redemption Camp, March 1, Ogun, Nigeria. Retrieved March 2002 (http://rccg.org/Holy_Ghost_Service/Monthly_Holy_Ghost%20Service/mar2002.htm).

Adeboye, Enoch A. 2003. *Open Heavens: A Daily Guide to Close Fellowship with God.* Vol. 4, *Levels of Breakthrough.* Cape Town, South Africa: Struik Christian Books.

Adeboye, Olufunke. 2007. "'Arrowhead' of Nigerian Pentecostalism: The Redeemed Christian Church of God, 1952-2005." *Pneuma* 29 (1): 24-58.

Addendum—Our Poise." N.d. Pp. 39-40 in *The Redeemed Christian Church of God, North America and Caribbean Statement of Fundamental Truths.* Greenville, TX: The Redeemed Christian Church of God.

Adenuga, Olaide. 2004. Interview by Afe Adogame, RCCG/RAPAC Project Manager and Coordinator, November 17.

Adogame, Afe. 2004. "Contesting the Ambivalences of Modernity in a Global Context: The Redeemed Christian Church of God, North America." S*tudies in World Christianity* 10(1): 25-48.

Adogame, Afe. 2007. "HIV/AIDS Support and African Pentecostalism: The Case of the Redeemed Christian Church of God (RCCG)." *Journal of Health Psychology* 12(3): 475-84.

African Missions North America Chapter (AMNA). N.d. "Some of Our Projects Worldwide." Retrieved May 23, 2013 (http://jfccenter.org/AMprojects.html).

Ajayi, Bosun. 2002. Interview by Afe Adogame, RCCG, Bonn, Germany, October 24.

Akande, Laolu. 2003. "Multi-million Dollar Redemption Camp Underway in U.S." *The Guardian*, April 8. Retrieved April 2003 (http://odili.net/news/source/2003/apr/3/100.html).

Akinyoye, Ajibike. 2004. Inteview by Afe Adogame, RCCGNA Headquarters, Dallas, TX, March 9.

Bruni, Frank. 2003. "The Changing Church: Faith Fades Where It Once Burned Strong." *New York Times*, October 13 and 14, p. A1.

Christ Against Drug Abuse Ministry (CADAM). N.d. (http://cadamonline.com/index.html).

Christ Redeemer's Ministry. 2011a. "CRM Hospitality." Retrieved May 23, 2013 (http://city.rccgnet.org/crm.html).

Christ Redeemer's Ministry. 2011b. "Facilities." Retrieved May 23, 2013 (http://city.rccgnet.org/facilities.html).

Christ Redeemer's Ministry. 2011c. "Haggai Estates." Retrieved May 23, 2013 (http://city.rccgnet.org/Haggai_estates.html).

ChristianEbooks.com. N.d. "Christian Disneyland." Retrieved December 6, 2007 (http://www.christianebooks.com/christiandisneyland.htm).

Disneyland Resort. 2013. "Homepage." Retrieved May 23, 2013 (http://www.disneyland.com/).

Farwell, Scott. 2005. "African Church Plans Christian Disneyland." *The Dallas Morning News*, July 17.

Grady, Lee. 2002. "Nigeria's Miracle: How a Sweeping Christian Revival is Transforming Africa's Most Populous Nation." *Charisma and Christian Life* 27(10): 38-41.

House of Joy. 2012. "Mission/Vision." Retrieved January 19, 2012 (http://houseofjoyng.org/theNGO.htm).

Jenkins, Philip. 2002. "A New Religious America." *First Things* (August/September): 25-28.

Jinadu, Comfort. 2011. "Recovery from Drug Dependence: Experiences of Service Users in a Christian Faith-based Agency." Unpublished PhD thesis. Department of Social Work, University of Edinburgh, Edinburgh, UK.

Jubilee Family Christian Center. N.d. "African Missions Projects Worldwide." Retrieved March 24, 2005 (http://jfccenter.org/africa_missions.html).

Lieblich, Julia and Tom McCann. 2002. "Africans Now Missionaries to U.S." *Chicago Tribune*, June 21, p. 1.

Miller, Lisa. 2008. "50 Most Powerful People in the World." *Newsweek Magazine* 153(1): 49.

Ojo, Matthews. 2001. *General Information and Church Planting Manual*, Fall 2001 ed. Greenville, TX: The Redeemed Christian Church of God North America, Inc.

Oyitso, Brown. 2004. Interview by Afe Adogame, RCCG Provincial Pastor, Victory House Parish, Festac Town, Lagos, Nigeria, September 6.

Redeemed AIDS Programme Action Committee (RAPAC). (http://www.rccgrapac.org/main.htm).

The Redeemed Christian Church of God (RCCG). 2002/2003. "A Brief History of the Redeemed Christian Church of God." *Sunday School Manual, The Redeemed Christian Church of God, 2002/2003 Edition*, p. 127.

The Redeemed Christian Church of God. 2004. Retrieved March 25, 2011 (http://www.rccg.org).

The Redeemed Christian Church of God. N.d. "RCCG Fundamental Beliefs." Retrieved March 2012 (http://home.rccg.org/ChurchHistory/Fundamental Beliefs3.htm).

The Redeemed Christian Church of God. N.d. "UK Parish Web Sites." Retrieved June 2012 (http://www.jesus-house.org.uk/ and http://www.rccgarea4.org.uk/).

The Redeemed Christian Church of God Internet Outreach. N.d. Retrieved October 4, 2012 (http://main.rccg.org/parish_directory/parish_directory_main.htm).

The Redeemed Christian Church of God, North America. 2003a. "RCCG: Past, Present and Future: The Structure, Administration and Finance of the Redeemed Christian Church in North America." 7th Annual RCCG North America Convention Program, Dallas, TX: RCCGNA Headquarters, June 18-20, pp. 15 and 30.

The Redeemed Christian Church of God, North America. 2003b. "The Latter Rain." 7th Annual RCCG North American Convention Program, Dallas, June 18-20.

The Redeemed Christian Church of God, North America. 2008. "Parish Directory." Retrieved September 5, 2008 (http://www.rccgna.org/login/pdirectory.asp?offset=0 and http://www.rccgna.org/bocus.asp).

The Redeemed Christian Church of God, North America (RCCGNA). 2012a. Retrieved April 10, 2012 (http://www.rccgna.org/zones.asp).

The Redeemed Christian Church of God, North America (RCCGNA). 2012b. "Church Origins." Retrieved April 10, 2012 (http://www.rccgna.org/TheChurch/Origin.aspx).

The Redeemed Christian Church of God, North America (RCCGNA). 2012c. "Find a Parish." Retrieved June 15, 2012 (http://www.rccgna.org/Provinces/Search.aspx).

The Redeemed Christian Church of God Parish Directory Worldwide. N.d. "Parish Directory Worldwide." Retrieved April 10, 2012 (http://www.rccgnet.org/dir/RCCG_World_Wide/).

The Redeemed Christian Church of God Redemption Camp. 2011. "About Redemption Camp." Retrieved May 23, 2013 (http://city.rccgnet.org/about_redemption.html).

Sengupta, Somini and Larry Rohter. 2003. "Where Faith Grows, Fired by Pentecostalism." *The New York Times*, October 13, p. A5. Retrieved May 24, 2013 (http://www.nytimes.com/2003/10/14/world/where-faith-grows-fired-by-pentecostalism.html?pagewanted=all&src=pm).

Shorimade, Samuel. 2003. Interview by Afe Adogame, RCCG Cornerstone Worship Centre for All Nations parish, Cambridge, MA, November 23.

The United Nations Office on Drugs and Crime (Nigeria). 2004. "Christ Against Drug Abuse Ministry." Retrieved August 2013 (http://www.unodc.org/ngo/showSingleDetailed.do?req_org_uid=1372).

Wellspring Rehabilitation Centre. 2003. "Curriculum for Recovery and Social Re-integration." Wellspring Rehabilitation Centre, Lagos, Nigeria.

Chapter 3
The Gulen Movement: Sunni Islam

Helen Rose Ebaugh

The Gulen movement is a faith initiated non-political, cultural, and educational movement that began in Turkey in the 1970s and is dedicated to providing opportunity for the new generation of youth in Turkey and in the Turkish diaspora. Today it is a vibrant transnational movement involving between 8 million and 10 million participants who have built quality schools, hospitals, media outlets, relief organizations, and interfaith dialog centers in over 180 counties on five continents. The movement focuses on the spiritual and intellectual consciousness of the individual, seeking to form an inner self that will empower the person to effect change in society. It stresses the role that technology and new global networks can play in articulating a Muslim consciousness. The Gulen-inspired network community, therefore, differentiates itself from other Islamic groups by stressing Turkish nationalism, the free market, modern education, democracy, and peaceful co-existence.

History of the Movement

Mr. Fethullah Gulen, the inspiration behind the movement, was an imam in Turkey who, in the 1960s and 1970s, began preaching in mosques, in coffeehouses, and public areas in Izmir, as well as throughout the villages in the Aegean region in Turkey. He was born in 1941 in Erzurum, a small village in eastern Turkey, into a very pious family. His father was an imam and a scholar who instilled in Fethullah a love for learning, not only of the Qur'an but also of literary and philosophical works (Ebaugh 2010). He was influenced by the Sufi master Said Nursi, who taught that Muslims should not reject modernity but find inspiration in the Islamist texts to engage with it. The basic goals of the Nursi movement were: a synthesis of Islam and science; an acceptance of democracy within the rule of law; raising an awareness of the connections between reason and revelation; and achieving salvation within a free market and through quality education. These Nursi ideas greatly influenced the thought of Fethullah Gulen.

Mr. Gulen grew up in the political and religious atmosphere created by Mustafa Kemal Ataturk who is credited as the "father" of the modern republic of Turkey, which he masterminded in 1923. One of the principles of Kemalism, as it came to be known, was secularism, based on the French model of state control of religion (Yavuz and Esposito 2003). Ataturk and his followers argued that the traditional customs of Islam, such as sharia law, the madrasas (Islamic schools), the covering of women and the fez of the men, as well as the use of the Arabic alphabet and language, were major factors prohibiting the modernization of Turkey. To counter these forces he argued that the state must take control of religion in society. He closed the traditional Sufi orders of monks, outlawed the fez and the veil, replaced the Arabic alphabet with Latin, closed the madrasas (religious schools), and removed Islam from the constitution as the official state religion of Turkey. Religion was outlawed from the public sphere and made a private matter. The principle of secularism replaced Islam in the Constitution (Ebaugh 2010).

This is the political and social atmosphere in which Mr. Gulen became an imam, hired and paid by the state, to service the private practice of Islam in the state-owned mosques, a situation that still exists in Turkey today. Even the sermons of the imams continue to be strongly regulated by a weekly brief from the state office of the Directory of Religious Affairs. In 1966, Mr. Gulen was assigned to Izmir, a thriving industrial city in the Aegean region of Turkey, where he was assigned a mosque. It was during these years in Izmir, at the same time that many youth movements—for example, nationalism, socialism, and communism—were attempting to recruit the youth in Turkey to their causes that Mr. Gulen began to develop his ideas on education and service. He did not restrict his preaching to the mosques but began to preach in coffeehouses, on town squares, and anywhere he could find an audience both in Izmir and surrounding villages. Over the course of several years, increasing numbers of people listened to Mr. Gulen's sermons and began to resonate with the ideas he advocated (Cetin 2009).

Goals of the Movement

The combating of ignorance and poverty through education became a major motif of Mr. Gulen's preaching and activism. Education, he argued, is the answer to becoming a productive and contributing individual in society. Likewise, it is the means by which people become the true beings that God created them to be.

He saw three forms of education that enhance and complement one another to create a whole human being: science, humanities, and religion (Aslandogan and Cetin 2006). Rather than seeing conflict between science and religion, he viewed them as complementary. A faith-based world-view provides a comprehensive and sound narrative that can support and give meaning to secular learning. The best knowledge, he argued, enables people to connect happenings in the outer world to their inner experiences (Gulen 1998). He also rejected religion as blind faith and criticized people who fail to use their reason to understand the observable universe. He therefore saw the necessity of combining faith and reason.

Mr. Gulen criticized the *madrasas* (religious schools) and the *takyas* (traditional Islamic institutions of education) for not meeting the needs of modern society as they fail to integrate science and technology into their traditional criteria. As a result, he repeatedly said that Turkey needed secular schools, not more *madrasas* or mosques. Likewise, the secular schools were failing their students by not providing them with spiritual and ethical values. He therefore proposed an educational system that integrates science and ethical values.

In the 1980s, Mr. Gulen also began emphasizing interfaith and intercultural dialog as a major need in modern society. He anticipated the rapidly emerging global aspect of Turkey, as well as the rest of the world, and argued for the need for various groups in society to understand one another and work together toward "common human values." He often referred to the harmonious inter-religious relationships that existed in the Ottoman Empire where Christians, Jews, and other religious groups, such as the Zoroastrians, lived together in peace. As a testimony to the importance of religious and ethnic tolerance and understanding, he met with Pope John Paul II and the Greek Orthodox Patriarch Bartholomew, even though some young Islamists criticized him for these actions. He quoted the Prophet Muhammed as saying there is no superiority of Arabs or non-Arabs but that Islam gives the same value to all humans who are called to be servants of the Most Compassionate One (Saritoprak and Griffith 2005).

Repeatedly, Mr. Gulen promoted the idea that Turkey could serve as a bridge between the Muslim world and the West. Just as Turks played an important role in the Ottoman Empire, Turkey is now poised to lead the Muslim world into the globalized twentieth and twenty-first centuries with emphasis on tolerance, dialog, science and education (Sevendi 2008). He promotes a progressive Islam in which Muslim nations are able to engage the world with science, education, philosophy, social sciences, and technology. Because of its strategic location between East and West, and its democratic system of government, he sees Turkey as the leader in the Muslim world to bridge the gap between East and West.

He also strongly criticized the use of Islam to justify terrorism. Ten days after the attacks of 9/11 on the World Trade Towers and the Pentagon, he took out an advertisement in the *Washington Post* condemning the attacks and asserting that terrorism is incompatible with the teachings of the Prophet and the religion of Islam (Gulen 2001). He argued that Islam abhors acts of terror and that a religion that professes "He who unjustly kills one man kills the whole of humanity" cannot condone the senseless killing of thousands. He maintained that no terrorist can be a Muslim and no real Muslim can be a terrorist.

While Mr. Gulen continuously advises his supporters not to become involved in politics and does not advocate an Islamic political system in Turkey, he firmly believes that religion should not be confined to the private sphere but should be part of public life. He sees that the domination of religious affairs by the state harms Islam and, hence, religion must be freed from state control and people should be free to worship openly as they choose. He openly accepts the legitimacy of the secular state while asking for religious freedom under it (Gulen 1995). His goal is not to reorient the state in terms of Islamic precepts but to stress a state that does not interfere in the free exercise of religion while taking advantage of the power of faith in combating social ills such as violence and drugs.

He is also a strong advocate of democracy and argues that democracy is the most appropriate and effective form of government in the globalizing world. In his view, democracy and Islam are completely compatible. He is quoted as saying, "Ninety five percent of Islamic rules deal with private life and the family. Only five percent deals with matters of the state, and this could be arranged only within the context of democracy" (Gulen 1995). He goes on to advocate that people respect the government and express opposition through the vote.

Services Provided

During his early years in Izmir, a group of local businessmen were inspired by Mr. Gulen's insistence on the importance of educating youth and offered to finance the projects he was advocating. First, summer camps were begun for middle and high school youth where secular subjects, for example, history and biology, were taught along with principles of Islam.

At this point in Turkish history, private schools were illegal and only public schools existed. Many Anatolian people, especially from rural areas of Turkey, feared to send their children to the high schools and universities in the cities because of the often violent youth movements that existed there, along with problems of drugs and crime. To encourage parents to allow their children to attend educational institutions, movement supporters began to establish "light houses," dormitories where children could attend school but live in an atmosphere that was removed from the politicized environment. Local university students were encouraged to tutor the students in the dormitories both in secular subjects and in living by Islamic principles. These service projects—for example, summer camps and "light houses"—had the consequence of introducing more young people to Mr. Gulen's ideas and goals for Turkey and were the solid beginnings of the global social movement inspired by him. Many of these same young people became the subsequent teachers in the schools and leaders within local groups that formed around his ideas.

Universal university exams were, and still are, required of all high school seniors in Turkey who aspire to attend university. Rates of passing these exams were very low and, hence, few students had the opportunity to be university educated. In 1974, Mr. Gulen was posted in Manisa, Turkey, where he began the first university preparatory courses in an attempt to prepare ordinary Turkish children for higher education. Until this time, it was almost totally the children of wealthy families who were given adequate preparation for these exams and who qualified to enter university.

In the early 1980s, Turgut Ozal was elected president of Turkey and initiated policies that stressed foreign investment and globalization of the Turkish economy. He also allowed the entrepreneurial skills of the Turkish businessmen to grow, leading to a growing middle class in Turkey. His neo-liberal policies allowed the expression of Islam in public places such as the media and resulted in the development of religiously sponsored radio and television stations, print media, and charitable, non-profit organizations. He deregulated broadcasting and empowered Islamic voices such as those in the Gulen movement to express themselves on radio stations and television, and in the print media. No doubt, these policies gave greater visibility to the movement with the evolution of *Zaman* newspaper, boasting today of having the largest newspaper readership in Turkey, the subsequent development of *Zaman Today*, the English version, and translations of the newspaper in numerous languages all over the world where Turks now live. In 1993, Samanyolu Television was launched with commitment to family-oriented programs with no explicit sexuality or violent crime.

Another policy change initiated by President Ozal was the establishment of private schools. In 1982, the first two Gulen-inspired high schools were opened, financed by businessmen in the movement. In the following decades hundreds more schools were opened throughout Turkey. These schools follow the state curriculum and teach only one hour of world religions per week. Many of the teachers are supporters in the movement who followed Mr. Gulen's advice to attend schools of education to provide the youth of Turkey a quality education. As a result, the teachers are highly motivated and routinely put in many more hours than a normal workday, tutoring and mentoring students, many of whom live in the dormitories that are attached to the majority of the schools.

The schools emphasize science, math, and the latest technological advances such as computer laboratories, as well as the inclusion of social sciences and fine arts. The fact that each year many students in these schools win the top prizes in the international science Olympiads attests to the quality of the schools. They have a reputation in Turkey for being among the best in the country. Because of the decentralized structure of the movement (to be discussed later), there is no accurate count of the number of Gulen-inspired schools in Turkey today, but the best estimates are that there are over 500 such schools, in addition to the hundreds that now exist outside of Turkey.

In 1994, Fatih University, located outside Istanbul, opened its doors, financed by a "founding foundation" that consisted of supporters of the Gulen movement. Today, tuition fees are sufficient to run the university in terms of operating costs. However, Turkish law is such that buildings cannot be constructed with tuition money, rather foundations must raise the money for such expenditures. Many Gulen supporters continue to make contributions to the foundation for the physical upkeep and expansion of the university. There are also universities today in other countries such as Azerbaijan and the United States.

There are also at least six private hospitals in Turkey that provide top quality health care. Even though Turkey has universal health care, it does not cover all expenses incurred in private hospitals. Some people are able to afford out-of-pocket expenses, but many others are not able to do so. For these patients, often their medical bills are covered by Gulen supporters. For example, recently doctors from these hospitals travelled to southeastern Turkey to provide medical exams and vaccinations for people there, especially to Kurds in need of health care. Those who required hospitalization were transported to one of the Gulen-supported hospitals where they were treated at no cost to themselves.

Organizational Structure

The Gulen movement has no central headquarters or formal organizational chart as is characteristic of bureaucracies. Rather, it is a non-hierarchical, networked group with locally organized groups of supporters who provide both the finances and labor involved in meeting organizational goals in the local area. The majority of supporters are united by diligently reading *Zaman* newspaper, watching Samanyolu Television and keeping abreast of the website that records the sermons and commentaries of Mr. Gulen. However, there is no equivalent of the Vatican or Aga Khan Foundation headquarters that sends out directives or organizes service projects around the world.

Each local group elects presidents and coordinators of various projects such as the local dialog society, the Turkish cultural center, a superintendent, and principals of local schools. These local organizations also have secretaries and project coordinators who organize meetings and events and solicit volunteers for different activities. However, while some individuals emerge with informal influence, there is no formal leader or president who is in charge of the local group. The organizational concept of "chapter" responsible to a "higher" formal authority is totally foreign in this movement. Rather, individuals stay connected with others in the movement largely through social networks that formed during university years in Turkey as friends during their formative history in Turkey or through attendance at Gulen conferences.

The success of Gulen-inspired projects relies on the *cemaats* and *sohbets* that were familiar to practicing Muslims in Turkey. After the formation of the Republic and the outlawing of Sufi orders and Islamic schools, practicing Muslims, who wanted to preserve the Islamic heritage while adapting to modernity, formed circles (*cemaats*) around scholars and intellectuals who promoted the practice of Islam in the new modern Republic. Within these *cemaats* were *sohbets* or "local circles" of people who met regularly to read Qu'ranic commentary, to share ideas and needs of people in the group, and to determine service projects that the group chose to support financially. It is in these local groups that individuals experience the solidarity of the movement and function both to demonstrate commitment but also to generate commitment of supporters (Ebaugh 2010).

Mr. Gulen encouraged *sohbets* for those inspired by his ideas to discuss their relevance for contemporary Turkish society. These circles were based either on residential location or on the sharing of education and/or jobs. These *sohbets* also had business repercussions, since assisting one another by networking is one reason the Gulen community in Turkey is one of the richest and most successful in the country. Being part of the movement often provides a ready-made source for both networking among businessmen and consumers of business products. In addition, organizing on the basis of professions, occupational groups, or people who share interests also promotes recruitment.

To further promote relationships and contacts among businessmen in the movement, the highly successful TUSKON organization that draws many Gulen supporters establishes contacts and networks of members around the world. In 2007, TUSKON invited hundreds of African businessmen to Istanbul to discuss best business practices and to help them network with businessmen in Turkey and globally where the movement has a strong business presence.

As the movement spread from Turkey to become a global movement, the same organizational model was replicated in each locale. The organization grew informally in each area as Turkish people who were inspired by Mr. Gulen discovered one another, joined together in *sohbets* for mutual support, and determined which local needs existed in each locale. The model was established in the early days of the movement in Turkey as Mr. Gulen and his earliest followers met together informally to address local needs, rather than to develop an elaborate organization to focus on service projects.

Many individuals whom I have met in my study of the group globally—such as people in Melbourne, Azerbaijan, Madrid, and Brussels—did not know anyone in the Houston, Texas community (United States), even though they knew that there was a vibrant group of Gulen supporters there who had built a new dialog center and were establishing the first North American University. This was gleaned primarily through a website. Everywhere I met the movement, people were very sophisticated in computer technology and maintained attractive and up-to-date websites. These websites are carriers of information for the entire networked group.

Finances

In order to finance the quality schools, as well as a growing number of private hospitals, private universities, a media conglomerate of over 35 outlets (the Journalists and Writers Foundation) and Kimse Yok Mu (a disaster relief non-profit association), Mr. Gulen called forth the spirit of giving and hospitality that is deeply embedded in Turkic-Islamic culture (Ebaugh 2010; Fuller 2008; Park 2007; Yavuz and Esposito 2003). He called on everyone inspired by his ideas to support the service activities according to their unique abilities. In particular, he advocated private enterprise and encouraged businessmen and entrepreneurs to grow their businesses, make them wealthy, and then use some of the proceeds to finance the service projects.

Financial giving is an inherent characteristic of participants in the movement. Motivated by traditional Turkish hospitality and by the requirement in Islam that one helps one's neighbor in need, everyone involved in the movement makes some kind of financial contribution. The amount of donations varies from 5 percent to 20 percent of yearly income, with 10 percent being an average (Ebaugh 2010).

A small group of businessmen give substantially more, frequently dividing their annual profits into thirds: one third back into the business, one third for living expenses, and one third as charitable contributions to projects of the movement.

Typically, local businessmen, both in Turkey and in the global diaspora, establish a non-profit foundation to meet the varying needs that are identified in the local population. They put up the initial money to build necessary buildings and launch the project, such as a local school or hospital. Gradually, through tuition or fees the project becomes more or less independent and the businessmen move on to another project either locally or in another country.

In addition to the amounts of money that are contributed by supporters, another important contribution is the volunteer labor of supporters to every project that is launched. Teachers in the schools provide many more hours of service than is required by their contracts, including tutoring, supervising in the dormitories, and preparing students for competitions. Doctors and nurses donate services for people who cannot afford them. Women spend endless hours preparing food for various gatherings, such as dialog events and festivals, and much of the labor for events is donated by volunteers in the movement.

Despite the fears of some critics who assert that the movement is financed by governments such as Saudi Arabia or Iran, or by the American CIA, my research (Ebaugh 2010) indicates, based on extensive interview materials, that it is the supporters within the movement who are financing the projects both in Turkey and globally. In some instances outside of Turkey, governments provide assistance to these projects, such as in Azerbaijan, where the government provided the land and dilapidated original building for the first school. Likewise, in Melbourne, the government provides some grant support to all private schools, and the Gulen-inspired schools get their share of these monies. However, with a few such exceptions, it is primarily the supporters themselves who provide both the financial support and the in-kind services that maintain the numerous projects.

Global Spread of the Movement

Until the late 1980s, the Gulen-related institutions were isolated to Turkey. However, with the fall of the Soviet Union in 1989, Mr. Gulen began to preach that it was now time to expand schools and other educational projects to the former Soviet countries, especially those with largely Turkic populations in Central Asia (Balci 2003). He argued that the collapse of the Soviet Union and the recent independence of these countries would leave a gap in influence, especially in terms of the youth, and that it was essential to instill in young people modern educational skills along with good human values. In 1992, the first Gulen-related private school opened in Azerbaijan where today there are 15 such schools, 11 *dershanes* or teaching centers, which prepare students for university exams, and a university that offers programs based on Mr. Gulen's philosophy and Azerbaijan national educational curricula.

Shortly after the beginning of the school in Azerbaijan, a school was opened in Kyrgyzstan (Keles 2007) and in 1993, the first of seven opened in Turkmenistan (Clements 2007). These schools stressed science, math, and computer technology. Throughout the former Soviet Republics, groups of Turkish people also began English courses, dialog societies, and, in the case of Turkmenistan, the International Turkmen-Turkish University (See also Balci 2003).

Due to the lack of central organization of the movement, it is impossible to count how many supporters there are around the world or how many schools/educational institutions/dialog societies or other service projects exist. I am currently tracing the movement in a number of countries (Azerbaijan, Denmark, Belgium, the UK, Australia, Spain, Germany, and Ireland) and what follows is a description of some patterns I have observed regarding the carriers of the movement globally, adaptations to local conditions and changes over time in the global movement.

In 1993, the first school associated with the movement opened in Copenhagen, Denmark, with nine schools now in operation, including one high school. Summer camps for youth, built on the Turkish model that Mr. Gulen initiated in the 1970s, are also now operative in Denmark. An active dialog society in Copenhagen provides programs for interfaith dialog.

In 1997, almost twenty-five years after the first wave of Turks migrated to Melbourne, Australia, the first Gulen-inspired school, Isik high school, opened there. Today there are 16 such schools in Australia with over 6,000 students enrolled, located both in Victoria and on the opposite coast (Adelaide and Perth). In addition, two major dialog societies exist: the Australian Intercultural Society (AIS) in Melbourne and the Affinity Intercultural Foundation in Sydney. There is also a *Zaman Australian* newspaper associated with the movement and the *Dialogue Australian Pacific*, an interfaith magazine inspired by Gulen supporters.

In Brussels, Belgium, there are four schools inspired by the movement, two Flemish-speaking and two French-speaking. In 2010, the Intercultural Dialog Platform was organized with the purpose of relating to the European Union and to the European Commission. The Golden Rose, a very active association of women involved in the movement, organizes daycare for women who want to be more active in programs offered by the movement, including seminars, workshops, and classes in, for example, computer technology, English, and parenting, not only for movement women but also for the larger public.

There is one main school in London, located in the Turkish subdivision with mostly Turkish students, 90 of them at present. It was opened in 1999 when the government first allowed private schools to open. Given that there are not a large number of wealthy Turkish businessmen in London but, rather, small shop owners and blue-collar workers, it has been difficult to garner enough financial resources to support more schools that are expensive to operative with an insufficient number of students who can afford private school tuition. Supporters in the movement are able to support supplementary courses such as tutoring, mentoring, and preparation for university exams. In 1999, the first dialog society was also organized in London with a current board with members from a variety of faith traditions as well as several proclaimed atheists/agnostics.

Germany follows a similar pattern as London since the early "guest workers" from Turkey who were lured to Germany after World War II (WWII) with assurances of jobs and incentives to work there had no intention of staying. However, some sixty years later, the third and fourth generations of Turkish workers are German citizens, speak German and often no Turkish, and have no desire to return to Turkey. However, because of the discrimination that Turks have experienced in Germany, and still are experiencing, in schools, and workplaces, the majority of Turks have found it impossible to achieve social mobility (Karakoyun 2009). Many of the young people who break out of the cycle and obtain university and higher degrees find it very difficult to get professional jobs and are forced to go to Turkey where such employment is possible. The 3.5 million Turks in Germany, therefore, have historically been of lower social status with limited financial means and unable to support schools. It was only in 2004 that the first Gulen-inspired school was opened in Berlin. Today, there are 26 such schools in Germany, with almost exclusively Turkish students, since Germans do not want their children attending a school with predominantly Turkish students.

While there is no Gulen-inspired school in Spain, there are several dialog societies, one in Madrid and one in Barcelona. The dialog society is attempting to work with public authorities to attract more Turkish businessmen to Spain which members hope will eventuate in the finances to open a private school inspired by the movement. A similar situation exists in Ireland where there are very few Turks living among the 6.4 million citizens (estimates vary from 750 to 2,500). The first Turks came in the late 1990s as workers for the GAMA construction company, which later went bankrupt and forced many of the workers to return to Turkey for employment. NITECA, the dialog society in Belfast, has fewer than 20 core members and the Ireland Dialog Society in Dublin, likewise, is small.

In the United States, the movement is growing mainly in terms of students who came to obtain graduate degrees and businessmen who see the United States as a favorable business environment. All of the major cities and many smaller places have active interfaith/intercultural dialog societies. In the past ten years the Gulen-related schools proliferated rapidly, especially in Texas where they first opened as charter schools, which are approved by state legislatures and publicly financed. Known as Harmony Schools, they are primarily located in disadvantaged neighborhoods, draw students from local neighborhoods, follow the state curriculum, and are frequently rated among the best schools in the area.

Based on my research on the global spread of the Gulen movement to the countries mentioned above (Azerbaijan, Australia, Denmark, Belgium, the UK, Spain, Ireland, and the United States), I will describe ways in which patterns differ in how the movement spreads across borders and how it adapts to local cultures.

Carriers of the Movement

How a movement is first introduced into a country makes a significant difference in the development of the movement in that country. In terms of my data, there are three patterns: In Azerbaijan and Belgium, businessmen came to the areas, opened businesses there, and began to meet with local politicians, power brokers, and neighborhood residents to talk about the needs of the community and how they could be addressed. In Azerbaijan, a wealthy merchant from Turkey heard Mr. Gulen preach about the need to open schools in the Central Asian countries once they gained their independence from the Soviet Union, sold everything he owned, bought an old bus, and drove, with his family, to Azerbaijan to open the first school. He solicited both funds from fellow Turkish businessmen and Turkish teachers to begin the school in 1992. The Azerbaijan government donated the land and an old building, but the Turkish community provided renovation funds and capital for the first several years. A local educational minister supported the businessman's efforts and facilitated the school project.

In the United States, it was graduate students who introduced the movement in the country and continue to constitute the leadership in the movement, even after graduating and becoming professors or white-collar workers. As a result, in the United States members of the movement are overwhelmingly professional workers.

In Melbourne, on the other hand, the second pattern was apparent. The first supporter of the movement arrived in Australia in 1981, along with the first wave of rural migrants from Turkey. He knew no one in the country who identified with the movement. However, by the end of the 1980s, he established the first small group who studied the ideas and works of Mr. Gulen and met in small local circles to form a community of supporters. In 1985, he met with local police officials and started the New Generation Youth Association to address the growing concerns of delinquency among second generation Turks in Melbourne. The association became well recognized and appreciated for its ability to lower the crime rate among youth in the area (Barton 2008). In 1987, the pioneer started the Light Training Center, a free tuition center in inner city Melbourne for Muslim students. Modest funds came from the local Turkish community with almost no assistance from businessmen in Turkey. In 1992, Mr. Gulen visited the community and brought some funds from Turkish businessmen. With the improved social status of the second wave of Turkish immigrants in the 1990s, more local contributions came forth and the first private school opened in Melbourne in 1997.

A similar pattern exists in London where the Turkish immigrants are the working poor and have few resources to contribute to movement activities. The merchants tend to be small kebob-shop owners with very few rich businessmen behind the movement. As a result, only one school currently exists in the city with only 90 students, all Turkish, from the local Turkish residential area. There are about 500 "supplementary" courses that focus on tutoring and mentoring for the university exam and charge minimal fees for attendance.

Spain and Ireland represent the third pattern in regard to the effects of different carriers on the process of global spread of a movement. The Gulen movement is definitely a Turkish-rooted movement that relies on the labor force, financial support, and involvement of Turkish people for its success. For various reasons, there are very few Turkish immigrants in Spain (estimates are approximately 500,000), and in Ireland, and, of those, even fewer are wealthy businessmen, due to the poor economy of Spain compared to other European countries and to the current depressed economic conditions in Ireland. In addition, during the reign of Franco, Spain was a closed country in terms of entrepreneurship. There is also little Spanish taught in Turkey, so immigrants are not prepared for language challenges. As a result, there are no Gulen-inspired schools in Spain or in Ireland, and the dialog societies are very small in terms of core members.

Variations in the carriers that transport the movement across borders, therefore, result in very different trajectories of the movement in different countries. These differences have implications not only for the success of the movement globally but also in ways in which adaptations occur in terms of local cultures, social and political structures, and local, community environments.

Adaptations to Local Environs

One major way in which the movement adapts to local environments relates to varying political structures. This is especially evident in the types of schools that are created as well as their financing. In Turkey, the Gulen-inspired schools are all private schools that utilize the state curriculum. In Azerbaijan, they are also private schools, even though the government helps to maintain their operation in terms of building upkeep and utilities. In Australia, all private schools are funded to get them started and then via grants for various projects. Likewise, in Denmark the government pays 80 percent of school expenses for students, and parents are responsible for the remaining 20 percent. In Germany, after the first 3-5 years of self-support, a school becomes a public school and the government provides 95 percent of funding. Currently, the private school in London does not receive any government funding even though the current school administration is applying for some government grant money. In the United States, virtually all the schools are charter schools that are publicly funded.

Interactions with local politicians also vary by regional context. In London, for example, the dialog society has significant relationships with members in the House of Lords and in the local government offices. During a recent visit to London, I spent several days meeting with government officials to discuss ways in which the Gulen movement can provide a model for local community organizing, a major thrust of the current Cameron government. Likewise, in Brussels the International Dialog Platform is organized to relate to members of the European Union and the European Commission. In Melbourne, the dialog society has close relationships with the provincial governor and the local enforcement agencies (Barton 2008).

In the United States, the movement often invites local and state officials to speak and be part of an intercultural trip to Turkey. The Gulen Institute in Houston, Texas (United States) also organizes a youth essay contest on a politically or socially relevant issue, along with United Nations sponsorship.

Critics of the Movement in the Media

A social movement, by definition, challenges the status quo and has to deal with media that are not sympathetic or sometimes hostile to the movement's message (Goodwin and Jasper 2009). There will be people, often in influential positions, that are threatened by protests or arguments for change in the system. Since movements are, by nature, ideological in that they are rooted in philosophies, political outlooks, or religious principles, there will be some individuals and interest groups that object to a movement that advocates change. Interest in new or unfamiliar movements also attracts media attention as newsworthy and often the media is especially alert to any potential problems that a movement might pose. Leaders in a movement often feel obligated to respond to media reports, especially to inaccuracies or accusations that are unwarranted.

The Gulen movement, both in Turkey and around the world, has its critics, often outspoken and vociferous, some of whom have gained the attention of major news media. Briefly, I will summarize the four major criticisms, based on my interviews with a sample of critics, in Turkey and Houston, Texas (United States), as well as my reflections on the criticisms based on my interviews with members in the movement and observations in the institutions supported by the movement.

Fear of an Islamic State

The most often repeated criticism, both in my interviews and in the media in Turkey and the United States, is the fear that Mr. Gulen is building a base of supporters to overturn the secularism introduced by Ataturk when the republic was created. Frequently, the fear is related to the overthrow of the Shah in Iran by Ayatollah Khomeini in 1979. Many critics point to an infiltration of top government and military positions by Gulen supporters with the aim of an eventual coup to take over the secular government.

Based on numerous of Mr. Gulen's speeches and writings, as well as interviews with over a hundred of his supporters, I saw no evidence of such a coordinated effort or intention on the part of the movement. Given that a significant percentage of Turkish citizens are supporters of the movement, there is no doubt that some people in government and military positions are attracted to movement goals and activities. However, I saw no concerted efforts to form a political party or interest group for political aims. Rather than a political movement, I view the Gulen movement as a social, civic movement that aims to change the hearts and minds of people toward greater tolerance, social responsibility, and modernization in terms of educational and scientific goals. Mr. Gulen advocates greater freedom to practice religion in public places rather than strict control by the state. However, he repeatedly argues that people must respect government, be loyal citizens, and be proud of their Ottoman heritage.

Mr. Gulen Is a Pawn of the United States

A second fear is that Mr. Gulen, who now lives in the United States and has been issued a "green card" that legitimizes his stay here, is supported financially by the United States government, especially the Central Intelligence Agency, in hopes that this "moderate" Islamic movement will dominate the Middle East and be a challenge to radical Islam. A major focus of my research in Turkey on the movement was on the finances of the movement. Based on empirical data (for example, interviews with CEOs and executive officers in Gulen-inspired institutions, review of financial records, and interviews with major donors to the movement), I found no empirical evidence to support this contention.

In addition, for six years a court case against Mr. Gulen was pending in the Turkish courts. Prosecutors pored over numerous documents in an attempt to bring evidence of wrong doing against Mr. Gulen and the movement. In 2007, the case was dismissed on the basis of lack of evidence. In addition, over the past several decades Mr. Gulen and the organizations associated with him have been vetted by numerous governmental agencies such as the Turkish Department of the Treasury and the state's prosecution office. No financial transgressions were discovered that would arouse the suspicion that foreign governments were funding the activities.

Taking Turkey Backwards in Its Move Toward Modernization

There is fear among the critics that Mr. Gulen, a devout practicing Muslim, is advocating traditional customs and values that do not support modernization, science, and democracy. However, Mr. Gulen's writings and sermons, as well as what is taught in the schools and practiced in the other Gulen-inspired projects, reflect just the opposite. Repeatedly, he advocates that people be educated, especially in the sciences, to advance democracy and the modernization of Turkey.

The issue of the status of women in the movement has also been the object of criticism since the public "face" of the movement is, in many countries, male dominated. Many women in the movement veil, which is also a controversial issue in some countries and supports a stereotype of the submissive Islamic woman in others. However, the role of women varies in each country in which the movement is active. For example, in Brussels, the Golden Rose Foundation is a leader in providing educational opportunities for women and providing advice to some members of the European Parliament in terms of women and Islam. In Madrid, an educated woman who works for a large computer firm is vice-president of the dialog society and very assertive in organizing public events. In Dublin, women are often more active in dialog and intercultural events than the men. Women serve as masters of ceremony in interfaith and intercultural events in many countries, especially where women speak the language fluently, an issue in those countries who have recently arrived Turkish immigrants in the movement and who have language difficulties.

Accusations of Lack of Transparency

A commonly voiced criticism is that the movement is not publicly transparent but involved in clandestine political activities that belie its stated intentions. However, the "secretiveness" of the movement has not been demonstrated by empirical evidence. Numerous researchers who have studied the movement attest to the fact that gaining access and cooperation has not been a problem. In fact, there is a rapidly expanding social scientific literature evolving on the history, goals, and activities of the movement and no objective evidence of nefarious or suspicious activities.

Changes in the Movement as It Spreads Globally

There is no doubt that the global spread of the movement is creating changes in the goals, membership, and structure of the movement. It is rapidly moving from a gemeinschaft group in which there is much face-to-face interaction among first-generation members who know Mr. Gulen to second- and third-generation youth who do not have the same awe of the founder. Many young people whom I met, for instance, in Germany, do not regularly read the sermons of Mr. Gulen posted on his website. They are not familiar with his biography or his early speeches in Turkey. Rather, they are concerned with current social issues such as education, tolerance, and dialog and want to be socially active in bringing about these goals in society. The fact that there are increasing numbers of such young people in the movement suggests that the death of Mr. Gulen in the not too distant future, given his poor health, will not have the same impact on the movement that frequently happens when a charismatic leader dies. Also, given his humility, his lack of day-to-day involvement in activities of the movement and his insistence that the movement is not "his" but belongs to all the caring people who are supporters, there are many people who have internalized Mr. Gulen's vision and who serve as informal leaders all over the world. Mr. Gulen, as far as anyone close to him knows, has not indicated a successor to his role in the movement and, given the non-hierarchical, network structure in the movement, such would be highly unlikely.

Increasing numbers of younger people in the movement who are second- and third-generation Turks do not have the same network ties to others from Turkey as do older supporters. Rather, they grew up together in the ethnic enclaves and cities where they are now located and, hence, many of them do not have the Turkish identity that is true of older members. Also, many of them were educated and socialized along with non-Turks and have friendship networks outside the Turkish community. This fact, along with the increasing numbers of non-Turks in the many countries in which the movement now has a presence, has implications for the future. One major challenge as the movement becomes more global and less Turkish relates to what I consider the core mechanism for building and sustaining commitment to its goals and values, namely, the *sohbets*, or local circles. All of the *sohbets*, to my knowledge, are conducted in Turkish or at least consist of people with Turkish backgrounds. As increasing numbers of non-Turks are becoming supporters of the movement around the world, the challenge is to open up the *sohbets* to include diversity of membership. This move would function to instill in supporters commitment to the values and goals of the movement.

The status of women within the movement remains an issue as long as organizational leadership is male-dominated, as is the case in many of the countries in which the movement is active. Despite insistence that the women are highly respected by men in the movement and that they are the "backbone" of the movement in so far as men could not do what they are doing without the women taking leadership roles in the family, until structural equality is achieved and the public sees women in top administrative positions, the image of female submission remains an issue. Some recent studies (Curtis forthcoming) show that women in the movement are increasingly engaged in professional careers and obtaining higher educational degrees. However, until women occupy leadership roles on boards and executive committees of Gulen-related institutions and organizations, become principals, university presidents, and heads of the Gulen-inspired hospitals, and are seen as leaders in public events, their public image as equal to men in the movement is jeopardized.

What started with small crowds inspired by the preachings of a humble imam in Turkey has grown into a large global movement that spans many countries on every continent. Inspired by his message, today there are hundreds of schools, dialog societies, newspaper and televisions outlets, relief societies, cultural centers, tutoring centers, and outreach groups attempting to achieve the vision that Mr. Gulen articulated in his numerous sermons, books, and video outlets of creating a world in which people who share "common human values" live together in dialog and peace. The fact that Mr. Gulen is a peace builder in the world today was recognized in 2001 when the World Parliament of Religions honored him, along with the Dali Lama, as outstanding religious leaders of world dialog and peace.

References

Aslandogan, Yuksel A. and Muhammad Cetin. 2006. "The Educational Philosophy of Gulen in Thought and Practice." Pp. 34-61 in *Muslims Citizens of the Globalized World: Contributions of the Gulen Movement*, edited by Robert A. Hunt and Yuksel A. Aslandogan. Somerset, NJ: The Light.

Balci, Bayram. 2003. "Fethullah Gulen's Missionary Schools in Central Asia and their Role in the Spreading of Turkism and Islam." *Religion, State & Society* 31(2): 151-77.

Barton, Greg. 2008. "How the Hizmet Works: Islam, Dialogue and the Gulen Movement in Australia." Paper presented at the Islam in the Age of Global Challenges Conferences, Georgetown, Washington. November, 2008.

Cetin, Muhammad. 2009. *The Gulen Movement: Civic Service Without Borders.* New York: Blue Dome Press.

Clements, Victoria. 2007. "Turkmenistan's New Challenges: Can Stability Co-Exist with Reform? A Study of Gulen Schools in Central Asia, 1997-2007." Paper presented at the Muslim World in Transition: Contributions of the Gulen Movement Conference, London, October 2007.

Curtis, Maria. Forthcoming. "Gender Dimensions of the Gulen Movement: Muslim Women's Public Spheres Yesterday, Today and Tomorrow." In *Gulen in Europe: The Western Journal of a Modern Turkish Muslim Movement.* Edited by Gurkan Celik, Johan Leman, and Karel Steenbrink. Boston, MA: Brill Publishers.

Ebaugh, Helen Rose. 2010. *The Gulen Movement: A Sociological Analysis of a Civic Movement Rooted in Moderate Islam.* Netherlands: Springer.

Fuller, Graham. 2008. *New Turkish Republic: Turkey As a Pivotal State in the Muslim World.* Washington DC: United States Institute of Peace.

Gulen, Fethullah. 1995. Interview by Nuriye Akman, *Sabah*, Borneo, January 27.

Gulen, Fethullah. 1998. *Towards the Lost Paradise.* Izmir, Turkey: Kaynak Basim-Yayin.

Gulen, Fethullah. 2001. Advertisement in the *The Washington Post*, September 21.

Goodwin, Jeff and James Jasper. 2009. "Introduction." Pp. 3-7 in *The Social Movements Reader: Cases and Concepts,* edited by Jeff Goodwin and James Jasper. Malden, MA: Wiley-Blackwell.

Karakoyun, Ercan. 2009. "The Gulen Movement's Contribution towards Integration of Muslims in Germany." Paper presented at the Parliament of World Religions Conference, Melbourne, Australia.

Keles, Ibrahim. 2007. "The Contributions of the Sebat International Education Institutes to Kyrgyzstan." Paper presented at the Muslim World in Transition: Contributions of the Gulen Movement Conference, London.

Park, W. 2007. "The Fethullah Gulen Movement as a Transnational Phenomenon." Pp. 46-58, in *The Muslim World in Transition: Contrbutions of the Gulen Movement*, edited by I. Yilmaz. Conference proceedings. London: Leeds University Press.

Saritoprak, Zeki and Sidney Griffith. 2005. "Fethullah Gulen and the 'People of the Book': A Voice from Turkey for Interfaith Dialog." *Muslim World* 95(3): 329-40.

Sevendi, Nevval. 2008. *Contemporary Islamic Conversations: M. Fethullah Gulen on Turkey, Islam and the West.* New York: State University of New York Press.

Yavuz, M. Hakan and John L. Esposito. 2003. "Introduction—Islam in Turkey: Retreat from the Secular Path?" Pp. xiii-xxxvi in *Turkish Islam and the Secular State: The Gulen Movement*, edited by M. Hakan Yavuz and John L. Esposito. New York: Syracuse University Press.

Chapter 4

Soka Gakkai International: Nichiren Japanese Buddhism

Daniel A. Metraux

Japan's Soka Gakkai is the largest of Japan's many New Religious Movements (NRMs) with a major presence not only in Japan, but also meaningful representation in nearly two hundred foreign countries and territories. This Japan-based Buddhist organization claims ten million members at home and has attracted two million followers abroad through its ability to assimilate into local cultures and to offer doctrines and practices that are universal in their application. Japanese as well as foreign members find the Soka Gakkai's form of Buddhism appealing because it is said to give them a sense of confidence and self-empowerment, permitting them to manage their lives in a more creative and fulfilling manner. Soka Gakkai bases its Buddhism on its interpretation of the doctrines of Nichiren (1222-82), the founder of Japan's only native school of Buddhism. It is largely an urban movement with chapters across every corner of Japan. Its international office, Soka Gakkai International (SGI), coordinates the activities of each of its many autonomous chapters abroad. Founded in the early 1930s, Soka Gakkai grew quickly in the early postwar era and by the 1960s began to sponsor chapters abroad in such areas as Korea, Taiwan, Southeast Asia, North America, and Europe. Today SGI is represented on every continent and has developed a wide following from a broad range of social and economic backgrounds.

SGI chapters abroad were generally started by Japanese members who migrated. The Australian chapter began through the instigation of several Japanese housewives who formed their own group in Sydney and attracted a number of Caucasian friends to join them. Japanese businessmen residing in Canada and Southeast Asia formed early chapters there and quickly found natives eager to join their group. Ethnic Chinese members who joined groups formed by Japanese members in Southeast Asia traveled elsewhere in the region and started new chapters in their new locales. Often Soka Gakkai leaders from Tokyo would travel abroad to areas with local groups to give them encouragement and advice on how to expand their new chapters. Over time, native members came to greatly outnumber ethnic Japanese in many of these international chapters.

There has been a vast expansion of Buddhism in North and South America, Southeast Asia, Europe, India, and Australia-New Zealand in recent decades. Generally there have been two very different forms of this Buddhism, Buddhism brought by ethnic Asian groups that have migrated to the West and groups of

Westerners who are attracted to Buddhism for a whole range of often esoteric ideals. Soka Gakkai International is rather unique in that its many international chapters generally attract a very multi-ethnic and multi-cultural following.

The goal of this chapter is to analyze the expansive growth of a lay Japanese religious organization in Southeast and South Asia, Australia and New Zealand, Europe, parts of Africa, and North America.[1] This paper attempts to address three points: The nature of Soka Gakkai Buddhism, why it has spread to so many different parts of the globe, and why it has attracted such a broad multi-cultural and multi-ethnic following. It is the contention of this writer that the Soka Gakkai movement and its form of Buddhism have become global because they successfully address universal issues that influence all people everywhere and that their emphasis on empowerment of the individual finds a receptive audience in many modern cultures.

After studying Soka Gakkai in Japan from the mid-1970s through the mid-1990s, I conducted research extensively in Canada in the mid-1990s, the early 2000s, and 2010. I made research trips throughout Southeast Asia in the late 1990s, to Australia in 2000, 2002, and 2003, to Cambodia in 2006, and to New Zealand in 2003 and 2011. I conducted modest written surveys in each area as well as in-depth interviews with individual members. It is important to note that these surveys and interviews were conducted with the full cooperation of SGI leaders and only involved a very small percentage of the overall membership. Furthermore, the sampling procedure itself was far from random and the results are not necessarily fully representative of the whole membership. Rather, the findings probably reflect the thinking of the most committed members and not the experiences of less active or disenchanted members. A more random sample might have yielded more statistically valid results, but limits on time and resources placed certain constraints on this research.

The Soka Gakkai Legacy

One of the most interesting developments in Japanese studies has been the widespread diaspora of many of Japan's new religions throughout the world since the 1960s.[2] They have achieved their greatest success in Korea, Taiwan, Hong Kong, Southeast Asia, Brazil, Peru, and the United States, but they also have a presence in Canada, Europe, Africa, and Oceania. SGI, which has the largest following of any Japanese NRM abroad, began organizing foreign chapters in the

---

[1]   Studies of SGI expansion include: Wilson and (1994); Hammond and Machacek (1994); Machacek and Wilson (1994); and Metraux, (1996; 1997; 2001).

[2]   Notably Tenrikyô, Sekai Kyuseikyô, PL Kyôdan as well as Soka Gakkai International have expanded outside of Japan. Work on the expansion of Japanese NRMs abroad includes Susumu (1991) and Inoue 1985).

1960s. Its largest chapters are in Korea, Southeast Asia and Hong Kong, South America, India, Australia, and the United States.[3]

Makiguchi Tsunesaburô (1871-1944), a Japanese educator and devout lay practitioner of Nichiren Shôshû ("True Sect of Nichiren"), founded Soka Gakkai in the 1930s as a support group for his educational ideas. However, by the late 1930s, he and his younger disciple Toda Jôsei (1900-58) had transformed the organization into a lay support group for Nichiren Shôshû, one of several Nichiren Buddhist denominations in Japan. Makiguchi and Toda were imprisoned in 1943 in Tokyo due to their refusal to participate in the government's attempts to rally Japan's religious organizations behind the war effort. Makiguchi died in prison in 1944, but Toda, released in July 1945, rebuilt Soka Gakkai into a major religious organization in the 1950s. Toda's successor, Ikeda Daisaku (b. 1928), expanded Soka Gakkai in Japan and played a key role in SGI's expansion abroad. Ikeda also organized a political party, the Kômeitô, which has maintained close ties to the Soka Gakkai since the late 1960s and has consistently ranked third among Japan's political parties. The Kômeitô was part of a coalition that governed Japan from the late 1990s to 2009.

The realization that Soka Gakkai had become a highly successful lay Buddhist movement with its own strong leadership, which had its independent social and political programs, did not sit well with Nichiren Shôshû, a conservative and traditional Buddhist sect. The fact that the sect's priesthood and Soka Gakkai were going in different directions caused a growing schism by the late 1970s that led to the formal separation of the two organizations by the early 1980s. Today Soka Gakkai, together with its SGI affiliates, is an independent lay religious movement devoid of temples and priests that is dedicated to the propagation of its version of Nichiren Buddhism.

Soka Gakkai grew rapidly in the immediate post-World War II era because its leaders focused on Buddhist teachings that stressed the happiness of self and others in one's immediate environment. Happiness was understood in very concrete terms for millions of dispirited and hungry Japanese: food, health, finding a mate, and securing employment. Later in the 1960s and 1970s, when Japan became more affluent, happiness was defined in more philosophical terms to include "empowerment, character formation, and socially beneficial work" (Seager 2001: 94) The fact that Soka Gakkai is an independent lay religious movement has probably broadened its appeal in an increasingly secular age.

---

[3] According to figures provided to this writer in 2009 by SGI, Soka Gakkai membership in some countries was: Australia, 4,000; Cambodia 1,600. Canada 6,800 (Quebec over 1,000), Taiwan (1998) 200,000, Hong Kong 24,000, Malaysia 60,000, New Zealand 1,800; Philippines 15,500; Singapore, 40,000; South Korea, 700,000-1 million; USA, 150,000-300,000.

The Doctrines of the Soka Gakkai

Soka Gakkai regards itself as the modern successor to Nichiren and sees as its goal the proselytization of Nichiren Buddhism throughout the world.[4] The Soka Gakkai, like other Nichiren denominations, is noted for its focus on the supposed saving powers of the *Lotus Sūtra*[5] and an attendant belief that all people have an innate Buddha nature within them which makes it possible to achieve enlightenment in their current form and present lifetime. Each person, Nichiren noted, carries both the potential for good (Buddhahood) or evil within him. The sad fact of life is that the evil aspects of human nature generally prevail, meaning that life in this world is dominated by greed, hatred, and violence. The goal of Nichiren and Soka Gakkai Buddhism is to bring out the Buddha nature inherent in all humankind, thereby realizing a peaceful and harmonious world. SGI Canada introduces itself on its web page with the following:

> Soka Gakkai International is a global organization devoted to peace, culture and education, based on the humanistic Buddhist philosophy of Nichiren Daishōnin. SGI members represent the full spectrum of society, with members of all ages, ethnic and social backgrounds …
>
> Nichiren Daishōnin[6] … is regarded as the Buddha of the essential teaching, who sought to return to the original spirit of Sākyamuni Buddha as taught in the Lotus Sutra. Its core message is that everyone has the potential to manifest their enlightened nature, as they are in this lifetime.
>
> Just as the lotus blooms in a muddy pond, all people can manifest the Buddha nature--inner resources of courage, wisdom and compassion that can equip them to overcome life's challenges and lead happy and fulfilling lives. As "engaged Buddhists," SGI members aim to create value in any circumstances and contribute to the well-being of others. Their practice sparks a process of ongoing inner transformation and empowerment known as "human revolution." The promotion of peace, culture and education is central to SGI's activities. (http://www.sgicanada.org/about/aboutsgi.html)

Like Nichiren, Soka Gakkai bases its worldview on the idea that humankind today is living in a world plagued by greed and evil and that its only hope of

---

   [4]   The Nichiren school of Buddhism today has over two dozen traditional sects and NRMs such as Soka Gakkai.

   [5]   The *Lotus (Saddharma-pundarīka) Sūtra*, known as *Myōhō-renge-kyō* in Japanese, dates from the first two centuries CE in northwestern India. It was circulated widely in China following Kumarajīva's famous translation into Chinese from Sanskrit in 406 CE and became the main text of the Tiantai school of Chinese Buddhism in the sixth century. It reached Japan by the end of the sixth century and became the key document of the Tendai school of Japanese Buddhism early in the ninth century.

   [6]   *Daishōnin* is an honorific title meaning roughly "great priest."

survival is through its form of Buddhism. Nichiren lived during the Kamakura era (1185-1333), one of the most turbulent periods of Japanese history, during which the country was beset by domestic strife, a series of natural disasters that included massive earthquakes, tsunami, storms, fires and famine, and two attempted invasions by Mongol armies. Many Japanese at the time believed that they were living in the age of *mappō*, understood as the period of the degeneration of the Dharma, when people moved away from the saving truths of Buddhist scripture and turned to evil and violent ways. Nichiren, who himself subscribed to the doctrine of *mappō*, devoted his life to a search for the solution to the ills that had befallen Japan. He predicted natural disasters and social disorder and later foreign invasions and domestic revolts, arguing that Japan was on the verge of catastrophe because of the failure of Japanese to follow the true teachings of the Buddha Śākyamuni found in the *Lotus Sūtra*. The Soka Gakkai insists that humankind is still experiencing *mappō*, but that a peaceful, prosperous, and harmonious world could be realized here and now if everybody everywhere subscribed to its version of Nichiren Buddhism.

SGI's practice centers on chanting the *daimoku*, the phrase *Namu-myōhō-renge-kyō*. This translates roughly as "I commit myself to the wonderful *dharma*," referring to the highest teachings of the Buddha found in the sacred *Lotus Sūtra*. Nichiren taught that chanting the *daimoku* will release the powers of Buddhism within each believer and that this chanting will bring positive benefits to the faithful. Nichiren knew that, while the promise of the Buddha, the salvation of all who honored the teachings of the *Sūtra*, could be readily understood, the actual teachings of the *Sūtra* were so complicated that they were well beyond the capacity of any person to comprehend, so he presented an essential and simple way that even the most illiterate person could demonstrate his faith and embody its glory. That is to utter the title (*daimoku*) of the *Lotus*, *Nam-myōhō-renge-kyō*, "Praise to the Lotus Sūtra of the True Dharma." This chanting of the *daimoku* lies at the core of every Nichiren Buddhist including followers of the Soka Gakkai.

Members daily perform a brief worship ceremony called *gongyō*, chanting the *daimoku* and short segments of the *Lotus Sūtra* before a copy of Nichiren's *Gohonzon* (a scroll on which is written the title of the sutra in Chinese characters). The *Gohonzon* is said to embody the teachings of the true Buddha and contains the power to bring true happiness to those who worship before it. Soka Gakkai describes the transformation of each individual follower as a "human revolution" (*ningen kakumei*). The cumulative effect of many people experiencing these "revolutions" would theoretically be a happier, peaceful, and more harmonious world. Soka Gakkai teaches that through chanting, studying the Lotus Sutra, and proselytizing this message everywhere, the entire world can save itself.

Soka Gakkai's Controversial History

The huge growth and power of the Soka Gakkai has drawn harsh criticism over the years, especially in Japan because of its aggressive proselytization in its early years, its decision to play an active role in politics, and what critics call a personality cult around leader Ikeda Daisaku. Soka Gakkai's practice of *shakubuku* contributed to their rapid growth but alienated many in Japanese society who decried such confrontational methods. *Shakubuku*, "break and subdue," is a very aggressive form of proselytization where the believer attempts to convert a person through forceful arguments and confrontations. SGI chapters in both Canada and the United States also drew criticism in their early years for this method of propagation. There have even been accusations of "brain washing" of new members in Japan and abroad.

Soka Gakkai's emphasis on exclusivity was seen by some as an anomaly by many religious leaders and groups in Japan. There is a tradition followed by some Nichiren schools of not having any relationship with other religious sects or organizations because of the supposed superiority of its own form of Buddhism. Soka Gakkai furthered this tradition of exclusivity in its earlier years, but this criticism has declined considerably since the 1970s when Soka Gakkai and its SGI chapters abroad largely abandoned *shakubuku,* started using gentler, less aggressive methods of recruiting new members, and became more socially engaged and "mainstream" in its recruitment and organizational practices.

Critics say that it is improper for a religious organization to play an active role in politics in that it breaches the separation of religion and state.[7] There have been accusations of political and financial corruption among the higher echelons of Gakkai leadership. Soka Gakkai counters that it uses its political power to enable it to actualize aspects of its social agenda. For example, it promotes itself as a movement fostering world peace and points to its successful efforts to protect Article 9 of Japan's "Peace Constitution" which prohibits rearmament. Nevertheless, Soka Gakkai's active participation in Japanese politics will continue to raise controversy as long as these practices continue. On the other hand, Soka Gakkai's prohibition of any direct political involvement in other countries outside Japan has made SGI far less controversial in other lands.

The adoration that many Soka Gakkai members have for Ikeda has raised many eyebrows. Ikeda is clearly admired by Soka Gakkai members not only in Japan but also in foreign chapters as well. Critics compare this practice to a personality cult. Whether this criticism is warranted or not, the fact remains that Ikeda's articles, lectures, study sessions, activities, and even his photography dominate Soka Gakkai publications often at the expense of news about other organizational members or activities.

Another criticism focuses on reports that early Soka Gakkai leaders such as Toda called the *Gohonzon* a "happiness-manufacturing machine" which could be turned on through chanting.[8] It was said that there were members both in Japan

---

[7]   Other religious organizations often endorse particular candidates or run individual or slates of candidates, but the Soka Gakkai is the only religious group that created its own political party.

[8]   For a discussion of this point, see SGI-UK Study Department, "The Gohonzon" (n.d.).

and in the United States who would "chant for a Cadillac." This criticism implies that Soka Gakkai followers are naive, that their desires are wholly materialistic and superficial, and that they believe in a kind of crude form of superstition.

These criticisms are not without foundation. When I began researching Soka Gakkai in the mid-1970s, there were many reports of members chanting for material goods. Soka Gakkai leaders told me that Toda was simply trying to illustrate the power and value of the *Gohonzon* using very simple terms that poorly educated members would readily understand. They also noted that unfortunately some members did not understand the profundity of Nichiren's teachings. The true purpose of the religion is to help people strive for happiness and to play a role in changing people's character for the better by enhancing their Buddha nature, and that material gains are not the sole benefits one should strive for.

Ikeda Daisaku, Soka Gakkai's spiritual leader, has borne the brunt of many attacks on Soka Gakkai. Ikeda, who is often viewed by both members and critics as a virtual personification of the Soka Gakkai itself, is regarded as a saintly figure by his followers and as a megalomaniac by his harshest critics. Nonetheless, in a 1993 issue of the *Tokyo Journal*, a critic wrote:

> Ikeda Daisaku—statesman, billionaire, god ... Ikeda Daisaku's followers believe he is the earthly incarnation of a saint; those who believe otherwise suffer his god-like wrath. Ikeda Daisaku should be powerful—he has karma on his side. Enough karma to lure over 12 million followers to his radical Buddhist sect ... He is also known as an arrogant and mean-spirited man who taunts Gakkai executives at meetings. Yet his combination of religious aura and political clout has proved devastatingly successful ... Japan's political map is being redrawn, and Ikeda Daisaku—statesman, billionaire, god—seems intent to play his part. (*Tokyo Journal*, 1993: 1)

Supporters of Ikeda, on the other hand, often portray him as a selfless statesman and humanitarian who has devoted his life to the causes of world peace, human understanding, and preservation of environment. They point to his many honorary doctorates from universities around the world, his speeches at the United Nations, and his many "dialogues for peace" with distinguished world leaders and intellectuals like Henry Kissinger and Arnold Toynbee as evidence of Ikeda's high stature (Metraux 1994).

Global Demographics of SGI

There has been a notable demographic change in SGI membership in the West including Canada and in Southeast Asia since the 1960s and 1970s. During the 1960s many members were older women, many of them ethnic Japanese with limited educational backgrounds, but since the early 1980s, SGI chapters in these areas have attracted many more non-ethnic Japanese young adult members in their late twenties and early thirties. Although they represent all socio-economic classes, they are now generally well educated and are split evenly between males and females.

Many of the younger SGI Canadian members I met are university educated and most had embarked on or were planning to enter professional careers. There seems to exist a strong affinity between a religious dogma that emphasizes "mental work" (attitudes and individual focus) and the well-educated who have to work very hard to attain their educational credentials. This phenomenon may also explain why this form of Buddhism is attractive to this particular social stratum and also helps to address why Soka Gakkai's Japanese origin does not seem to matter much to many of its non-Japanese converts. As Wilson and Dobbelaere (1994) found in their research in Great Britain, as Hammond and Machacek (1994) also saw in the United States, and as I found among a largely ethnic Chinese SGI following in Southeast Asia, the ethic of individual success and self-determination has a certain affinity with the experiences of white-collar professionals.

The emphasis of the Soka Gakkai's teachings has shifted somewhat since the immediate postwar era in Japan. At that time many Japanese joined Soka Gakkai because it provided a positive outlook, a promise of happiness, and a sense of community to a fluid, dismayed, and impoverished population, much of it from rural areas but looking to start a new life in cities like Tokyo and Osaka. Members learned that they could find hidden strengths within themselves and that these gains would enhance their ability to get better jobs and a higher standard of living. Today the focus is much more psychological. There is more emphasis on developing the self-confidence of members and on encouraging them to engage themselves more in their activities and communities for the betterment of society.

Today there are perhaps several hundred thousand SGI members in South Korea, between 150,000 and 300,000 members in the United States, 60,000 in Malaysia, 24,000 in Hong Kong, and 40,000 in Singapore. Virtually all of the members in Singapore, Hong Kong, and Malaysia are ethnic Chinese. There are very few ethnic Japanese in any of the SGI chapters I have studied outside of Japan. Membership in the United States includes high numbers of Whites, Blacks, and ethnic Chinese, but only a small number of ethnic Japanese. The same is true for Canada. SGI Australia (4,000 members) and New Zealand (1,000 members) began as mainly white organizations, but today have large numbers of ethnic Southeast Asian Chinese, Koreans, Polynesians, and Indians, as well as white Australian devotees. Indeed, the great ethnic diversity of a great many of SGI's foreign chapters is one of its most notable features.

A critical question is the following: If the Buddhism offered in all foreign chapters is identical in form to that in Japan, why has SGI attracted so many non-ethnic Japanese members abroad? Professor Shimazono Susumu of Tokyo University has suggested several reasons for the success of Japanese NRMs abroad including SGI:

One of the common characteristics of the New Religions is their response to strongly felt needs of individuals in their daily lives, their solutions to discord in interpersonal relations, their practical teachings that offer concrete solutions for carrying on a stable social life, and their provision, to individuals who have been cut off from traditional communities, of a place where congenial company and a spirit of mutual support may be found. As capitalistic industrialization and urbanization advance, large numbers of individuals are thrown into new living environments, thus providing conditions that require spiritual support for the individual … Japanese religions are abundantly equipped with cultural resources that answer the needs of just these people in treading the path towards the urban middle class. (Susumu 1991: 1163)

Soka Gakkai is very unusual in that, of the many new forms of Buddhism now found in the West, it alone breaks the "Two Buddhisms" paradigm—the idea that there are two distinct groups who join Buddhist groups or become Buddhists— ethnic Asians living in the West and Westerners who are attracted for a variety of reasons. Soka Gakkai stands out because it is strikingly multi-ethnic and has had success in many parts of the world among native populations including such places as Korea, Malaysia, Brazil, Europe, parts of Africa, India, and North America. SGI is unique because it is able to bring a variety of ethnic groups together to practice.

Peter Clarke (2000) suggests several reasons SGI has been especially successful in attracting a multi-ethnic following. SGI in particular has succeeded in developing a strong following in many countries because, "though a very Japanese form of Buddhism, it appears capable of universal application; no one is obliged to abandon their native culture or nationality in order to fully participate in the spiritual and cultural life of the movement" (Clarke 2000: 281). Soka Gakkai leaders, while maintaining the essential elements of their faith, have released their form of Buddhism from its inherently Japanese roots by skillfully adapting their religious practices to each culture that they seek to penetrate. They recruit local leaders who direct the foreign chapter free of any direct control from Tokyo, conduct all religious exercises and publish all documents in the native languages, and emphasize those traits that are important to the host culture. Clarke, for example, notes that SGI practices in the United States that appeal to many American members are "the absence of moralizing, the stress on individual choice, and the need to take responsibility for one's own actions" (2000: 285). SGI appeals to ethnic Chinese in Southeast Asia and North America because of its emphasis on individual self-empowerment—the idea that each person is responsible for his/her own happiness and success. Wherever one encounters SGI members throughout the world, one always hears how important the sense of self-empowerment is for individual members.

Soka Gakkai places great emphasis on the concept of *human security*. The goal of the Soka Gakkai is to provide greater human security by having more people experience its "human revolution," the transformation of their own character whereby each individual becomes a more self-confident, self-empowered, and more compassionate person. Members in Japan and abroad are then to go out into society and work to improve the human condition in whatever field they choose to enter. Soka Gakkai International also seeks to improve human security through its activist involvement in education and in community projects in conjunction with other local organizations.

The idea of human security is also important within the organization itself. Members in each chapter in Japan and abroad meet at least twice a month in each other's homes where they study Nichiren Buddhism and tell each other about their own problems and worries. Members provide each other with moral support, advice, "a shoulder to lean on," and encouragement. This mutual support of members is a critical reason for SGI's worldwide growth and success. On the other hand, I have found little evidence of the Soka Gakkai itself giving material support to members, though there are many instances where individual members will help each other out on a very private basis.[9]

Soka Gakkai has adapted itself to each cultural context in which it finds itself. At the same time, it has particular characteristics that make it attractive to potential converts. This is despite much anti-Japanese prejudice left over from World War II (WWII) in some of these areas. For many countries with a Buddhist tradition, Soka Gakkai's presentation of Nichiren Buddhism is not only comfortable but also potentially life transforming because it offers a new approach to that ancient faith. SGI members in these countries maintain that SGI's emphasis on individual responsibility and initiative, together with the organization's ability to provide them with a strong sense of optimism and a community of believers and supporters, made membership in the organization very appealing. As in the United States, the founding members of Soka Gakkai in Southeast Asia were older women, but the membership has become younger as rapid social and economic changes have made this movement, with the characteristics noted above, attractive to a wider circle of people.

Cultural adaptation of a non-indigenous religion in an alien culture is a very complex but necessary step if that religion is to survive in a new habitat. Much of the Soka Gakkai's success in foreign cultures is due to its ability to find a balanced method of adaptation. The human problems addressed by SGI and its solutions are universal in their scope and are not attached to any one culture or nationality. SGI is also very adept at bringing people together in small distinct groups that work together on a frequent basis. A large number of SGI members I have interviewed in Canada, Southeast Asia, and elsewhere state that the social bonds made possible through SGI are an important factor in their joining and staying in SGI.

---

[9] The Soka Gakkai has used its political power in Japan to force the Japanese government to keep Article 9 of the nation's Constitution which forbids the creation of an active Japanese military. The Soka Gakkai argues that preserving Japan's "Peace Constitution" is critical in keeping Japan out of foreign wars, thus enhancing the human security of the Japanese people. SGI groups outside Japan are not allowed to participate in politics in any manner.

The fact that there is uniformity in the Buddhist teachings of SGI worldwide helps to provide a sense of uniformity and unity worldwide among SGI members and chapters. Religious tracts produced in and transmitted from Tokyo are read and studied by followers everywhere. The spiritual leader Ikeda Daisaku is revered and studied in every Gakkai chapter I have visited from Montreal to Singapore. SGI chapters around the world are also structured in a fairly uniform manner. Every foreign chapter I have visited has, for example, a youth division, and men's and women's divisions, as well as small district groups whose few members meet twice a month as individual units for discussion and study meetings.

National SGI organizations are autonomous on an organizational level. They are run and manned by local nationals, and all business is conducted in the local language. Meetings in Quebec, for example, are in both English and French. National organizations make their own decisions, typically raise their own funds, and choose their own leaders. Links with Tokyo are generally informational. Strong efforts are made to show the community that SGI follows the culture and customs of its host nation. Its international success also stems from the fact that it does not promote itself or its doctrines as being inherently Japanese, emphasizing instead a form of Buddhism that, though founded in Japan, is applicable to everyone everywhere.

The fact that SGI is a Buddhist movement has won it support from many Chinese in Southeast Asia. Many Chinese who migrated to Southeast Asia during the latter part of the nineteenth century and throughout the twentieth century come from Buddhist backgrounds in their native land. Many of those who have joined SGI in such places as Singapore, Malaysia, and the Philippines told this writer that their families no longer practiced Buddhism in their new countries, but that Soka Gakkai offered them the opportunity to practice Buddhism again. They found the very modern aspects of Soka Gakkai, especially in promoting the empowerment of the individual, to be added inducement for membership.

The Global Reach of Soka Gakkai International

Soka Gakkai International is a global movement with chapters and members in every region of the world (see Table 4.1 below). The greatest concentration of members is in East Asia with smaller chapters throughout Southeast Asia. There are large South American chapters in such countries as Brazil, Argentina, and Peru as well as a strong following in the United States and Canada. There are smaller but very active chapters across Western and Eastern Europe and Russia, India and South Asia, Australia and Oceania, and the Middle East and sub-Saharan Africa. In China, there are a few individual members but no active chapters.

SGI chapters throughout the world have become very involved in their respective local communities. Their goal is to work together with other community groups to promote such values as peace, respect for the environment, improved education, and relief for people suffering from a variety of natural disasters. SGI-South Africa

Table 4.1   Soka Gakkai International Membership Worldwide by Region

Region	Members
North America	352,000
Central America	20,000
South America	236,000
Europe	105,000
Middle East and Africa	25,000
Asia and Oceania	1,017,000
Japan	8,270,000 (Households)

Note: Figures derived by Soka Gakkai International as of 3 November 2011.

Source: http://www.sgi.org/about-us/sgi-facts/sgi-membership.html (accessed February 12, 2013).

in 2012 was engaged in a "Victory over Violence" campaign and a series of other initiatives with other community groups to promote nonviolence and to preserve the legacy of Gandhi in South Africa. SGI in India hosts various exhibitions promoting a culture of peace, nonviolence and sustainability at community and school levels. SGI in Brazil actively has volunteers in over 100 schools to improve literacy while SGI in the Dominican Republic has been active in developing a reforestation program. The British branch of SGI is actively working with Muslim and black Christian communities to foster better understanding between them and the broader spectrum of British society.[10]

SGI's Finances and Ties to the Japanese Soka Gakkai

All of the SGI national chapters are independent autonomous units that govern themselves, choose their own leaders, develop their own programs, and finance their own activities. SGI Canada is no different from any other national SGI group. There is a small paid staff that works out of its main headquarters in Toronto, but much of the work there and in other chapters across Canada is done by volunteers who commit massive amounts of time, energy, and devotion to their cause. SGI Australia had only one or two paid staff members in its Sydney headquarters—the entire operation is basically run by volunteers.

Finances are a key component of any organization's success. Money is needed to construct or purchase buildings, keep the electricity running, and pay for staff

---

[10]   See the following sites to get a broader view of SGI chapter activities throughout the world: http://www.sgi.org/about-us/activity-hightlights/africa.html; http://www.sgi.org/about-us/activity-hightlights/asia.html; http://www.sgi.org/about-us/activity-hightlights/europe.html; http://www.sgi.org/about-us/activity-hightlights/latin-america.html

to maintain the day-to-day operations of the organization. Soka Gakkai in Japan is noted for its great wealth, but many of the international chapters live on fairly lean budgets. Most of these chapters raise their own money for daily operations through member contributions, but there are often major expenses that cannot be procured locally by smaller chapters. When Malaysia SGI needed a new cultural center, its large and comparatively wealthy membership quickly raised the necessary funds locally, but when the very much smaller SGI chapters in Australia and Canada needed money to purchase land for major building projects, they received generous funding grants from the Tokyo office of SGI.

The funds for the day-to-day operations of SGI Canada come from member contributions, publications, and other local resources. There are electric bills and phone bills to be paid, journals to be published, and so on, and the funds for these matters are received from member and local sources. There have been subsidies from SGI Tokyo, however, for big ticket projects and items such as the purchase of the land and buildings at the Caledon Centre for Culture and Education.

Connections between SGI chapters and SGI Tokyo, however, are very strong. All of the doctrines and methods of worship are identical worldwide. Many of the teaching materials as well as the guidance lectures of Soka Gakkai's spiritual leader Ikeda Daisaku are sent from Tokyo. SGI leaders in each chapter travel to Tokyo for occasional meetings and exchange information and ideas with one another and the Tokyo office on a frequent basis even though local autonomy is also very important.

Daily Lives of Members

Every SGI member has daily, monthly, and other occasional matters in which they are supposed to participate. It is important to note that SGI members come from all walks of life and have very normal personal and professional lives that extend beyond their SGI membership. While the amount of time and effort that each individual puts into SGI differs with each member and family, in general the average SGI member puts in about as much time each month as does a reasonably active member of many Christian churches.

Just how much time and effort each SGI member puts in is entirely up to the individual member. Each member is supposed to do some chanting alone or with other family members every morning and evening, but some members chant longer than others. The key element is personal practice at home. Twice a day, once in the morning and again in the evening, the believer sits in a formal posture facing the Gohonzon in his/her home, chants *Nam-myôhô-renge-kyô* and recites from the *Lotus Sūtra*. The sections of the *sūtra* which are recited are the *Hobe* and *Juryo*,[11] which constitute the heart of the sutra. The goal of this practice is

---

[11] The second and sixteenth chapters of the *Lotus Sūtra* where Shakyamuni reveals that all people without exception can gain enlightenment—that all people have the Buddha

to energize the Buddha nature /life force that is said to exist in every person. One who does this personal *gongyo* practice regularly supposedly will become endowed with compassion and wisdom.

The key group function is the district meeting. For example, each SGI Canada region is divided into small districts with about 10-15 members. These groups meet at each other's homes twice a month, once for a discussion meeting and again for a study meeting. The local district meeting constitutes the chief forum for introducing newcomers to the practice and in building strong personal bonds between members living in each district. SGI Canada leader Tony Meers notes:

> All of our activities, from one-to-one meetings to large-scale events, exist for the purpose of helping people live happy and fulfilled lives. We have experienced what is possible with a united spirit and effort. There is something truly wondrous about working for the sake of others. When we apply this kind of solidarity to our district activities, taking time to visit and meet with each individual and making new friends, we can create joyful discussion and study meetings where everyone will feel revitalized. (Meers 2010: 11)

SGI Canada, like SGI chapters in Japan and other countries, is also divided into groups such as the women's division, the men's division, the young women's and the young men's divisions. These meetings provide additional opportunities for study, discussions, planning special events, and the chance to develop personal friendships and relationships.

There are often activities that involve members from a region or the whole country. For example, Soka Gakkai has always put great stock in what it calls "cultural festivals" where followers, especially younger members, sing, dance and engage in other activities. These festivals are largely designed to bring members together, to promote a sense of cooperation, and to have fun. Annual festivals in Japan can involve as many as 15,000 performers in a massive auditorium, but festivals abroad are on a much smaller scale.

SGI Chapters as Family-based Organizations

Although there are many, especially new members, who have no other family in the organization, SGI chapters are very family-based. Many of the younger faithful interviewed in recent years were second- or even third-generation members. Their parents, or even grandparents, had joined SGI before they were born or when they were very young. These younger members had grown up in the faith, but that did not automatically mean their unswerving devotion to the movement. Many had brothers, sisters, or cousins who were not members, but those who stayed often

nature innately within them.

encountered some major crisis and received help, advice, or strong support from other SGI members which renewed their commitment to the organization.

When revisiting SGI Canada's cultural center in Toronto in June 2010, I requested the opportunity to meet with a focus group of young adult members to learn why and how so many young Canadians had made Soka Gakkai Buddhism an essential part of their lives. Toronto is one of the most cosmopolitan and multicultural cities anywhere with a population that is nearly half Asian including a large mix of South Asians and Chinese. SGI membership in Toronto certainly matches this multicultural multi-ethnic mix and my five-person randomly selected focus group reflected this mix. Two young men and three young women—one of whom had just become a medical doctor—spent over two hours talking about their lives in SGI Canada.

Four of the five came from families whose parents were SGI members. They grew up participating in SGI events in Canada and chanting with their parents, often on a daily basis, yet as children they had very little understanding of the movement and its teachings. As young teenagers they all began to question the practice. They all moved away from SGI and launched their own search for satisfaction and meaning in life, but later they all returned to the movement.

Their reasons for returning to SGI were varied. They had all experienced some degree of hardship, anxiety, and loneliness. Chanting, alone or with others, and participation in SGI meetings, activities, and festivals brought them a greater sense of confidence, energy, and purpose in life. One young woman, whose family is from Taiwan, had been brought up in Canada in a wealthy family, but while in elementary school, the family business in Taiwan went into temporary decline. Her family members chanted fervently, never giving up hope, and in time the business recovered. When she saw her family chanting, she joined and soon noticed a change within herself. She felt stronger and more composed and all of her close friends said how she looked different, stronger, and more confident. Another young woman said that as a teenager she was confused and lacked direction in life, but when she started chanting, she felt a surge of energy within. "I suddenly understood my mission in life and felt determined to lead others to happiness in life." The young woman who became a doctor realized her goal in life when as a teenager she began chanting. She participated in a Buddhist club at university and saw working as a family doctor as a way to contribute to the welfare of society. A young man, now a successful musician, was having difficulty focusing as a teenager—suffering nightmares, having difficulty sleeping, and experiencing fits of deep depression. His mother suggested several times that he try chanting and eventually he did just that. It took a while, but in time he felt a change coming over his personality. He felt a surge of energy and suddenly felt creative as a musician. His nightmares and depression disappeared and he felt true joy in life. All four found happiness through Buddhism and said that this Buddhism fit in very well with Canada's culture of caring.

Soka Education

The Soka Gakkai began in the 1930s as an educational movement. Its founder, Makiguchi Tsunesaburô, was a teacher who wished to refocus Japanese education away from an emphasis on rote learning. He demanded that schools should pay more attention to the needs and interests of individual students and that students should have internships in their communities to learn about the "real world" while still young. He also advocated greater study of the world outside Japan. He felt that the key to education should be helping to guide each student to "create value" in their lives. He formed the Sôka Kyôiku Gakkai ("Value-Creating Educational Society") in 1930. It was not until the late 1930s and early 1940s that he and his successor, Toda Jôsei, shifted the emphasis to religion as a means to find greater happiness in life.

Education remains at the heart of the Soka Gakkai movement. It established its own primary and secondary school systems in Tokyo and Osaka in the late 1960s. These schools, which are open to all applicants including Soka Gakkai members, are noted for their high educational standards and excellent facilities. Soka University, located in Hachioji City outside of Tokyo, is highly regarded for its undergraduate and graduate programs. Soka Gakkai has opened Soka University of America (SUA) near Los Angeles, California. SUA, which has received high praise from *US News* for the high quality of its academic program, has about 500 students drawn from both the United States and Japan. There are Soka kindergartens in Brazil, Hong Kong, Malaysia, and South Korea.

Soka schools, both in Japan and abroad, are managed as private independent entities. While each school may receive substantial assistance from Soka Gakkai for the construction of new buildings or the purchase of new property, they are all tuition driven. When visiting Soka kindergartens in Asia, I was struck by the high quality of the facilities and the close interaction between young students and their teachers. Many of the students were not from Soka Gakkai families but were attracted by the excellence of the schools. Tuition is certainly not cheap; tuition at SUA in 2012 was about $30,000.

Public Reaction to SGI Abroad

Since the Soka Gakkai in Japan encountered significant anger and hostility during the 1950s and 1960s, it is fair to ask if it has met with hostility from non-members abroad. There was some hostility in the United States in the 1960s when some SGI members tried to recruit new members through some of the same over-exuberant methods of proselytization as practiced in Japan. However, Soka Gakkai in Japan and global SGI dropped these practices by the 1970s and have adopted quieter and "gentler" forms of recruitment. SGI members are urged to invite non-member family members or friends to meetings or festivals and some, like SGI Canada, hold "Buddhist seminars" in libraries and universities.

The fact is that SGI has gone mainstream. Its member chapters keep a very low profile, avoid any form of public confrontations, and, where possible, work on community projects with other local groups. This approach has allowed it to function very quietly and to draw very little attention and thus no hostility from non-member locals. When I attended frequent Sunday meetings of SGI in Canberra, Australia, the chapter rented a room for a couple of hours in a public hall and conducted the gathering virtually unnoticed except for a few friendly and curious onlookers.

Soka Gakkai International, however, is a highly socially engaged lay Buddhist movement. Soka Gakkai in Japan is active socially not only in politics[12] but also in a variety of environmental, educational,[13] and cultural activities. SGI organizations abroad are prohibited any form of direct political engagement,[14] but involvement in social welfare, educational or other community action programs, commonly in conjunction with other local groups, is very common. SGI Canada, for example, is no exception to this rule.[15] Since its founding in the 1960s, SGI Canada has been quite active across the country raising money for worthy causes and working with other local, national, and international organizations to promote the social good. SGI chapters, however, generally avoid public scrutiny because they keep a very low profile. A search of major American, Canadian and

---

[12]   The Soka Gakkai in Japan, working through its party, the Kômeitô, has an active political agenda to support its Buddhist aims including social welfare proposals, promoting closer peaceful relations with neighboring countries such as China, and with great success protecting Japan's "peace constitution" from conservative forces who wish to eliminate or alter Article 9 which forbids rearmament for Japan.

[13]   Soka Gakkai began as an educational reform movement in the 1930s and still retains a strong interest in education. It has its own educational system in Japan from kindergarten through Soka University near Tokyo. There is also Soka University of America in California.

[14]   While all non-Japanese SGI branches totally abstain from any direct political action, some chapters such as SGI Singapore or Malaysia have close ties with their governments and on occasion will participate in government-sponsored events or social welfare-educational programs.

[15]   Concerning Soka Gakkai social engagement, an SGI Canada brochure notes: "SGI is a Buddhist organization devoted to peace, culture and education based on the humanistic philosophy of Nichiren Buddhism ... [T]he movement is characterized by its emphasis on individual empowerment and inner transformation or "human revolution," which enables individuals to take responsibility for their lives and contribute to building a world where people of diverse cultures can live in peace ... Education and dialogue are crucial for the advancement of peace and the SGI sponsors various exhibitions as a means of public peace education. The promotion of cultural activities and exchange on an international scale is also an integral part of SGI's activities ... Working as a global citizen means working at a grass-roots level within our own communities. SGI Canada members participate as volunteers in a variety of community-based cultural and humanitarian activities. An example of this is the promotion of the Earth Charter as an important movement for positive change in the community" (Meers 2010).

Australian newspapers in recent years indicates virtually no coverage or even mention of SGI—evidence of the ability of the various SGI chapters to avoid public controversies and thus "bad press."

Concluding Notes

Soka Gakkai International has found a small but growing niche in many different cultures throughout the world. A key factor in its success is the feeling of self-confidence and self-control many of its members feel they derive from this practice. They feel empowered to manage their own lives in a creative manner and to participate in what they regard as helping to create a world where peace, prosperity, harmony, and creative spontaneity are to be enjoyed by all. A small community within a nation made up of different communities, SGI provides its members companionship with like-minded people, a direction to channel their spirituality, and a growing sense of confidence and direction. SGI chapters often find a niche because its members feel that the religion fills a spiritual void. They claim a higher degree of happiness, self-confidence, peace of mind, and self-fulfillment.

A factor in SGI's success is its emphasis on community. The fast pace in a rapidly changing society, constant movement from one job or location to another, and the sizable growth of immigrant groups, especially from Asia, have left many people in industrial societies in Asia and the West with the sense that they are without strong community roots. SGI's practice of creating small chapters whose members meet twice or more monthly in each other's homes creates a tightly bonded group of individuals who share much in common with each other. The neighborhood newcomer or recent immigrant can find a ready-made group of friends or concerned individuals who can ease the lonely transition into a new area.

The increasingly complex nature of multicultural societies in the West has meant greater tolerance and acceptance of Eastern religions. Soka Gakkai might have had a harder time assimilating into Western societies before 1960, but today's growing tolerance of multiculturalism and massive Asian immigration gives it fertile ground for slow expansion. SGI chapters avoid partisan political issues and campaigns and also keep a low profile, but their participation in community events and exhibitions makes its presence more welcome and acceptable to its neighbors.

References

Clarke, Peter B. 2000. "'Success' and 'Failure': Japanese New Religions Abroad." Pp. 272-311 in *Japanese New Religions in Global Perspective,* edited by Peter B. Clarke. Richmond, Surrey, UK: Curzon Press.

Hammond, Philip and David Machacek. 1994. *Soka Gakkai in America: Accommodation and Conversion.* Oxford: Oxford University Press.

Inoue, Nobutaka. 1985. *Umi o watatta Nihon shukyô* (Japanese Religions Overseas). Tokyo: Kobundo.

Machacek, David and Bryan Wilson, eds. 1994. *Global Citizens: The Soka Gakkai Buddhist Movement in the World*. Oxford: Oxford University Press.

Meers, Tony. 2010. "Let's Return to Basics." Interview with Daniel A. Metraux. *New Century* 14 (June): 11-12.

Metraux, Daniel A. 1994. *The Soka Gakkai Revolution*. Lanham, MD: University Press of America.

Metraux, Daniel A. 1996. *The Lotus and the Maple Leaf: The Soka Gakkai Buddhist Movement in Canada*. New York: The University Press of America.

Metraux, Daniel A. 1997. *Soka Gakkai Buddhist Movement in Quebec: The Lotus and the Fleur de Lys*. Lewiston, NY: Edwin Mellen Press.

Metraux, Daniel A. 2001. *The International Expansion of a Modern Buddhist Movement: The Soka Gakkai in Southeast Asia and Australia*. Lanham, MD: University Press of America.

Seager, Richard Hughes. 2001."Soka Gakkai—the next Ten Years." *Tricycle* 41 (Fall): 91-98.

SGI-UK Study Department. N.d. "The Gohonzon." Retrieved August 27, 2011 (http://www.sgi-uk.org/resources/The%20Gohonzon%20-%20Notes.pdf).

Soka Gakkai International. 2013a. "Africa." Retrieved June 2, 2013 (http://www.sgi.org/about-us/activity-hightlights/africa.html).

Soka Gakkai International. 2013b. "Asia." Retrieved June 2, 2013 (http://www.sgi.org/about-us/activity-hightlights/asia.html).

Soka Gakkai International. 2013c. "Europe." Retrieved June 2, 2013 (http://www.sgi.org/about-us/activity-hightlights/europe.html).

Soka Gakkai International. 2013d. "Latin America." Retrieved June 2, 2013 (http://www.sgi.org/about-us/activity-hightlights/latin-america.html).

Susumu, Shimazono. 1991. "The Expansion of Japan's New Religions into Foreign Cultures." *Japanese Journal of Religious Studies* 18(2-3): 105-32.

Tokyo Journal. 1993. "Daisaku Ikeda: Statesman, Billionaire, God." Retrieved July 11, 2011 (http://www.mombu.com/religion/religion/t-tokyo-journal-jams-up-the-news-god-hell-evil-history-religion-3166068-last.html).

Wilson, Bryan and Karel Dobbelare. 1994. *A Time to Chant: The Soka Gakkai Buddhists in Britain*. Oxford: Clarendon Press.

Chapter 5
BAPS Swaminarayan Community: Hinduism

Arun Brahmbhatt

Pramukh Swami Maharaj,[1] the administrative and spiritual leader of the Bochasanwasi Shri Akshar Purushottam Swaminarayan Sanstha (BAPS), on the occasion of the first blood donation drive organized in 1976 by BAPS's service arm, the Akshar Purushottam Public Charitable Trust, reflected:

> According to the principles of Shriji Maharaj, we have accepted *seva dharma*. We have been born to engage in this *seva*. Whenever there has been hardship in society, Shriji Maharaj and *santo*[2] have helped … [Today,] *santo* and youth have enthusiastically taken great interest in giving blood, and Shriji Maharaj has become pleased … I pray that all lives are bettered, that all are liberated, and that people are inspired to do good.[3] (BAPS 1976: 224)

These blessings reveal the multiple dimensions and configurations of service—here referred to as *seva*—in BAPS, including its legacy, motivations, and centrality to life. Frequent reference is made to Shriji Maharaj, also known as Sahajanand Swami and Bhagwan Swaminarayan, who was the founder of the Swaminarayan *sampradaya*, a Hindu *bhakti* (devotional) community. The Swaminarayan *sampradaya* has seen the formation of independent sects or branches, including BAPS, which was established in 1907.

Since its inception in India in the 1950s, the Akshar Purushottam Public Charitable Trust has been joined by BAPS Charities, an international nonprofit organization engaged in over 160 humanitarian activities (BAPS Charities 2012). Though a comprehensive examination of all the service initiatives undertaken by BAPS and its charitable organizations is not possible in this chapter, an analysis of some of these activities will shed light on the global operations of a service-oriented organization with roots in a specific regional and religious context.

---

[1] All proper nouns are transliterated according to their standard convention, without diacritics. Sanskrit and Gujarati words, unless their use is common in English, are italicized, and transliterated without diacritics.

[2] *Sant* (plural *santo*) and *sadhu* refer to ordained ascetics or monks in the Swaminarayan tradition.

[3] All translations from Gujarati and Hindi texts are my own.

Members of BAPS and its charitable organizations describe their involvement in the following types of social service activities: medical, educational, disaster relief, welfare, environmental, community, and rural development services (BAPS Charities UK 2010a; BAPS 2013g). Although "*samaj seva*" is a close translation of "social service" into Gujarati, two main terms found within academic literature to convey these concepts are: *seva*, or physical service, and *dana,* or charitable and philanthropic giving. For members of BAPS, *seva* and *dana* are both undergirded by a "spirit of service." Functioning as the motto of BAPS Charities, this "spirit of service" is described as "selfless service" (BAPS 2013g); the nuances of this spirit, particularly as it manifests globally, will be explored in detail.

Theorists of globalization take as their starting point the fact of the world being characterized by the motion of objects, ideas, images, and people (Appadurai 2000; Levitt 2012). It is a world of accelerating flows, though the cause, nature, extent, and results of these flows are disparate (Appadurai 1996). Globalization may be addressed from a broad range of disciplinary, methodological, and theoretical groundings,[4] and while many such discussions are based on an analysis of global capital, scholars such as Appadurai (1996) and Levitt (2005) have pointed to the salience of culture in understandings of globality. Appadurai (1996: 33) describes various interrelated landscapes that serve as the sites for "global cultural flows," including the "ethnoscape," or "the landscape of persons who constitute the shifting world in which we live." To Appadurai's system, Dwyer (2004: 196) appends the category of "religioscape" to think through the dynamic landscape of religious space and practice. Since scholars have variously described BAPS as a global (van der Veer 2002), diasporic (Vertovec 2000), transnational (Williams 2001), cosmopolitan (Brosius 2010) and deterritorialized (Kim 2008) community, I seek to examine the ethnoscape and religioscape of BAPS as conduits for global cultural flows as enacted through social service.

I start this chapter by sketching, in broad strokes, the inception of the Swaminarayan Hindu tradition in the nineteenth century and BAPS in the twentieth century. This will provide a backdrop to examine the history of service in the Swaminarayan *sampradaya* generally and BAPS specifically.[5] Examining these specific enactments of social service will provide an important site for the exploration of religion in various global contexts: first, the colonial period, and subsequently, the present period of modern transnationalism. Analyzing social service in the Swaminarayan *sampradaya* allows us to tease out the complexities of the global condition, revealing how individual members and the community as a whole navigate the various

---

[4]   For a wide-ranging index of such methodological and theoretical starting points, see Srinivas (2010: 25).

[5]   It is important to note that among Swaminarayan organizations, BAPS and its various charitable organizations are not alone in performing social service. For example, the International Swaminarayan Satsang Organization (ISSO) Seva is another Swaminarayan service organization with a substantial international presence. See www.issoseva.org (ISSO Seva n.d.).

demands of the local and translocal. I will further investigate service activities in terms of the ways of belonging generated, including through complex citizenships and participation in diasporic public spheres. Throughout this discussion, I will explore how Swaminarayan articulations of social service as devotional endeavor are integral to our understanding of globalized religious practice.

Regional Roots, Transnational Routes: An Overview

The Swaminarayan Sampradaya

Sahajanand Swami (1781-1830) was born in the north of present-day India, but leaving his family and home as a young peripatetic renunciant (*bal-brahmachari*), his travels through the Indian subcontinent led him to western India, to the region that would eventually become the state of Gujarat. He arrived in the hermitage (*ashrama*) of a Vaishnava religious leader named Ramanand Swami, who had a sizeable following of monks and laypeople, and four small temples spread throughout the regions of Gujarat, Kathiawar, and Kutch (Parekh 1936). A short two years later, in 1801, Ramanand Swami conferred leadership of his *ashrama* upon the young and charismatic Sahajanand Swami, who spread his teachings through the same regions of Gujarat, Kathiawar, and Kutch for nearly thirty years. Very early on, he was revered as a divine figure by his followers, most of whom worshipped him as a direct manifestation of God (Parekh 1936).

The community grew steadily over the three decades of Sahajanand Swami's teachings. Various sources provide a range of estimates in terms of the *sampradaya*'s reach: British sources indicated that, in the 1820s, Sahajanand Swami had at least 100,000 followers, while some within the community suggest that the following had grown to 1.8 million during his lifetime (Williams 2001), and that there were at least 3,000 *sadhus* initiated. Much of the institutionalization of the community took place during the last ten years of his life, which saw the construction of six temples, the production of a variety of texts, and the establishment of offices of administration (Schreiner 2001).

In terms of texts, particularly important are two that have scriptural status among his followers. The first is the *Vachanamrut*—a collection of 274 of Sahajanand Swami's sermons, rich in theological content and delivered in Gujarati between 1819 and 1829, which were transcribed by four of his senior *sadhus*. The second is a text called the *Shikshapatri*, a collection of 212 Sanskrit verses attributed to Sahajanand Swami himself and completed in 1826. Both texts are considered to be the "essence of all authoritative texts" that precede them (Schreiner 2001). In terms of the administration of the *sampradaya*, Sahajanand Swami drew up a line of demarcation separating a northern diocese based in Ahmedabad and a southern diocese based in Vadtal. Each diocese was to be administered by an *acharya*, or "preceptor," an office of succession held by two of Sahajanand Swami's nephews. Due in large part to what Schreiner (2001) calls an "institutionalization of charisma," the *sampradaya* continued to grow after Sahajanand Swami's passing, so that by 1872, a British government census indicates that the *sampradaya*'s membership neared 288,000, which was roughly 4 percent of the overall population of the area (Williams 2001).

The BAPS Swaminarayan Sanstha

In 1905, about 100 years after the inception of the Swaminarayan *sampradaya*, a *sadhu* named Shastri Yagnapurushdas left the Vadtal diocese due to attempts on his life precipitated by key doctrinal differences (Dave 2007). Shastri Yagnapurushdas—later known as Shastriji Maharaj—established a new community in 1907, which would become the Bochasanwasi Shri Akshar Purushottam Swaminarayan Sanstha (BAPS). Though he left Vadtal with only a handful of *sadhus* and householder devotees, by the time of his passing in 1951, he had built five large, spired, stone temples (Kim 2009) and initiated fifty *sadhus* (Williams 2012).

During this time, BAPS also saw its first sustained migration outside of Gujarat and the Indian subcontinent. Patterns of the spread of BAPS and the Swaminarayan *sampradaya* loosely follow patterns of Indian migration and, more specifically, Gujarati migration. While Gujaratis had taken advantage of Indian Ocean trade travel to Africa even during the premodern period, migration took a different tenor in the nineteenth century when India's position as a British colony allowed for the transfer of labor to other sites of colonial influence, most predominantly, in Africa (Dwyer 2004; Sidel 2004). Due to prolonged periods of famine and plague as well as economic hardship in Gujarat, East Africa became a viable option for the immigration of skilled workers, many of whom thrived on the creation and maintenance of the railway system (Williams 2001). Though Shastriji Maharaj himself never visited East Africa, his encouragement of the development of a BAPS community was facilitated through the ease of communication as well as travel of a few devotees between East Africa and India (Williams 2001). Additionally, a small temple in Nairobi, Kenya, opened in 1945, for which Shastriji Maharaj performed the image installation rituals in India (Amrutvijaydas 2007: 31).

The BAPS community continued to develop in East Africa under Shastriji Maharaj's successor, Yogiji Maharaj. Over three visits to East Africa in 1955, 1960, and 1970, Yogiji Maharaj opened five more temples in Kenya and Uganda (Amrutvijaydas 2007). During this time, there was also a shift to the United Kingdom. This followed the displacement of Gujaratis and other ethnic Indians to the United Kingdom under the policy of "Africanization" after the independence of Kenya, Tanzania, and Uganda from the British Empire in the early 1960s (Dwyer 2004). Gujarati migrants to Britain joined a smaller number who had already migrated directly from India. While a few such migrants from India had been guided to establish a BAPS community in Britain in the early 1950s, it was not until the momentum gained by the East African migration and Yogiji Maharaj's visit to London in 1970 that the first temple was opened (Amrutvijaydas 2007).

Indian migration to the United States—and the consequent spread of the BAPS community—has followed a slightly different pattern. A few thousand Indian migrants, primarily from Punjab, arrived in the late nineteenth and early twentieth centuries, as well as immediately after Indian independence. However, Indian immigration increased significantly due to the Immigration Act of 1965. While there were only 6,000 Indians in the United States before 1965, by 1980 there were over 380,000 (Sidel 2004). These numbers have continued to increase into the present period, so that, according to the 2010 United States Census, the "Asian Indian" population is 2.84 million (United States Census Bureau n.d.). In terms of religious affiliation, according to the Pew Forum on Religion and Public Life (2012), as of 2010, there were 1.79 million Hindus in the United States, comprising 0.6 percent of the overall United States population; in the United Kingdom, there were 800,000, comprising 1.3 percent of the overall population. Membership in BAPS has seen similar growth. In 1971, there were fewer than 30 members of BAPS spread out in various parts of the United States (Williams 2012). At present, of an estimated total of one million members worldwide, there are an estimated 40,000 members of the BAPS community in the United States and 30,000 in the United Kingdom (Kim 2009).

The rapid development globally of the BAPS Swaminarayan community during the final quarter of the twentieth century and the start of the twenty-first is in large part due to the efforts of the current spiritual leader and Yogiji Maharaj's successor, Pramukh Swami Maharaj. In 1971, there were 190 temples and centers combined, including 7 spired, stone temples[6] (Williams 2001); at present, there are over 1,100 temples and 3,300 centers worldwide, including 34 spired, stone temples (BAPS 2013a). The first temple in the United States was inaugurated in New York in 1974; by 1990, there were eight temples around areas with high concentrations of Gujarati immigrants; at present there are roughly 70 temples, including five spired, stone temples (Amrutvijaydas 2007; BAPS 2013f). In review, the transnational spread of BAPS has followed patterns of Gujarati migration. It has been promoted by frequent trips abroad by the spiritual leaders of BAPS. Pramukh Swami Maharaj himself has taken 27 trips outside of India, and he has often sent senior *sadhus* as well (Amrutvijaydas 2007:190). Also, starting in the mid-1990s, there has been a contingent of *sadhus* based permanently outside of India. This overseas residence of *sadhus* has also been facilitated by an increase in the overall number of *sadhus* in the community, from roughly 200 in 1980 to almost 900 only 30 years later (Williams 2012).

---

[6] By "temple," I refer to the *mandir*—a site where images of Swaminarayan, his spiritual successors as maintained by the BAPS community, and other Hindu deities have been ritually consecrated. Temples vary in size and type: by "spired, stone temple," I refer to the *shikharbaddh mandir*, a temple constructed according to traditional architectural manuals. "Center" corresponds to any site where members of the BAPS community congregate, and many not necessarily have ritually consecrated images.

Organizational Structure

Much like the administrative structure instituted by Sahajanand Swami that was needed to meet the demands of his growing *sampradaya*, an organizational structure was necessitated by the growth of the BAPS community at home and abroad. BAPS was founded in 1907 and, under developing legal guidelines, became an officially registered and certified trust in 1947 (Amrutvijaydas 2007). The trust was managed by an administrative committee with a defined structure headed by a president; since 1950, this office has been held by Pramukh Swami Maharaj[7] (Williams 2001). In the 1950s, with the further establishment of temples and an increase in membership, and after visits by Yogiji Maharaj, a similar administrative apparatus, though on a smaller level, and only with lay leaders, was set up in East Africa (Dwyer 2004; Williams 2001). With continued development overseas, a highly rationalized system of organization and hierarchical management (Kim 2008) has been set up in the United States, Britain, and other areas. For example, North America has been divided into six regions, which in turn report to a national headquarters, which then may take guidance from the international headquarters in Ahmedabad (Levitt 2005). Such a system has been integral to effectively managing the diverse efforts of an estimated 55,000 lay volunteers and 900 *sadhus* worldwide (BAPS 2013e).

Rather than one overall structure in BAPS administrative organization, there are several trusts that have been established in order to support activities, including social service activities, across various national legal contexts. Williams (2001: 62) enumerates five tax-exempt charitable trusts in India alone:

> Bochasanwasi Shree Akshar Purushottam Swaminarayan Sanstha for general activities, Swaminarayan Aksharpith for publications, Gnanyagna Vidyapith for educational institutions, Bochasanwasi Shree Akshar Purushottam Gaushala Trust for animal husbandry, and Bochasanwasi Shree Akshar Purushottam Public Charitable Trust for medical clinics and hospitals.

In North America, a charitable organization by the name of BAPS Care International was established in 2000 to oversee humanitarian activities in the United States and Canada; this was renamed as BAPS Charities in 2007 (BAPS Charities 2007). BAPS Charities was registered in the United Kingdom in 2008 (Charity Commission n.d.) and is in the process of being registered in parts of Africa and New Zealand (Viratswarupdas 2013). Though these various charities and trusts, each with separate boards of trustees to oversee their operations, function as independent entities, they do not operate in isolation and often complement each other.

---

[7] It is important to distinguish between spiritual leadership and administrative leadership. Pramukh Swami Maharaj was the administrative president under two separate spiritual leaders (*gurus*)—Shastriji Maharaj until 1951, and Yogiji Maharaj between 1951 and 1971—before he became both spiritual and administrative leader. In fact, "Pramukh" is translated as "president."

Social Service as Religious Practice

Service in the Nineteenth Century

Having explored the transnational trajectory of the Swaminarayan *sampradaya* and BAPS, I will now sketch a history of the specific practice of social service within the broader milieu of religious practices in the Swaminarayan tradition. Members of the BAPS community actively engaged in social service activities consider themselves to be following in the footsteps of Sahajanand Swami. Prior to analyzing current global social service projects, it is useful to examine the nature and scope of social service carried out by the founder of the Swaminarayan *sampradaya*. En route to Gujarat, when Sahajanand Swami, then known as Nilkanth, was in the southern part of the Indian subcontinent, he encountered a traveler who had fallen ill with dysentery. Since this man had no one to care for him, Sahajanand Swami served him for two months by procuring food, cooking, and cleaning (Parekh 1936). Then, when Sahajanand Swami entered the *ashrama* of Ramanand Swami in Loj, he immediately became involved in the daily upkeep of the *ashrama*, including the almshouse set up to feed pilgrims en route to the nearby sacred site of Dwarka in western Kathiawar. Manilal Parekh (1936) observes that running an almshouse was a time-honored and centuries-old practice. Sahajanand Swami maintained these almshouses after taking over leadership of the community in 1801. In 1803, Sahajanand Swami learned that these almshouses were under attack, possibly by figures opposed to his community and teachings. He guided the *sadhus* in charge of them to "maintain the center even if you are hit, abused, insulted, robbed, or made to fast" (Dani 1980: 11-12). Williams (2001) notes these almshouses were particularly useful during frequent famines. Furthermore, during a particularly harsh famine in Kathiawar in 1813-14, Sahajanand Swami himself collected and distributed grains to those who were suffering, and he sent his *sadhus* to unafflicted South Gujarat to beg for further food and grains.

These above efforts are manifestations of the two boons requested by Sahajanand Swami to Ramanand Swami when he took over leadership of the *ashrama*: "any miseries destined for members of the satsang [community] should be borne by Sahajanand himself, and that Sahajanand should bear any scarcities of food or clothing in place of any members of the community" (Beckerlegge 2006: 192). In addition to scarcity of food, scarcity of water was a major problem plaguing the people of Kathiawar, and not just in periods of extended famine. Very early on, after taking over leadership of the *sampradaya*, during a tour of Kathiawar in 1802, Sahajanand Swami came to a town called Mangrol, in which a large stepwell lay dry and unused. He instructed his followers, both *sadhus* and laypeople alike, to dig the stepwell deeper in an attempt to get water; furthermore, he worked alongside them. Ten days later, water was struck (Dave 2009a). A few years later, Sahajanand Swami had a reservoir dug in the village of Kariyani; during the monsoon season, the reservoir would fill up and provide water to the residents for months afterwards (Satyaprasaddas 2000). In 1806, he again had a dry well dug deeper to reveal water in the town of Budhej (Dave 2009b). Furthermore, when Sahajanand Swami composed the *Shikshapatri* in 1826, he enjoined his followers to engage in various social service activities. There are injunctions to be charitable towards the poor; to help others during periods of natural disaster, human calamity, or plague; to feed those who come to the temple in search of food; to establish schools; and to serve those afflicted with illness (Parekh 1936).

What is notable in these examples of social service is Sahajanand Swami's exhortation that even though *sadhus* are renunciants, "they should freely mix with the masses and try to mitigate their sufferings" (Dani 1980: 34). In this respect, social service in the Swaminarayan *sampradaya* is reminiscent of that of another more well-known community, Swami Vivekananda's Ramakrishna Math and Mission, in which an order of ascetics was actively engaged in administering service to the surrounding community, particularly around the issue of famine. Swami Vivekananda (1863-1902), who is best known for his address at the 1893 World Parliament of Religions in Chicago, postdated Sahajanand Swami by a few decades. However, Beckerlegge (2006) suggests that it is reasonable to assume that Vivekananda came into contact with social service projects in the Swaminarayan *sampradaya* when he spent some time in Gujarat in the last part of the nineteenth century. Beckerlegge (2006: 192) makes clear that while no causal link between the ideologies can be made with extant information, "the apparent similarities that have been identified, however, do indicate the existence of common underlying sentiments that could prompt individuals in different regional traditions to undertake substantial and organized philanthropic activity beyond the limits of conventional alms-giving." Furthermore, this could be evidence these efforts are rooted in an ethos common to Hindu and Indian religious traditions.

Seva *as* Sadhana

As will be discussed in subsequent sections, the conscious and unconscious motivations behind and ramifications of social service are multiple; but one of the principal common underlying sentiments guiding social service projects from the nineteenth century onwards alluded to by Beckerlegge (2006) is that of service as a religious practice. Members of the Ramakrishna Math and Mission consider themselves to be engaged in a "practice of a spiritually motivated discipline (a *sadhana*) of service to humanity" (Beckerlegge 2006: 53). In his emphasis on *seva* as *sadhana*, Vivekananda drew upon his *guru* Ramakrishna's teaching that human beings (*jiva*) should be treated and served as divine (*Shiva*). In effect, one could serve God through serving humans. Vivekananda further developed a system of "practical *Vedanta*," a reinterpretation of the classical orthodox Hindu system of *Advaita Vedanta*,[8] which saw ethical implications of the nonduality between humans and *brahman* (the ultimate reality) (Halbfass 1995).

This understanding of service as one element of religious practice is not unique to self-described Hindu movements but is also applicable to other religious traditions in India. For example, Anne Murphy (2004), in describing the historical and theological significance of *seva* in the Sikh tradition,[9] explains the central place of *seva* in Sikh practice and theology, particularly as a means of humbling oneself and serving God through serving others. Similarly, while discussing the Sri Sathya Sai Seva Organization,[10] Srinivas (2008: 144) explains that an understanding of *seva* as "spiritual praxis" is predicated on a model wherein "care of others is simultaneously a cure of the self," which is an anthropocentric, humanistic model "insofar as the understanding of humanity is that divinity is inherent within." While keeping in mind the relative chronology of these service initiatives—*seva* in the Sikh tradition preceding the Swaminarayan articulation, and the Ramakrishna and Sai instantiations as following it—this mapping of spiritual practice onto social service appears to be a widespread phenomenon.

A configuration of *seva* as religious practice can also be seen in the Swaminarayan *sampradaya*, most conspicuously in the *Vachanamrut*. *Seva* is discussed by Sahajanand Swami no less than 27 times in the 274 individual sermons that comprise the *Vachanamrut* (*The Vachanamrut* 2001). At one point, citing several sections of the *Bhagavata Purana* and the *Bhagavad Gita*, important sacred texts in Vaishnava traditions, Sahajanand Swami concludes that "a devotee should not wish for anything except the service of God" [Gadhada 1-43].[11] Elsewhere, the conceptualization of *seva* extends to serving God and the *Sant*. Here, *Sant* refers not to ordinary ascetics or *sadhus*, but to the figure of the *guru* or

---

[8]   *Vedanta* is numbered among the six schools of classical Hindu philosophy. Though its categorization as a system of philosophy or theology is contested, it is a system surrounding the commentarial exegesis of three canonical texts: the *Upanishads*, the *Bhagavad Gita*, and the *Brahma Sutras*. There are several schools of *Vedanta*, including the *Advaita* or "nondual" school of Shankara (788-820 CE), and the *Vishistadvaita* or "qualified nondual" school of Ramanuja (1017-1137 CE). For an overview of the distinctions between the two, see Flood (1996: 238-45). While Sahajanand Swami draws explicit ties to Ramanuja in contradistinction to Shankara, members of BAPS argue that Swaminarayan *Vedanta* is its own independent system (Shrutiprakashdas 2004).

[9]   The Sikh tradition is a religious tradition that traces its origins to the teachings of Guru Nanak (1469-1539) in Panjab. The tradition venerates a lineage of ten *gurus*, which was sealed off with the consolidation of the chief Sikh sacred text, the *Guru Granth Sahib*.

[10]   The Sri Sathya Sai Seva Organization is part of a transnational religious movement founded by Sathya Sai Baba (1926-2011). With roots in devotional *bhakti* and Sufi (Islamic mystic) traditions of South Asia, Sai Baba's movement is alternatively termed a New Religious movement or a New Age movement, blending teachings from various world religions and traditions.

[11]   This, and other similar annotations, refers to the particular section in the *Vachanamrut* cited.

spiritual leader.[12] To this end, Sahajanand Swami extols developing an "addiction" to *seva*: "if one becomes addicted to serving God and His *Sant* to the extent that one would not be able to stay for even a moment without serving them, then all … impure desires … will be destroyed" [Gadhada II-25]. To draw this out further, *seva* can encapsulate even service to the devotee of God. Sahajanand Swami repeatedly commends one who performs the menial service of devotees of God, explaining that the "method for a person to please God is to serve devotees of God by thought, word and deed" [Gadhada II-19], and further indicating that, "there is no spiritual endeavor that benefits a person and gives as much happiness" as this type of *seva* [Gadhada II-40]. This sampling of Sahajanand Swami's discussion of *seva* in the *Vachanamrut* suffices to demonstrate the importance of the spiritual practice of service to God, *guru,* and devotees.

Beckerlegge (2011) contends that the narrower understanding of service as directed towards God, *guru*, and devotees in time was broadened to incorporate an organized service to humanity. In Sahajanand Swami's teachings, while the *Vachanamrut* spends less time on the topic of humanitarian services as defined today, there is evidence that indicates that service to humanity was also incorporated under the rubric of religious practice. When Sahajanand Swami had his *sadhus* dig the first stepwell in Mangrol in 1802, he explicitly linked the exertion of effort for the good of others with *bhakti* (devotion) (Dave 2009a). This notion of service as *bhakti*, Mangalnidhidas (forthcoming) explains, is the link by which members of BAPS understand the spiritual benefits of *seva* to humanity from the explicit discussions of the spiritual benefits of *seva* to God, *guru* and devotee of God. This comes from the interpretation of fulfilling God's command as *bhakti*. As discussed above, Sahajanand Swami enjoined his followers in various sections of the *Shikshapatri* to serve humanity, and the faithful completion of these activities at the behest of Sahajanand Swami, Mangalnidhidas explains, is *bhakti*; once again, serving humanity is a means to serve God. This imbrication of service and devotion is a common feature of *bhakti* traditions (Beckerlegge 2006).

Antecedents: Pre-Nineteenth-Century Service

Though the foregoing discussion stresses the nineteenth-century expansion of the term *seva* to include service to humanity alongside service to God, the *guru*, and devotees, this does not imply that social service was absent in Hindu traditions prior to this time. Srinivas (2008) observes that the expansion of the connotations of *seva* was a *semantic* expansion, not necessarily ideological. Searching for antecedents of modern Hindu social service is not a project of constructing an

---

[12]   BAPS's English translation of the *Vachanamrut* defines *Sant*, which is synonymous with *satpurush*, as the "guru for a spiritual aspirant," and the person "through whom God remains ever-manifest, passing on His divine energy and experience, love and guidance to all beings on earth. The continuing lineage of God-realised *Satpurushes* ensures that the gateway to liberation and God is forever open for all seekers" (*The Vachanamrut* 2001: 751).

unbroken tradition of service in "Hinduism." Any such project takes as its basis the understanding that "Hinduism" is an umbrella term, and that it is more accurate to refer to discrete yet related Hindu traditions (van der Veer 2002).[13] Similarly, there is no one single tradition of service in Hindu traditions, but it is nonetheless fruitful to examine various textual articulations of what constitutes service.

References to physically engaging in social service are not frequent, and mainly occur in classical normative accounts of proper action. For example, in her discussion of early articulations of social service, Varadappan (2003) cites a commentator on the *Upanishads*, a set of Hindu sacred texts, who enumerates five great *yajnas* (sacrifices) required of all men: to *brahman* (the ultimate reality), to the *pitr*-s (ancestors), to *daiva*-s (gods), to *bhuta*-s (living beings), and to *nara* (other men). She thus extrapolates social service from "sacrifice to men." Among the *Dharma* Shastras, a set of texts prescribing behavior for various categories of people, the *Yajnavalkya Smriti* enjoins *shranta-samvahana*, or "affording relief to the weary" and *rogi-paricharya*, or "the tending of the sick" (Vidyarnava 1918). In a text called the *Nyayabhashya*, Vatsyayana, in describing action (*pravritti*), enumerates proper bodily action as *dana* (charity), *paritrapa* (protection), and *paricharana* (service) (Potter 1989). "*Paricharana*," here, carries the connotation of physical service.

This passage from the *Nyayabhashya* is also noteworthy for its emphasis on *dana*, which literally translates to "giving." *Dana* is a concept that is much discussed in Hindu texts and has consequently received much scholarly attention.[14] Some trace the antecedent of charitable gifting back to the most ancient of Hindu sacred texts, the *Rig Veda* (1500 BCE), which exalts those who donate (Bano and Nair 2007). Subsequently, in the *Taittiriya Upanishad*, a teacher includes exhortations to his students at the conclusion of their education to engage in *dana*, "You should give with faith, and never without faith. You should give with dignity. You should give with modesty. You should give with trepidation. You should give with comprehension" [verse 1.11.3] (Olivelle 1998: 299). In the *Dharma Shastras*, while *dana* receives sustained exposition in sections on moral conduct, there is a further subgenre of lengthy manuals composed between 1000 CE and 1300 CE solely dedicated to *dana* (Heim 2004). In her study of these manuals, Heim describes various purposes of gift-giving, including the teleological and soteriological purposes of merit-making for the donor that mark the act as a religious endeavor, as well as the social purposes. The compendia enumerate royal gifts, gifts to the gods, and gifts of public welfare. This last category listed gifts of security, learning and health, including building hospitals and dispensing medicine (Heim 2004). In this way, though there are antecedents for social service and charitable giving in

---

[13]   There is a spirited debate in the study of Hindu traditions about the extent of the colonial construction or invention of "Hinduism"; for a survey of the various perspectives, see Lorenzen (1999: 630-31).

[14]   It must be stressed that *dana* is not solely a Hindu phenomenon and also plays heavily into Jain and Buddhist practices (see Heim 2004).

Hindu prescriptive texts, it must be reiterated that these do not appear in a singular concatenation and are expanded considerably in the nineteenth century.

A Global Overture: The Colonial Encounter

Having explored some examples of social service in the nineteenth-century Swaminarayan *sampradaya* and the religious motivations for such service as explained by Sahajanand Swami, as well as the prehistory of service in Hindu textual archives, we now turn our attention to the development of service, both in terms of the *seva* and *dana*, as effected by global flows during two distinct moments: colonial globalization and contemporary globalization. Each of these moments represents a remarkable shift in global interactions. As Appadurai (1996: 28) observes, although there has always been much "long-distance (and long term) cultural traffic," the colonial period "set the basis for a permanent traffic." In the past few decades, postcolonial scholarship has articulated the multifarious ramifications of the colonial encounter in British India; for the purposes of assessing the effects of colonialism on social service, it would be useful to look at: (1) the missionary encounter, and (2) colonial governance.

It has long been understood that, especially in the nineteenth century, Christian missionaries sought to cast Hinduism as a backward and primitive religion and insisted on the superiority of Christianity (van der Veer 2009). Specifically, it was alleged that Hinduism lacked the capacity for dynamic and beneficial social change (Beckerlegge 2011). The indigenous response was to claim the spiritual superiority of Hindu religious traditions, and to advocate reform within Hindu traditions to meet the specific challenges posed by the missionaries. Consequently, movements stressing reform have been branded by scholars as reactionary and mediated by the colonial encounter. Many have argued that Vivekananda's emphasis on social service was an adoption of ideas presented by Christian missionaries, and that Vivekananda's interpretation of Hindu texts was conditioned by his Western-influenced education and reading of German idealists' romanticization of these texts (Beckerlegge 2011). Thus, the nineteenth century "recasting" of *seva* is in part explained as the adoption of a Christian ethos.

Dana is also conceived of as being influenced by the colonial encounter, specifically with respect to colonial governance. While the depictions of *dana* in the *Dharma Shastra* compendia discussed above were textual exhortations, studies have shown that merchants in the western Indian city of Surat (Haynes 1987) and Marwari merchants in Rajasthan (Birla 2009) did in fact follow these patterns of *dana*, which were made both for religious merit but also as symbolic investments in establishing relationships with those around them in power. In the nineteenth century, however, there was a considerable shift in the focus of donations from the construction of almshouses and wells to schools, colleges, hospitals, and other public works and causes (Haynes 1987). In tracing the genealogy of this change, Haynes argues that, as the British increasingly implemented a bureaucratic form of government, *dana* took on the form of large-scale philanthropy to earn symbolic capital with colonial officials, who privileged public charity (Haynes 1987). While prior patterns of donation continued, there was an increased emphasis on the types of projects espoused by the British. Birla takes this argument further by looking specifically at the standardization of legislation around charitable endowments and the creation of public trusts in the late nineteenth and early twentieth centuries. Legislation around charity was fleshed out in Victorian England in the latter half of the nineteenth century, which, in turn, led to significant legislation in British India. Birla (2009: 68-69) references: the Indian Income Tax Act of 1880, which defined charity as "activity *exclusively* for public benefit" and conferred a tax-exempt status on such charities; the Charitable Endowments Act of 1890, which further defined public charitable trusts; and the Charitable and Religious Trusts Act of 1920, which created a separate category for religious trusts deemed of public import—the public religious trust. This change in legislation facilitated the creation of a specific type of religious and charitable trust, privileging a specific kind of *dana*.

The colonial encounter had some important ramifications on the conceptualization and practice of *seva* and *dana* in nineteenth-century colonial India, but the Swaminarayan case is more complex. First, it must be made clear that the colonial influence on Gujarat was minimal until the third decade of the nineteenth century. Though many aspects of religiosity emphasized by Sahajanand Swami are similar to those of the reform movements which come afterwards, many (for example, Dwyer 2004; Schreiner 2001) have pointed to the lack of evidence that Sahajanand Swami's teachings were influenced by the West or Christianity. His interactions with colonial agents and Christian missionaries were limited and came towards the end of his life, well after the establishment of the fundamental principles and practices of his religious movement. This is in clear contrast to Vivekananda who received a Western education in Calcutta before taking up ascetic practice, and who traveled to the United States (Beckerlegge 2006). However, even in the case of Vivekananda, it is argued that accounts claiming Vivekananda's emphasis on *seva* was a strictly Western imposition are false, and fail to factor in the role of his *guru* Ramakrishna's emphasis on *seva* (Beckerlegge 2006). It is important, then, not to overstate colonial influences, and certainly in the early periods of the Swaminarayan *sampradaya*, these influences are notably absent.

The legacy of colonial legislation on charitable trusts is, however, felt in the Swaminarayan *sampradaya*. As delineated earlier, BAPS became a religious trust in 1947, and established a separate charitable trust in 1950. Though social service activities did not begin in earnest until Pramukh Swami Maharaj became the spiritual leader (likely due to the resource limitations of the fledgling organization), the infrastructure had already been established. As described above, BAPS saw visible growth in the 1970s, and increased resources, both in terms of membership as well as finances—allowed for more attention to be paid to social services. A review of the social service activities taking place in the 1970s reveals a commitment to types of public works privileged by colonial legislation: namely, activities related to medical and educational welfare. In 1976, the first blood drive was organized in conjunction with the Indian Red Cross Society to supplement one-day medical camps (BAPS 1976). In these medical camps, free medical check-ups were performed and medicine dispensed. The charitable trust also donated funds to hospitals and schools (Anandswarupdas 1979; BAPS 1978). This was in addition to more traditional types of social service including relief work. In the aftermath of famine and other natural disasters such as floods and cyclones, BAPS volunteers arrived at disaster sites as soon as possible to offer food and other support (BAPS 2003a). It is worth revisiting, in this context, the speech delivered by Pramukh Swami Maharaj on the occasion of the first blood donation camp, quoted at the start of this chapter. Pramukh Swami Maharaj draws an explicit connection between the blood donation activities and those carried out by Sahajanand Swami, and he also mentions pleasing Sahajanand Swami. Pramukh Swami Maharaj and members of BAPS envision themselves carrying out the same social service activities as in Sahajanand Swami's time, and the understanding that these activities are religiously inflected is still present. However, an increase in a specific type of public charitable work can be seen as a change dictated in part by the changes in legislation influenced by the colonial encounter.

The "Transnational Optic"

Navigating the Local and Translocal

I will now turn to global flows in the era of contemporary transnationalism. I will apply what scholars such as Levitt (2007) call a "transnational optic," which de-emphasizes the boundaries of nation-states and emphasizes a world with no set borders and boundaries. Applying such an optic reveals a tension between cultural homogenization and the universalism of globalization on the one hand, and cultural heterogenization and contextual particularism on the other (Appadurai 1996; Srinivas 2010). The view of universalism and homogenization has been criticized for implying a teleology of the West; a center-to-periphery approach by which globalization is understood as Westernization (Srinivas 2010). As a corrective, these above scholars advocate understanding the various directions, trajectories, and speeds of global flows in a disorderly, complex system.

Migration studies are based on the logical assumption that immigrants maintain significant connections to their countries of origin (Levitt 2007). This is certainly observed with members of the BAPS community who migrated across political borders, specifically with respect to the transmission of the impetus to engage in social service activities. In the early years of social service outside of India, namely, in the 1980s and 1990s, the patterns of engagement followed the early years of service in India in the 1970s. For example, there were efforts in aiding in relief activities after natural and human calamities: following a famine in Ethiopia in 1984, an earthquake in California in 1994, and a terrorist attack in Nairobi, Kenya in 1998 (BAPS 2003a). In California, food and water were supplied, and members of the BAPS community also canvassed affected areas to assess and report damage (BAPS 1994). In Kenya, members volunteered at understaffed hospitals (BAPS 1998). The community also organized multiple blood donation drives (BAPS 1992) and free health fairs offering a range of services, including influenza vaccines, diabetes testing, and standard medical check-ups (BAPS 1999). Following a push to further organize the drives in 1997 in India, including various specialty camps for the screening of specific conditions (BAPS 2013d), BAPS Charities (at the time BAPS Care International), began a drive to have regular, annual health fairs in 2000 (BAPS Charities 2005). In these ways, members of the BAPS community outside of India have maintained a connection to India by bringing patterns of social service practices with them.

Focusing on one-way flows implies a false homogenization and uniformity of practice; but to take it one step further, it is important to move beyond "home" and "return" (Levitt, Lucken, and Barnett. 2011) and beyond the simple "push and pull" of migration theory (Appadurai 1996). Instead, we must pay attention to the local instantiations of translocal ideas or "how global facts take local form" (Appadurai 1996: 18). Srinivas (2008) observes that, though there is considerable transnational organization in the Sri Sathya Sai Seva Organization, decisions about the specific service activities in which a local chapter will engage are made locally, a product of local needs and available resources. Kim (2012) makes similar observations with respect to BAPS. While social service activities outside of India mirror those inside India, there are considerable context-specific differences in the expressions of BAPS's commitment to social service.

Before assessing the nature of these differences in various diasporic contexts, it is necessary to briefly describe the social service activities that take place in India. Since the 1990s, as the BAPS community in India continued to grow, there was a continuation of the same activities carried out earlier, but in a more structured, institutionalized format. This parallels a similar trend in the Ramakrishna Math and Mission, which has gradually invested resources into institutions such as schools and hospitals from an earlier focus on providing relief for human and natural calamities (Beckerlegge 2006). The various charitable trusts associated with BAPS in India have thus institutionalized previous commitments. For example, instead of simply donating funds to other schools, they have started up various residential and day schools, mostly in Gujarat (see Table 5.1 below). These schools vary greatly in their grades of instruction; some are in English while others offer instruction in Gujarati with occasional classes in English. Most offer significant tuition discounts and remissions for those who cannot afford it.

In the realm of health care, the project of organizing blood donation drives and free medical clinics is on-going, though in a more organized fashion since 1997. In addition to these efforts, BAPS currently operates twelve mobile dispensary units traveling to underserviced parts of Gujarat and neighboring areas, as well as seven hospitals and treatment centers (see Table 5.2 below). Furthermore, unlike with the Ramakrishna Math and Mission, BAPS has, in fact, increased its disaster relief efforts (see Table 5.3 below). In this arena, however, they have expanded their commitment by engaging not just in immediate relief following disaster but also in large-scale

Table 5.1   BAPS Schools in India

Town and state	Grades of instruction	Type of school
Atladra, Gujarat	Kindergarten-10th	Residential
Bakrol, Gujarat	11th-12th	Day
Bhadra, Gujarat	8th-10th	Day
Chansad, Gujarat	8th-10th	Day
Gondal, Gujarat	8th-12th	Day/Residential
Karamsad, Gujarat	4th-12th	Residential
Mount Abu, Rajasthan	Kindergarten-5th	Residential
Nagpur, Rajasthan	Kindergarten-12th	Residential
Raisan, Gujarat	Nursery-9th	Day/Residential
Sarangpur, Gujarat	5th-12th	Residential
Silvassa, Dadra and Nagar Haveli	Kindergarten-10th	Day
Tithal, Gujarat	Kindergarten-9th	Residential

Source: BAPS (2013c).

rehabilitation efforts. This includes rebuilding homes in one village and schools in three others in Maharashtra after an earthquake in 1993; three entire villages in Orissa after a cyclone in 1999; and two villages in Tamil Nadu after a tsunami in 2004 (BAPS 2003a; 2006). This list does not include BAPS's most extensive rehabilitation project to date, following the devastating earthquake in Gujarat in 2001, in which it rehabilitated 15 villages and colonies and 39 schools (BAPS 2003b). These massive projects required coordination, cooperation, and participation with external entities, including architectural and engineering firms like the Vastushilpa Foundation.

Table 5.2   BAPS Hospitals and Clinic in India

Place	Name	Date opened
Botad, Gujarat	T. M. Vadodaria Medical Center	1992
Mumbai, Maharashtra	Pramukh Swami Eye Hospital	1996
Chansad, Gujarat	Pramukh Swami Prathmik Arogya Kendra	2000
Dabhoi, Gujarat	Pramukh Swami General Hospital	2000
Atladra, Gujarat	Pramukh Swami Hospital	2001
Surat, Gujarat	Pramukh Swami Hospital	2005
Ahmedabad, Gujarat	Yogiji Maharaj Hospital	2012*

* A smaller health-care center was originally opened here in 2003.

Source: (BAPS 2013d).

Table 5.3   BAPS Relief Work in India

Year	Place	Type of Disaster
1974	Maharashtra & Gujarat	Famine
1975	Morbi, Gujarat	Flood
1976	Maharashtra & Gujarat	Famine
1977	Andhra Pradesh	Cyclone
1982	Saurashtra, Gujarat	Flood
1983	Saurashtra, Gujarat	Flood
1987-1988	Gujarat	Famine (Cattle Camps)
1992	Jamnagar, Gujarat	Famine
1993	Maharashtra	Earthquake
1994	Surat, Gujarat	Pneumonic Plague
1995	West Bengal	Flood
1996	Andhra Pradesh	Cyclone
1997	Gujarat	Flood
1998	Kutch, Gujarat	Cyclone
1999	Orissa	Cyclone
2000	Gujarat	Famine
2001	Kutch & Saurashtra, Gujarat	Earthquake
2004-2005	Tamil Nadu	Tsunami
2005	Maharashtra & Gujarat	Flood
2007	Saurashtra, Gujarat	Flood
2008	Bihar	Flood

Source: BAPS 2003a:35, 2013b.

BAPS Charities, and its predecessor BAPS Care International, are also heavily engaged in social service activities but not to the extent of BAPS in India. One of the principal activities organized in both North America and the United Kingdom, which is unique to these contexts, is that of the "walkathon" or "sponsored walk" in which participants raise money in anticipation of a five- to ten-kilometer walk. Started in 1994 in the United Kingdom and 1997 in North America, these became more organized and widespread in the following years. For example, in 2010, 12,000 participants in 45 centers across North America took part in the "BAPS Charities Walk" in the month of September; each individual center had chosen its own local, regional, and/or national charities as beneficiaries (BAPS Charities 2011). In the same year in the United Kingdom, 3,500 participants in 15 centers took part in the "BAPS Charities Annual Challenge" on one Sunday in April, each center again having its own local beneficiary, while also collectively supporting a national charity (BAPS Charities UK 2010b). In this way, while there is considerable overlap in terms of the social service activities in which members of BAPS engage, there are also significant context-driven specificities. In North America and the United Kingdom, there are fewer institutions set up to support social service than in India, but there is a great emphasis on collaborating with other charities, including BAPS's public charitable trusts in India engaging in social service activities.

The Purchase of Social Service: Ways of Belonging

Having described some of the translocal and local factors contributing to the expression of social service in the BAPS community, it is important to analyze what particular role social service plays within the community, both as a whole and for individual members. Theoretical understandings of transnationalism can help us understand how BAPS's social service activities allow members to participate in various social fields. First, we will examine various notions of citizenship. In this context, there is another tension generated by the transnational optic: though some speak out against a "methodological nationalism" in social sciences where the nation-state is seen as "the natural, logical container within which social life takes place" (Levitt et al. 2011: 469), others contend that transnational studies has become excessively "post-national" which obfuscates the "enduring capacity of the nation state to adapt to rapidly developing conditions" (Zavos 2012: 213).

Zavos argues that in grappling with changing contexts of multiculturalism and an ethnically plural society, the British state has put forward an "ethnic citizenship," one in which ethnicity is "reflected in the performance of religious identity as a kind of model minority" and is marked by an agenda of "community cohesion" (2012: 219-20). By espousing these principles of cohesion and enacting "civic virtue," communities can gain considerable social capital. In fact, Zavos (2012) points to the fact that the BAPS temple in Neasden, London, has often been visited by agents of the state as corroboration of the fact that, in its performance of civic virtue, BAPS is well-suited to function in accordance with the state's strategy of community cohesion.

The social service efforts of BAPS and the Swaminarayan community can be seen as enactments of civic virtue and have gained a lot of attention for the community. In Sahajanand Swami's time, his efforts sparked the interest of Sir John Malcolm, Governor of Bombay, and Reginald Heber, Lord Bishop of Calcutta (Williams 2001). This type of engagement and recognition has also continued recently. In India, BAPS has been involved in several government-sponsored social service initiatives, including literacy campaigns in rural Gujarat in 1991 and 1993 (BAPS 2013c). In the United States, BAPS Charities has become involved in President Barack Obama's "United We Serve" service initiative (BAPS Charities 2009). In England, BAPS Charities has been awarded the Queen's Award for Voluntary Service (Brosius 2012). In this way, members of BAPS located in various national contexts evoke a sense of citizenship.

Internationally, BAPS has been granted consultative status to the United Nations Economic and Social Council in recognition of its multi-level and expansive social services program (BAPS 1996). This last recognition dovetails with Zavos's argument that, though the nation-state does shape citizenship, citizenship is also *flexible*. According to Zavos (2012: 228), "citizenship is invoked as a general mode of responsibility, a general feature of global society, which [BAPS] is ideally placed to deliver precisely because of its transnational character." Social service activities thus become a way for members of BAPS to take part in transnational social fields (Levitt 2005) and diasporic public spheres, which are in turn developed by modern electronic media (Appadurai 1996). BAPS's social service activities are publicized in a variety of media: monthly magazines including the Gujarati and Hindi-language *Swaminarayan Prakash* and English *Swaminarayan Bliss,* as well as well-developed websites. These various websites allow for a variety of publics, both members of the community and beyond, to "gain knowledge of the transnational network and activities as if they were face-to-face neighbours and distance and time did not matter" (Brosius 2012: 446-47). Social service activities and their publication through media are linked to the imagining of a transnational "moral community" whose image as "stable yet flexible" is "projected for the consumption of non-*satsangis*"; this, in turn, is a consumption driven by a desire to partake in something of great global and historical importance (Brosius 2012: 441). By this analysis, social service in BAPS is one means to the development of a new form of cultural citizenship through which people can aspire to be both globally and nationally confident (Brosius 2010). This articulation suggests that social service is a public means to generate various ways of belonging in national and transnational contexts.

Global Community of Faith

Social service allows for members of BAPS to develop an additional way of belonging; however, an analysis of "belonging" must not stop at examining participation in a diasporic public sphere through a flexible citizenship rooted in various civic engagements. Srinivas (2010: 145) observes that, for members of the Sathya Sai Seva Organization, "citizenship is cast primarily in local terms within immediate social collectives such as the neighborhood or the city." At the same time, devotees, regardless of local context or even nationality, felt bound to each other through a common practice and the figure of Sathya Sai Baba. In much the same way, social service helps bind members of BAPS together in a transnational community of faith—a point that can be acknowledged only if we take seriously the express motivations of members of BAPS. Kim (2012: 435) points to the fact that "what is perhaps less resonant with its publics, and sometimes easily dismissed, are the ways in which BAPS's flexible interventions and its confidence in interacting with its publics are from the devotee standpoint guided and inspired by devotional motivations." Acknowledging the self-identified motivations of those engaged in social service in BAPS is not to negate completely the social ramifications of service discussed above. However, even in her discussion of these social ramifications, Brosius (2010) concedes that members of BAPS would not share in her analysis. It is a matter, then, of balancing what Williams (2001) calls the latent and manifest social function, the latter being what members of the community themselves suggest is the function of their actions. An analysis of social service, then, cannot stop short at social capital.

Conclusion

Members of the BAPS community are actively engaged in social service activities across the world, and I have sought to demonstrate how this engagement is mediated by the experience of globality. I have identified two moments of transnational transfer of people and ideas: one in the colonial period and one more recent. The modern expressions of social service in BAPS are certainly affected by these global contexts. Further, in navigating these contexts, BAPS "must remain attuned to the political, legal and governmental logics that inform its multiple publics" (Kim 2012: 433). This sees its expression in the fact that, organizationally, there is a separation between social service activities and religious activities. Studies of faith-based social service indicate that such a separation is essential; Anand (2004: 53) cites BAPS as an example of an organization engaged in social service that does not project a Hindu religious identity and, instead, "focuses on philanthropy that arises from a religious motivation for the greater good of the society." While social service is religiously motivated and seen as an act of devotion on the part of the actor, the expression of this service is not tied to a religious or proselytizing mission.

My analysis of social service in BAPS is animated by Vertovec's (2000) emphasis on paying attention to approaches of structure (in this case, the effects of global flows on social service) and agency (in this case, the meanings that social actors derive from their actions). Furthermore, in following Kim (2008), it is important not to suggest that conditions of globalization alone are responsible for expressions of social service activities in BAPS. Murphy's description of service in the Sikh tradition stands as a useful parallel for understanding the BAPS case: service is situated in a "historical past … reconstituted in the present through the production and reproduction of Sikh historical narratives in relation to contemporary practices," which bind the "community together in a shared past and theology" (Murphy 2004: 342-43). Though the specific types of service activities in which members of BAPS are engaged have been developed by various global flows of people and ideas, members of BAPS come together in a community bound by global expressions of a "spirit of service" dictated by a shared history and theology.

References

Amrutvijaydas, Sadhu. 2007. *100 Years of BAPS: Foundation, Formation, Fruition.* Ahmedabad, India: Swaminarayan Aksharpith.

Anand, Priya. 2004. *Hindu Diaspora and Religious Philanthropy in the United States.* Toronto: Center on Philanthropy and Civil Society, New York. Retrieved November 25, 2012 (www.istr.org/resource/resmgr/working_papers_toronto/anand.priya.pdf).

Anandswarupdas, Sadhu. 1979. "News and Flashes." *Swaminarayan Bliss* (April).

Appadurai, Arjun. 1996. *Modernity at Large: Cultural Dimensions of Globalization.* Minneapolis: University of Minnesota Press.

Appadurai, Arjun. 2000. "Grassroots Globalization and the Research Imagination." *Public Culture* 12(1): 1-19.

Bano, Masooda, and Padmaja Nair. 2007. *Faith-based Organisations in South Asia: Historical Evolution, Current Status and Nature of Interaction with the State.* Birmingham, AL: University of Birmingham. Retrieved October 1, 2012 (http://www.religionsanddevelopment.org/files/resourcesmodule/@random454f80f60b3f4/1202734559_WP12.pdf).

BAPS. 1976. "Dvitiya Tabibi Shrey Yagna—Raktadan Yagna." *Swaminarayan Prakash* (June): 224-25.

BAPS. 1978. "Swamishri in the Benefit of Mankind." *Swaminarayan Bliss* (April): 37.

BAPS. 1992. "Back Cover." *Swaminarayan Bliss* (October).

BAPS. 1994. "Earthquake Relief: Los Angeles." *Swaminarayan Bliss* (March): 14.

BAPS. 1996. "United Nations Approval." *Swaminarayan Bliss* (December): 4.

BAPS. 1998. "Aiding the Bomb Victims of Nairobi." *Swaminarayan Bliss* (September): 15.

BAPS. 1999. "Medical Services: 1998." *Swaminarayan Bliss* (April): 9-11.

BAPS. 2003a. "BAPS Relief Work." *Swaminarayan Bliss* (October): 35.

BAPS. 2003b. "Rehabiliation of Adopted Villages." *Swaminarayan Bliss* (October): 12-26.

BAPS. 2006. "Swamishri and Governor of Karnataka Dedicate Homes in Pattipulamkupam and Mahabalipuram." *Swaminarayan Bliss* (October): 17-18.

BAPS. 2013a. "BAPS Swaminarayan Sanstha—Global Network." Retrieved January 28, 2013 (http://www.baps.org/Global-Network.aspx).

BAPS. 2013b. "Disaster Relief." Retrieved January 19, 2013 (http://www.baps.org/humanitarianservices/DisasterRelief.aspx).

BAPS. 2013c. "Education and Research." Retrieved January 19, 2013 (http://www.baps.org/humanitarianservices/Education-and-Research.aspx).

BAPS. 2013d. "Hospitals and Clinics." Retrieved January 19, 2013 (http://www.baps.org/humanitarianservices/Health-and-Medical/HospitalsandClinics.aspx).

BAPS. 2013e. "Humanitarian Services." Retrieved January 24, 2013 (http://www.baps.org/humanitarianservices.aspx).

BAPS. 2013f. "North America." Retrieved January 10, 2013 (http://www.baps. org/Global-Network/North-America.aspx).

BAPS. 2013g. "The Spirit of Service." Retrieved January 23, 2013 (http://www. baps.org/humanitarianservices/The-Spirit-of-Service.aspx).

BAPS Charities. 2005. "Health Fair: Clifton, NJ." Retrieved November 23, 2012 (http://www.bapscharities.org/mediacenter/announcements/2005/clifton healthfair.htm).

BAPS Charities. 2007. "Name Change Announcement." Retrieved November 23,2012(http://www.bapscharities.org/mediacenter/announcements/2007/baps charitiesnamechange.htm).

BAPS Charities. 2009. "BAPS Charities Health Awareness Lecture Supporting President Obama's Service Initiative." Retrieved November 23, 2012 (http:// www.bapscharities.org/mediacenter/announcements/2005/cliftonhealthfair. htm).

BAPS Charities. 2011. "Walk 2010 Check Presentations." Retrieved November 23, 2012 (http://www.bapscharities.org/services/community/walkathon/2011/ index.htm).

BAPS Charities. 2012. "About Us." Retrieved October 10, 2012 (http://www. bapscharities.org/aboutus/index.htm).

BAPS Charities UK. 2010a. "Our Services." Retrieved December 24, 2012 (http:// bapscharities.org.uk/our_services.php).

BAPS Charities UK. 2010b. "Over 3,500 take part in the 'BAPS Charities Annual Challenge'." Retrieved December 24, 2012 (http://bapscharities.org.uk/news details.php?newsId=14).

Beckerlegge, Gwilym. 2006. *Swami Vivekananda's Legacy of Service: A Study of the Ramakrishna Math and Mission.* New Delhi, India: Oxford University Press.

Beckerlegge, Gwilym. 2011. "Seva (Service to Humanity): A Boundary Issue in the Study of Recent and Contemporary Hindu Movements." *Man in India* 91(1): 39-56.

Birla, Ritu. 2009. *Stages of Capital: Law, Culture, and Market Governance in Late Colonial India.* Durham, NC: Duke University Press.

Brosius, Christiane. 2010. *India's Middle Class: New Forms of Urban Leisure, Consumption and Prosperity.* London, UK: Routledge.

Brosius, Christiane. 2012. "The Perfect World of BAPS: Media and Urban Dramaturgies in a Globalised Context." Pp. 440-62 in *Public Hinduisms*, edited by John Zavos, Pralay Kanungo, Deepa S. Reddy, Maya Warrier, and Raymond Brady Williams. New Delhi, India: Sage Publications.

Charity Commission. n.d. "Charity Framework." Retrieved January 3, 2013 (http://www.charitycommission.gov.uk/Showcharity/RegisterOfCharities/Charity Framework.aspx?RegisteredCharityNumber=1123367&SubsidiaryNumber=0).

Dani, Gunvant. 1980. *Bhagwan Swaminarayan: A Social Reformer.* Ahmedabad, India: Bochasanwasi Shri Aksharpurushottam Sanstha.

Dave, Harshadrai T. 2007. *Shastriji Maharaj Jivan Charitra, Part 1*. 6th ed. Ahmedabad, India: Swaminarayan Aksharpith.

Dave, Harshadrai T. 2009a. *Bhagvan Shri Swaminarayan Bruhad Jivancharitra*. 5th ed. Ahmedabad, India: Swaminarayan Aksharpith.

Dave, Harshadrai T. 2009b. *Bhagvan Shri Swaminarayan Bruhad Jivancharitra*. 5th ed. Ahmedabad, India: Swaminarayan Aksharpith.

Dwyer, Rachel. 2004. "The Swaminarayan Movement." Pp. 180-99 in *South Asians in the Diaspora: Histories and Religious Traditions*, edited by Knut A. Jacobsen and Pratap Kumar. Leiden, Netherlands: Brill.

Flood, Gavin. 1996. *An Introduction to Hinduism*. Cambridge, UK: Cambridge University Press.

Halbfass, Wilhelm, ed. 1995. *Philology and Confrontation: Paul Hacker on Traditional and Modern Vedanta*. Albany, NY: State University of New York Press.

Haynes, Douglas E. 1987. "From Tribute to Philanthropy: The Politics of Gift Giving in a Western Indian City." *Journal of Asian Studies* 46(2): 339-60.

Heim, Maria. 2004. *Theories of the Gift in South Asia: Hindu, Buddhist, and Jain Reflections on Dana*. New York: Routledge.

ISSO Seva. n.d. "ISSO Seva: Serving Humanity." Retrieved October 3, 2012 (http://www.issoseva.org/MainHome.aspx).

Kim, Hanna H. 2008. "Managing Deterritorialisation, Sustaining Belief: the Bochasanwasi Shree Akshar Purushottam Swaminarayan Sanstha as Ethnographic Case Study and Theoretical Foil." Pp. 225-42 in *New Religions and Globalization: Empirical, Theoretical and Methodological Perspectives*, edited by A. W. Geertz and M. Warburg. Aarhus, Denmark: Aarhus University Press.

Kim, Hanna H. 2009. "Public Engagement and Personal Desires: BAPS Swaminarayan Temples and their Contribution to the Discourses on Religion." *International Journal of Hindu Studies* 13(3): 357-90.

Kim, Hanna H. 2012. "The BAPS Swaminarayan Temple Organisation and its Publics." Pp. 417-39 in *Public Hinduisms*, edited by John Zavos, Pralay Kanungo, Deepa S. Reddy, Maya Warrier, and Raymond Brady Williams. New Delhi, India: Sage Publications.

Levitt, Peggy. 2005. "Building Bridges: What Migration Scholarship and Cultural Sociology Have to Say to Each Other." *Poetics* 33: 49-62.

Levitt, Peggy. 2007. "Redefining the Boundaries of Belonging: The Transnationalization of Religious Life." Pp. 103-20 in *Everyday Religion: Observing Modern Religious Lives*, edited by Nancy T. Ammerman. New York: Oxford University Press.

Levitt, Peggy. 2012. "Religion on the Move: Mapping Global Cultural Production and Consumption." Pp. 159-76 in *Religion on the Edge: De-centering and Re-centering the Sociology of Religion*, edited by Courtney Bender, Wendy Cadge, Peggy Levitt, and David Smilde. New York: Oxford University Press.

Levitt, Peggy, Kristen Lucken, and Melissa Barnett. 2011. "Beyond Home and Return: Negotiating Religious Identity across Time and Space through the Prism of the American Experience." *Mobilities* 6(4): 467-82.

Lorenzen, David N. 1999. "Who Invented Hinduism?" *Comparative Studies in Society and History* 41(4): 630-59.

Mangalnidhidas, Sadhu. Forthcoming. "Service as Spiritual Endeavor in the BAPS Swaminarayan Tradition." in *Engaged Hinduism: World Engagement and Service in Hindu Thought and Practice*, edited by Rita D. Sherma and Arvind Sharma. Palgrave.

Murphy, Anne. 2004. "Moblising seva ('Service'): Modes of Sikh Diasporic Action." Pp. 337-72 in *South Asians in the Diaspora: Histories and Religious Traditions*, edited by Knut A. Jacobsen and Pratap Kumar. Leiden, Netherlands: Brill.

Olivelle, Patrick. 1998. *Early Upanisads: Annotated Text and Translation*. New York: Oxford University Press.

Parekh, Bhai Manilal C. 1936. *Sri Swami Narayana: A Gospel of Bhagwat-Dharma or God in Redemptive Action*. Rajkot, India: Sri Bhagwat-Dharma Mission House.

The Pew Forum on Religion and Public Life. 2012. "The Global Religious Landscape." Retrieved December 31, 2012 (http://www.pewforum.org/global-religious-landscape-hindu.aspx).

Potter, Karl H. 1989. "Metaphor as Key to Understanding the Thought of Other Speech Communities." Pp. 19-35 in *Interpreting Across Boundaries: New Essays in Comparative Philosophy*, edited by Gerald James Larson and Eliot Deutsch. Delhi, India: Motilal Banarsidass Publishers.

Satyaprasaddas, Swami. 2000. *Samajsudharak Bhagvan Shri Swaminarayan*. Bhuj, India: Sadguru Mahant Purani Swami Harisvarupdas.

Schreiner, Peter. 2001. "Institutionalization of Charisma: The Case of Sahajānanda." Pp. 155-70 in *Charisma and Canon: Essays on the Religious History of the Indian Subcontinent*, edited by Vasudha Dalmia, Angelika Malinar, and Martin Christof. New Delhi, India: Oxford University Press.

Shrutiprakashdas, Sadhu. 2004. "Shri Swaminarayan Sampraday Ke Darshanik Siddhant Aur Bhakti Sadhana ki Vikasan Prakriya." Pp. 1-60 in *Shri Swaminarayan Darshan: Ek Chintan*, edited by Sadhu Anandswarupdas. Ahmedabad, India: Swaminarayan Aksharpith.

Sidel, Mark. 2004. "Diaspora Philanthropy to India: A Perspective from the United States." Pp. 215-58 in *Diaspora Philanthropy and Equitable Development in China and India*, edited by Peter F. Geithner, Paula D. Johnson, and Lincoln C. Chen. Cambridge, MA: Harvard University Press.

Srinivas, Smriti. 2008. *In the Presence of Sai Baba: Body, City and Memory in a Global Religious Movement.* Hyderabad, India: Orient Longman Private Limited.

Srinivas, Tulasi. 2010. *Winged Faith: Rethinking Globalization and Religious Pluralism through the Sathya Sai Movement*. New York: Columbia University Press.

United States Census Bureau. n.d. "Race Reporting for the Asian Population by Selected Categories: 2010." Retrieved January 7, 2013 (http://factfinder2. census.gov/faces/tableservices/jsf/pages/productview.xhtml?pid=DEC_10_ SF1_QTP8&prodType=table).

The Vachanamrut: Spiritual Discourses of Bhagwan Swaminarayan, An English Translation. 2001. 2nd ed. Ahmedabad, India: Swaminarayan Aksharpith.

Van der Veer, Peter. 2002. "Religion in South Asia." *Annual Review of Anthropology* 31: 173-87.

Van der Veer, Peter. 2009. "Global Breathing: Religious Utopias in India and China." Pp. 263-76 in *Transnational Transcendence: Essays on Religion and Globalization*, edited by Thomas J. Csordas. Berkeley: University of California Press.

Varadappan, Sarojini. 2003. *The Concept of Social Service in the Philosophy of Sri Svami Narayana*. Chennai, India: Sarojini Varadappan.

Vertovec, Steven. 2000. *The Hindu Diaspora: Comparative Patterns*. London: Routledge.

Vidyarnava, Rai Bahadur Srisa Chandra, tran. 1918. *Yajnavalkya Smrti, Mitaksara and Balambhatta: Book I-Achara Adhyaya*. Allahabad, India: The Panini Office.

Viratswarupdas, Sadhu. 2013. Personal Interview with Arun Brahmbhatt, January 25.

Williams, Raymond Brady. 2001. *An Introduction to Swaminarayan Hinduism*. Cambridge, UK: Cambridge University Press.

Williams, Raymond Brady. 2012. "Representations of Swaminarayan Hinduism." Pp. 176-89 in *Public Hinduisms*, edited by John Zavos, Pralay Kanungo, Deepa S. Reddy, Maya Warrier, and Raymond Brady Williams. New Delhi, India: Sage Publications.

Zavos, John. 2012. "Transnational Religious Organisation and Flexible Citizenship in Britain and India." Pp. 212-39 in *Citizenship and the Flow of Ideas in the Era of Globalisation: Structure, Agency and Power*, edited by Subrata Mitra. New Delhi, India: Samskriti.

Chapter 6
The Gawad Kalinga Movement: Charismatic Catholicism

Stephen M. Cherry

Shortly after 8 a.m. on a rainy Saturday morning, a group of twelve first-generation Filipino Americans arrived at the Mercado[1] home in Houston, Texas (United States), after traveling in separate cars from around the state. Some had been driving for several hours but most lived within an hour of the Mercados in the metropolitan area. John Mercado and his wife Nana, both of whom are first-generation Filipino Americans, called the group together to pray, eat, and talk about their progress on raising money for a community development project in the Philippines known as Gawad Kalinga (GK—meaning "give care" in Tagalog). All of the members of the group are active members of the Catholic charismatic family renewal group Couples for Christ (CFC). They are also active in their parish churches. They have known each other for years, in some cases twenty or more, through shared times in their religious fellowships and through friends or family connections back in the Philippines. Although each member of the group learned about GK at different points in their lives and under differing circumstances, as GK is one of several social ministries of CFC, they all see Gawad Kalinga as a vital part of CFC's mission and an important way to put their faith into action.

After sharing camaraderie and food, each of the members took turns giving reports on their fundraising activities. Gloria, for example, talked about raising $2,000 in sponsorship money for a marathon she planned to walk in the coming months. Virgil talked about selling $1,000 of squares on a football bingo he started at his office. Sally pulled out a newspaper clipping about her ten-year-old son Bert who raised several thousands of dollars selling his art sketches door to door. Presenting checks to Danny, the treasurer, the group started to talk about their future plans.

As sponsors for building or razing and rebuilding several villages in the Philippines, the group had already raised enough funds for 20 out of the 50 planned homes in the first village. In some cases, they had also made trips to the Philippines to help with the housing construction. While some had not visited the village yet, others had made trips to other GK villages throughout the Philippines

---

[1]   *Note*: Pseudonyms have been used in place of real names for all those interviewed to ensure anonymity and confidentiality. The only time this is not the case is for respondents whose names are in public print or are the authors of editorials and articles themselves.

or sat in on strategic meetings to build GK villages in other countries. Highlighting this, Rose explained:

> What we are doing is not just for us [Philippines]. It is a matter of grace for all. Neighboring countries like Korea, Malaysia, and Papua New Guinea have seen this transformation in the Philippines and they cannot believe what GK is doing so they are asking us to help them get it started there too. I just sat in on the meeting in PNG [Papua New Guinea] last month. With God's help, what we are doing is going to continue to grow beyond the Philippines. Presidents and universities around the world are already studying our successes … (Interview 2005)

Agreeing, the group began to talk about how they need to stay focused on one community at a time but should be mindful of this bigger picture. John, for example, stated, "The big picture is simple, we are doing God's work here and as we move forward we need to remember that this is for all people through him." Continuing, John explained:

> GK is now our greatest export [Philippines]. More than a product, it is a beacon to the world. God has chosen us [Filipinos] to be a light among nations. He has given us GK as a show of love and a lesson. If he can transform the poorest of the poorest nations through us, his faithful, then all will come to know his grace. In time people will look back and ask themselves how the Philippines rose up? We will testify for the Lord and then we will move on to end poverty in every nation. (Interview 2005)

From Diaspora Philanthropy to a Nation Building Movement

Every year over a million workers leave the Philippines to work overseas in an estimated 190 countries. They join roughly 8.7 million Filipinos, who have already left the Philippines, making them one of the largest diaspora or migrant populations in the world (Agunias 2009). Feeling an intense sense of obligation to give back to their country of origin, many Filipinos send money and goods to the Philippines annually, if not monthly. In 2007, for example, Filipinos overseas sent home an estimated $14.5 billion (United States currency) in remittances. These remittances make up roughly 10 percent of the Philippine gross national product annually and in 2008 helped drive economic growth to over 7 percent, a thirty-year high (Newland 2009). Although the Philippines is increasingly becoming dependent on its diaspora communities, the Philippine government has done very little to capitalize on potential resources. As Patricia Tomas, the former Secretary of Labor and Employment and the current Chairman of the Development Bank of the Philippines, has noted, the Philippine government has been more concerned with managing the employment of overseas workers than bridging ties with its larger diaspora as a tool for development (Agunias 2009; Newland 2009).

Hometown associations have attempted to fill part of this void but remain a largely untapped resource (Orozco and Rouse 2007; Somerville, Durana, and Terrazas 2008). Organizations such the Ayala Foundation USA (AFUSA), founded in 2000 by Filipinos in the United States, have also attempted to fill this void by encouraging diaspora philanthropy. With the aim of connecting Filipino Americans to non-profit organizations in the Philippines as a means to alleviate poverty, AFUSA has raised over \$3.75 million for public school programs (Newland, Terrazas, and Munster 2010). From 2004 to 2006, AFUSA also operated a youth volunteer program for second- and third-generation Filipino Americans but the program was only able to mobilize 21 youth over this period and was eventually terminated due to a host of complications (Terrazas 2010). Outside of these attempts, other non-profit and non-governmental agencies such as Habitat for Humanity have also attempted to fill the void in Philippine development needs with varying degrees of success.

What has largely been missing from many attempts to develop and sustain the Philippines has been the collective mobilizations of Filipinos themselves. A single act of giving or a one-time trip to the Philippines to volunteer for a project is rarely linked to a sustained mobilization towards development projects that make sense within the Philippine context. However, Gawad Kalinga (GK) represents one such movement. While numerous transnational NGOs outside of the Philippines have initiated development projects throughout the islands, they have, for the most part, not been successful at mobilizing Filipinos. Additionally, these outside attempts have also failed on some level because they do not fully understand the unique situation in the Philippines. Pointing to this, Tony Meloto, a chief architect of GK and its programs, suggests:

> This is our dilemma with development initiatives by rich countries in a third world setting like the Philippines: We cannot depend on borrowed dreams of foreigners who, despite sincere intentions, do not understand the nature of poverty and the aspirations of our people. Ours is a story of how hope was lost and how it can be regained. (Meloto 2009: 9)

Gawad Kalinga is not just an indigenous expression of a desire to help others but a sustained movement that seeks to radically transform the Philippines from a developing nation to a so-called first world nation by 2024. What started as a mobilization of Filipinos for the Philippines rooted in the charismatic Catholic renewal movement, Couples for Christ, is not only spreading across the Philippines, however, but becoming a model of development in other countries. Exploring this transformation in greater detail, this chapter retraces the rise of the GK movement in the Philippines from its Catholic charismatic roots to its eventual split and reformation over the question of cooperate partners and sponsors. The chapter also describes the GK model and approach to development and explores its various projects being carried out in countries around the world. Although it is not possible to comprehensively examine every current GK project and program in this single chapter, the cases presented here highlight how Gawad Kalinga has become a truly global movement and explores the challenges and issues GK faces as it continues to spreads beyond the Philippines.

Religious Roots and the Spread of the GK Movement

Couples for Christ began in the early 1980s in Metro Manila in the Philippines with sixteen couples as part of an outreach to evangelize married couples within the charismatic community (called Ang Ligaya ng Panginoon's [LNP], "Joy of the Lord" in Tagalog). Among the pioneering couples of the movement were Frank Padilla and his wife. In 1993, a group led by Padilla severed ties with LNP over differences on how to approach evangelization. CFC emerged as a new organization and subsequently developed the Christian Life Program (CLP) to recatechize Filipino Catholics. Throughout the 1990s Filipinos couples around the world, including those interviewed in Houston, joined the movement. By the end of the 1990s, CFC had spread well beyond the Philippines and in 2005 was recognized by the Vatican's Pontifical Council as one of 122 International Associations of Faithful.

As a global movement, CFC began to set organizational goals beyond the CLP program. One of these goals was social development, labeled Gawad Kalinga (GK). Social development quickly spread as a major focal point of CFC members globally including first-generation Filipino Americans living in Houston, Texas (United States). The movement developed out of a series of social experiments in the early 1990s led by Tony Meloto and a group of likeminded friends. As a group, largely connected to the early pioneers of CFC, they had become increasingly aware of several disruptive behaviors they thought made impoverished conditions in the slums of Metro Manila worse. Highlighting issues such as gambling and gang involvement, the group founded Serving in God's Army (SIGA—Tagalog for "light" or "fire"), as a rehabilitation program to break the cycle of these conditions (Meloto 2009). Supported financially by successful and affluent philanthropists in the community, the group began to study the slums. At the same time, members of SIGA along with others from CFC began to organize a series of peer and faith events for their own children. By 1993, the ideas flowing in both programs began to merge.

In 1995, CFC, together with Youth for Christ and other members of SIGA began a series of camps for out-of-school youth in Bagong Silang in Caloocan City, one of the largest slums in Metro Manila. After two successful camps, the membership of SIGA rose from just a few to over 500 (Meloto 2009). With this success, the group formed the ANCOP foundation (meaning "Answering the Cry of the Poor"), to serve more youth in the area. By 1998, ANCOP decided that in order to successfully meet the needs of the youth in Bagong Silang it would need to take a more holistic approach to community and literally rebuild the slums. In 1999, ANCOP built its first house for the Adduro family. In 2000, under the emerging leadership of Meloto, the name Gawad Kalinga was coined to describe the movement and eleven teams were organized to build a series of homes, soon to be villages, outside of Bagong Silang. Also that year, ANCOP USA was founded as a Diaspora extension that could further fund the movement.

In 2001, CFC ministries officially launched Gawad Kalinga (GK). The following year GK also picked up its first major partner. President Gloria Arroyo allocated 30 million pesos, roughly $686,100 United States dollars, to build 1,000 GK homes in Dumaguete City in Negros Oriental (Meloto 2009). In 2003, GK was formally registered with the Securities and Exchange Commission as the Gawad Kalinga Community Development Foundation Inc. with the stated mission of:

> Advancing and upholding an integrated, holistic, and sustainable community development program, especially in depressed areas, addressing shelter, livelihood, education and health issues in the spirit of nation building, to strengthen the development and improvement of human and spiritual formation of couples and their children and to foster cooperation with others in the pursuit and realization of the objectives for which GK has been established. (http://www.gk1world.com/)

It was an ambitious mission but one built on growing momentum. During that same year GK held its first GK Expo and launched the GK777 campaign to build 700,000 homes in 7,000 communities (in the Philippines) in seven years.

What started as a CFC mission quickly expanded to a multi-sectored partnership with secular sponsors, such as McDonald's, Pepsi and Coke, Proctor & Gamble, Pfizer, Gillette, and Colgate Palmolive, to name a few. All were driven by a vision of a new Philippines with no more slums, violence, or corruption. During this time, British millionaire Dylan Wilk also began to give generously to the movement and eventually became a full-time member of its global team. More than charity work or simply building homes, GK established itself as a nation-building movement. Explaining this approach, Mark, a first-generation 28-year-old Filipino American in Houston, stated in 2006:

> This task of nation building comes with comprehensive and proven programs for education, health, livelihood, and community empowerment. Everything is integrated and holistic. "No more slums!" is the resounding battle cry of this full-scale war against poverty. (Interview 2006)

Continuing, Mark points out:

> No loans are given, no interest is charged, no profits are made. Only the spirit of giving provides. The enormity of this task makes it foolish to think it can be done ... well, not by 2010! But the foolishness of God is wiser than human wisdom [1 Cor 1:25]. And day after day, everyone witnesses the impossible. No movement gathers momentum this fast—no revolution or upheaval of this kind. This is wildfire. This is the blaze of the Holy Spirit. (Interview 2006)

Mark's words are typical of those who describe the early momentum of GK777. By 2006, the realization that a 2010 goal was going to need greater support and efforts led to GK launching the "One Million Builders" campaign (GK1MB—or Isang Milyong Bayahi in Tagalog), as a means to rally more volunteers to GK sites. Subsequently, GK launched the GK1MB Challenge as a one-week national volunteering drive.

During this time, Meloto, who was now the face of GK, received both the Ramon Magsaysay Award and the Gawad Haydee Yorac Award from the Manila Electric Company and the University of the Philippines for his efforts through GK. As news began to travel, the Massachusetts Institute of Technology (MIT) sent a team to the Philippines to study the GK model of development. In 2007, Singaporean President S. R. Nathan, having heard about GK's successes both from Filipinos in his country and from emerging Asian development reports, launched a series of sponsoring programs in Philippine GK villages. Also that year, GK expanded to build the GK Rafaella village in Phnom Penh, Cambodia through the leadership of Filipino Americans. Seeing distinct parallels to conditions in the Philippines, these Filipinos brought GK to Cambodia through a local partnership with a community of garbage collectors who earned their living by scavenging through junkyards. Although the GK Rafaella village started with Filipinos who saw a need in Cambodia, the project was widely supported by local Cambodians and, hence, quickly became a Cambodian-led initiative.

In 2009, under growing external pressure and internal politicking CFC relinquished its control over the GK board. Given differences and power struggles within GK, it was clear that GK777 would not meet its goals by 2010. Pointing to a host of setbacks and organizational restructuring, the GK Global Summit held in Boston of that year re-established its momentum with the launching of the 2024 Vision campaign. A new goal was set to move beyond GK777 and bring the Philippines to First World status by 2024 while continuing to extend the GK brand into other impoverished nations. Calling on a "global army," GK relaunched its GK1MB challenge and today appears to have emerged from its organizational restructuring stronger.

GK now claims that from 2003 to 2010 the movement was in its "social justice" phase, a time of challenges that inspired others to help the Philippines. GK leaders also now suggest that the movement has moved into a "social artistry" phase, a time of learning, developmental experimentation, and partnerships, that will last until 2017 in which time the movement will enter its last phase of "social progress." During this social progress phase, GK believes that it will not only achieve measurable sustainability in the Philippines and move those who were once impoverished to prosperity but those in other so-called Third World nations as well. With this new vision and a reinterpretation of the movement's past, GK is once again building momentum both in its international scope and the number of programs and projects it has undertaken.

GK Projects and Programs

GK programs and projects are centered on a seven-point developmental model. This model includes: (1) child and youth development; (2) community building; (3) environment; (4) food sufficiency; (5) healthcare; (6) infrastructure; and (7) centers for social innovation. Each GK village is built with this model in mind. The villages themselves are organized and constructed around clustered housing. In some cases villages are built over existing villages, essentially a massive community remodeling. In other cases, villages are built on open parcels of land. Whatever the case may be, these villages can be found within metropolitan areas, in adjacent slums, and barrios or even in rural spaces well outside major cities.

Like Habitat for Humanity, each house is linked through "sweat equity" to its neighbor—each member of the village helps to build her neighbor's house. The houses are brightly painted and built to be energy efficient and durable during seasonal storms. However, unlike Habitat for Humanity or similar projects, no loans are given and no interest is charged for GK homes. Residents move into the homes with no debt. Given that at least 4.5 million Filipinos are homeless and 70 percent are landless, these villages are built for a vastly different population than what many transnational NGOs have experienced elsewhere. Groups such as Habitat for Humanity, for example, have built homes in the Philippines; however, according to Meloto, Habitat has not been very successful at building entire communities (Meloto 2009).

Gawad Kalinga distinguishes itself through its holistic approach. Beyond physical structures, GK provides value-based education for pre-school children and vocational education for street children up to thirteen years old. Scholarships are also provided for some who may pursue higher education. For many who do not pursue higher education and the majority of adults outside of these programs, GK conducts livelihood and skills training seminars, provides start-up capital and materials for micro-finance and micro-enterprise, and assists in the marketing of GK communities' products such as food from backyard farming and poultry raising. This is part of GK's Center for Social Innovation (CSI) program that seeks to build a culture of social entrepreneurship. The result of these efforts is what many have called GKnomics.

GK has also established the Bayan-Anihan program in partnership with the Agricultural State Universities as the first family-based sustainable farm program in the Philippines. Each family is given roughly ten square meters of land to garden which is expected to yield, with training and help, enough vegetables each month to provide thirty meals per family. Corporations and individuals help fuel the growth of the program by adopting farms and actively participating in the communities' journey to self-sufficiency. Among several corporate sponsors, Selecta, Globe, Shell, and Wyeth were the first to support the program (Meloto 2009). As a direct result of the corporate sponsorship, community members commit their labor to establish and maintain the farms. The process also gives them pride and self-worth as they feed their families and communities.

Given that roughly four million children in the Philippines are malnourished and 50 percent of the population has no health care, the SIGLA, SERBISYO, and SISTEMA initiatives log health profiles of every family in a GK community and monitor their status through a volunteer team of doctors and paramedical practitioners (Meloto 2009). SIGLA also empowers people in each community to monitor their own health with regular interaction with these professional health providers. SERBISYO, as part of this outreach, focuses on parent education regarding proper nutrition and hygiene which is a requirement for all living in a GK village. It also focuses on services for those with tuberculosis. Since roughly six out of every ten Filipinos die without getting medical attention, these culminating initiatives, directed through SISTEMA, are working towards creating the nation's first sustainable preventative health system for those who need it most. GK Kalusugan, in partnership with a host of volunteers and corporate sponsorship, is now in 384 GK villages in the Philippines and has trained over 1,000 GK village residents to provide care in their communities as health-care workers. Many of these volunteers are youth who have also benefited from GK's larger educational programs and aspire to go to medical school and train as nurses.

In a nation where seven out of ten youth are unable to go to school because they must scavenge for food or are too sickly to concentrate or attend regularly, GK has put a great deal of emphasis on education. The GK Child and Youth Development program, briefly alluded to earlier, includes three specific sub-programs for children and youth ages three to twenty-five years old. GK SIBOL (meaning "to grow" in Tagalog), serves children ages three to six years old. It is a community-based pre-school program which envisions instilling each child with positive Filipino values and academically preparing them for formal schooling. Classes are held in a full-time Sibol school located in each GK community. GK SAGIP (meaning "to save" in Tagalog), is also an acronym for Sagipin Ang Galing Isip at Pangarap ng mga Kabataan—"save the talents, minds, and dreams of the youth." It caters to children ages seven to thirteen years old and seeks to nurture the new found hope and dreams of the youth through weekly values-formation activities that promote the values of love for God, country, family, and fellowmen. In some cases these schools supplement existing public schools, but in most cases they are the only schools these children attend. GK SIGA, for example, is established for young people 14 to 21 years old. It seeks to empower the youth in GK communities to initiate and model change in self, family, community, and society and become a light to the nation. Through the weekly *barkadahan* (group of friends) sessions, the youth are provided with opportunities to hone their skills and talents that will make them patriotic and productive citizens of society (www.gk1world.com).

In general, GK villages are built around a seven-point vision:

1. Each GK village aspires to become a model community that is, first, a faith community where residents are free to practice their religious belief in an atmosphere of mutual respect and reverence. No religious vows or membership is required.

2. Each community is expected to be a peace zone where neighbors live in harmony with each other and where conflicts are justly settled based on the higher principles of neighborly love and the common good.

3. Through communal living, harmony, and brightly painted homes, GK villages are also expected to be tourist centers where the sense of beauty and order is regarded as an indispensable part of dignified human dwelling.

4. Each village is expected to be a productive center where the potential of both human and natural resources is utilized to sustain the growth and development of the community.

5. GK villages are expected to be "green." That is, they are to be environmentally healthy communities where residents practice the principles of proper utilization and preservation of the environment. This is known as Green Kalinga.

6. Villages are to be places that empower individuals to actively participate in governing the daily life and activities of their village.

7. Villages are expected to be "secure communities" where residents are safe and well prepared to preserve lives and property in the event of a natural or man-made disaster.

To empower its communities further, GK assists in the founding of neighborhood associations in each community to inculcate stewardship and ensure accountability, cooperation, and unity. Guidelines for community living are decided upon by the members themselves and again, no religious vow of faith is required, despite the charismatic Catholic origins of the movement.

During the building process and up until the point where a community has established sustainability, "caretaker teams" oversee each village. The caretaker team is essentially GK's lifeblood "on-the-ground." The empowerment of the community rests in their hands through their daily interaction and guidance. They ensure the delivery of GK programs and activities at the village level. Members of the caretaker team are selected on the basis of willingness to embrace the vision and mission of GK and to live out its values of faith, patriotism, and *padugo* (Tagalog for "heroic sacrifice and service"). This voluntary group is led by a project director and community organizer. They are responsible for organizing communities into GK Kapitbahayans (GK neighborhood associations) to: (1) deliver the values-formation program; (2) implement the community development plan and GK programs; and (3) mentor the community leaders towards self-governance. All of this is built on the early foundational experiments in Bagong Silang. Although CFC has established numerous chapters in these villages, this has been by the choice of the villagers themselves, not a requirement for aid or continued participation in GK programs.

Perhaps the most striking example of this absence of religious control can be seen in Mindanao in the southern Philippines where CFC and GK are building villages for Muslim Filipinos. The joint project in over thirty Muslim communities in the Autonomous Region of Muslim Mindanao (ARMM), including Basilan and Sulu, has gone a long way towards bridging the long historic and violent divide between a Christian majority and a Muslim minority across the southern regions of the Philippines. Civil war and local strife have largely been set aside to give care to the region's most impoverished regardless of religious affiliation. This is particularly true of places like Basilan, where rebels in the late 1990s openly killed Christians living or working in the area. Today, a memorial for peace stands at the crossroads where these attacks took place and GK workers, predominately Catholics, are welcomed with open arms. Although historic animosities are still present among some, GK workers are some of the few trusted Christians in the region. Part of this is due to the enormous work GK has undertaken in rebuilding war-torn villages in the area. However, given the fact that GK has rebuilt mosques in these villages and has earned a reputation for working in partnership with Muslims without proselytizing, their reputation as so-called "peace workers," now speaks louder than anything they have done towards rebuilding homes in these villages. It is a more holistic approach and one that clearly demonstrates a genuine care for the people themselves. This case highlights the type of model GK envisions working around the world. Yet, given GK's charismatic Catholic roots, the de-emphasizing of religion in these efforts has not been without controversy. Religion has presented certain internal conflicts over who is selected as corporate partners and caused many to question the overall aim of the movement.

Partners, Finances, and a Splitting of the Evangelical Foundation

In 2007, Couples for Christ (CFC) split into two organizations, after several years of very public contentious politicking (see Cherry 2014). At the center of this conflict was Gawad Kalinga. As GK began to grow and spread, there was a certain amount of concern among many CFC members that GK had overemphasized the social development goals of the organization and had become the only thing driving the faithful. Interviews suggest that this was indeed the case, at least among first-generation Filipino Americans living in Houston. As one Filipino in his mid-forties explained, "Gawad Kalinga put a meaning to the CFC community … I believe that my wife and I would not have stayed in the CFC community if we did not see that it is meant for the good of the less fortunate brethren" (interview 2006). As sentiments such as these grew, questions over power and authority began to rise, especially with regards to the centrality of Meloto to the GK movement. CFC began to take a more direct role in managing GK in fear that Meloto had grown excessively strong. By the time the board took action, Meloto had exceeded its jurisdiction and was now the charismatic leader of a global movement.

Meloto and others had ardently insisted that GK villages were not CFC villages. From the very beginning, Meloto, a charismatic Catholic himself and a member of CFC, had feared that evangelization would destroy any efforts at alleviating poverty. Pointing to the role of religion in Philippine colonial rule, Meloto did not want to use religion as a tool but as an example (Meloto 2009). A number of key members in CFC did not like this approach and insisted that evangelization should be a key part of GK's mission. These demands grew stronger as GK spread. CFC saw GK as an opportunity to spread the gospel, whereas Meloto and others had other aims in mind.

Although the temporal ordering of the events that transpired in 2007 are confusing and subject to opinion depending on whom you ask, it is clear that the rise of two leaders, Meloto and Padilla, coupled with a growing GK movement sparked internal tensions. The relationship between religion and finance also came to the forefront of these tensions (see further Cherry 2014). In 2006, Pfizer was taken on as a corporate sponsor of GK projects. This proved to be the tipping point among those in CFC concerned with the nature of religion in GK's overall mission. Pfizer, one of the largest pharmaceutical manufacturers in the Philippines, produces condoms. Given the Catholic Church's stance on contraception, tempers began to flare. Meloto insisted that taking money from Pfizer was not an endorsement of contraception use and that a great deal of good could be done with their support. Many in CFC did not see it this way and the rift began to grow deeper. While GK was not the only source of contention for members of CFC, it was crucial to the eventual split (Alayon 2009; Cherry 2014).

After a series of articles in the *Philippine Daily Inquirer*, the most widely circulated newspaper in the Philippines, began to challenge Meloto and question the direction of GK, it was clear that a split was imminent (see, for example, *Philippine Daily Inquirer*, January 28, 2007). In February, during the International Council meeting of CFC, Meloto resigned from the board as did Padilla. Jose Tale was appointed Executive Director replacing Padilla. On April 8, Easter Sunday, Padilla released a statement about the future of CFC and summarized what he saw as *the* key issues in the dispute:

> Now here is the basic problem as I see it. GK IS SLIDING AWAY FROM GOD'S PLAN FOR IT ... The question is: is GK fulfilling God's plan for it? In other words, the basic danger is that GK will become a SOCIAL work that has lost its SPIRITUAL foundation ... (Note emphasis is original; see www.cfcffl. org/documents/documents.htm)

Continuing, Padilla questioned Meloto, the direction of GK, and the sponsorship of partners such as Pfizer:

> To call Tony [Meloto] or anyone else the founder, father, or driving force is to put the person in place of God ... If partners are not on the same page, simply explain things to them. If they tie their help with aspects that violate our pro-God agenda, then say goodbye to them. (www.cfcffl.org/documents/documents.htm)

The message was clear. After this statement, Padilla, who had originally split from LNP to form CFC, initiated the Easter Group as a new group seeking to get back to the evangelical foundations of CFC.

In June, Meloto wrote Bishop Reyes of the Diocese of Antipolo apologizing for the International Council's neglect of him as a Spiritual Advisor. Later that month, Bishops Villagas and Reyes, in addition to Archbishop Lagdameo of the Archdiocese of Jaro, wrote the elders of CFC on behalf of the Catholic Bishops Conference of the Philippines (CBCP): "It appears that certain CFC principles and way of life are giving way to Gawad Kalinga ... the spiritual and pastoral culture of CFC must not be sacrificed for the sake of GK" (www.cfcffl.org/documents/ documents.htm). It was clear that the bishops had sided with Padilla. However, in response, CFC told the bishops that they would move forward with the election after creating a separate GK board. The Easter Group, led by Padilla, claimed that by ignoring the recommendations of the bishops to shift the focus of CFC away from GK, CFC had disobeyed the Church.

In August, Padilla's Easter restoration group was officially recognized by Bishop Reyes as "a private association of the faithful" in the Dioceses of Antipolo. In the United States, Padilla was removed as national director and CFC-USA, a separate legal entity, and CFC-USA voted unanimously for a state of "status quo." In effect, they refused to recognize the split. In April of 2008, just one year after Padilla and CFC-FFL announced their split from CFC, the Vatican sent a letter to Tale, the new Executive Director of CFC, voicing the Church's disapproval of CFC's "overemphasis" on social work through GK as well as GK's partnering practices.

In September of 2009, under growing pressure, CFC relinquished its control over the GK board. That same year, the outspoken Archbishop Cruz of Pangasinan, instructed his parishes to have nothing to do with Gawad Kalinga—directly or indirectly. Today, CFC and CFC-FFL operate as separate organizations, and GK is independent from both, although supported by CFC through ANCOP as part of its broader social ministry. In the United States, Filipino Americans were left to decide which side they would take. Most, like those interviewed in Houston, Texas (United States), sided with CFC. Yet at the grassroots level, Filipinos in the Philippines and in global diaspora in both CFC camps (CFC and CFC-FFL) continue to work together on GK projects. This is especially true of Filipinos in the United States who are the largest international contributors to GK projects. Roughly 68 percent of all international GK funds in 2010 came from GK USA. However, despite the continued support of Filipino Americans, a shift in GK financing did occur after the split of CFC. Where diaspora philanthropy once drove GK projects, it now accounts for only 20 percent of all contributions. Corporate funding has dramatically increased and now accounts for roughly 42 percent of all GK contributions—the largest contributor to these projects. Filipino Americans clearly continue to raise money for these projects, as they did prior to the split, but GK has increasingly become less dependent on them. At the same time, as GK continues to pick up corporate and governmental sponsorships, the movement has spread more internationally in its scope as it moves forward on its 2024 aims and aspirations.

Moving Forward and Globally Around the World

Although GK successes in the Philippines over the last several years have increasingly carried its development model around the world, in some ways GK has always been international in its scope. In 2004, prior to the CFC split and only five years after the first GK home was built in the Philippines, GK had already garnered the interest of its neighboring nations both by word of mouth from Filipinos living abroad and through increasing media coverage and exposure of GK through Asian development reports. Indonesia was the first country to adopt part of the GK development model. Looking to create better conditions and opportunities for youth in Joglo, Jakarta, local partners in Indonesia invited a team of GK planners to the nation to help them build youth-based programs similar to the original youth programs that had been started by GK (then SIGA) in Bagong Silang in Caloocan City in Metro Manila. The programs were a tremendous success. As a result, GK Indonesia was launched that same year as a local development movement for impoverished and/or landless families in the nation. Initially, the programs were led by a team of Filipino advisors, but as things progressed, the caretaker team turned the projects over to its local partners.

One year later, GK was launched in Papua New Guinea (PNG) and the first of several houses was built. The program was launched, in part, by Houstonian Filipino Americans then living in PNG. Recalling the early stages of the project's development, Sally explained:

> Through the project I really came to know myself and the things I had been missing in my life, especially my relationship with God. Things just really took off in PNG and they became my family. Wherever I go I seem to run into people from PNG. It's really cool. Now that I am in Texas I work with GK to build in the Philippines but I still travel to do work in PNG. We are blessed to be in this community and it is a real inspiration to get involved deeper in this project. We are going to change the world. (Interview 2006)

Although the ensuing split in CFC temporarily halted the international spread of GK, it continued to build international partnerships with Austria, Germany, England, Ireland, and at least ten other nations in Europe throughout 2006. During that same year, GK also continued to extend its partnerships with Canada, Australia, and India.

In 2007, the same year CFC split, Singapore President S. R. Nathan, intrigued by development reports coming out of the Philippines and inspired by stories coming from Filipinos both in Singapore and Philippines, visited the GK village Baseco in Tondo, Manila to present a check for one million pesos, roughly $24,000 in United States dollars, raised by the LaSalle schools in Singapore for their "little brothers and sisters" in the Philippines (www.gawadkalinga.org). That same month, as Singapore became a major sponsor of GK in the Philippines, Rose and Bong Cabrera, both Filipino Americans, began to seek out a partnership with local groups in Phnom Penh, Cambodia. The Cabreras saw the slums of Cambodia as a natural fit for the GK model that had worked so well in the slums of the Philippines and hence established GK Rafaella in 2007 as a safe sanctuary for 20 families in the region. It became the first of several planned villages in Cambodia. In 2008, GK Cambodia was officially launched. Although the Cabreras remained important movers in the projects, and still are today, like GK Indonesia previously, GK Cambodia entered a new phase in 2008 and became increasingly managed by local Cambodian partners.

In 2008, GK also spread as a brand and a set of development ideas that were not only increasingly talked about in development circles but studied broadly. Both the Massachusetts Institute of Technology (MIT) and Harvard University completed their initial studies of the GK model at this time. A group of South Africans and Kenyans also visited the Philippines for the first time in 2008 and began talking to GK leaders about adopting the model for their own nations. Much of this interest came as a result of GK successes in the Philippines, not necessarily the expanse of the Filipino diaspora. As of September of 2008, GK had built over 30,000 homes and 2,000 communities in 64 of the Philippines' 80 provinces. It had also housed over 500,000 people in a nation in which 70 percent of the population was landless (ANCOP 2006). These successes were widely reported in development circles and fueled increasing interest in GK, particularly in Asia and Oceania.

In 2009, the GK Hope initiative (GKHi) was registered as an international charity organization in Singapore with the plan to start building GK villages and programs in the nation. That same year, GK India built its first village in the Philippines and visited the slums of Metro Manila to begin its study of the GK model for its own impoverished communities. Indian interest in GK, while still somewhat inspired by Filipinos living abroad, was primarily sparked by the increased exposure of the GK model in Asian development circles. GK was making a name for itself and no longer needed the Filipino diaspora to carry it forward. At the Asia-Pacific Economic Cooperation Summit (APEC CEO Summit) held in Singapore, for example, the GK model was highlighted to a group of 800 world business leaders as a viable and emerging solution to sustainable development. Drawing on evidence from several international studies of GK in the Philippines, Meloto suggested to the summit group that GK villages were making dramatic progress. Self-confidence and self-respect had risen among residents of the villages from 17 percent before GK to 99 percent after; 93 percent of residents said that they had a better quality of life; and 96 percent believed that their economic and life situations would improve in the future (Meloto 2009).

Two years later, at the 2011 World Economic Forum held in Jakarta, Indonesia, Meloto reiterated these successes and continued to offer GK as the model to end global poverty. However, while several studies pointed to the success of GK in the Philippines, much less was and is known about the impact of GK on village residents outside of the Philippines. In some ways, GK is far too young outside of the Philippines to measure any successes. At the same time, it is important to highlight the fact that interest in GK, particularly among Filipinos in diaspora,

GK Backbone Organization Structure

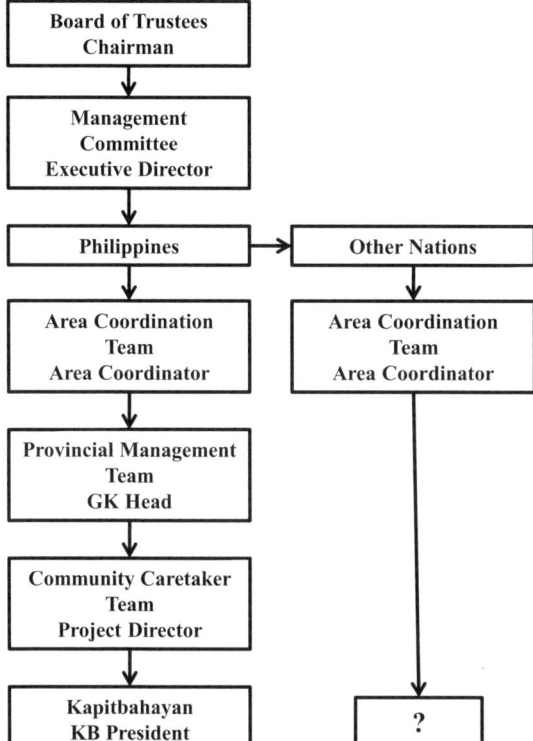

Figure 6.1   GK Organizational Chart

remains very focused on the Philippines itself. As GK has spread it has become something new and unique in each and every country. While strongly supported by Filipinos in diaspora and still largely under Filipino advisement, GK in Cambodia, Indonesia, and Papua New Guinea, for example, are not part of a monolithic top-down NGO housed in the Philippines so much as they are rooted in the same ideals and philosophy. They are married to a development model they believe can be molded and adapted to fit their own needs and see Filipinos and the Philippines as an ally in solving poverty in their nations.

Institutionally, GK, since the CFC split and reorganization, has operated within a fairly top-down model of organization (see Figure 6.1). However, while this model is adhered to strictly in GK operations in the Philippines, this is not necessarily the case in other countries where GK has turned over its management to local partners and governmental agencies. In both cases, at the top of the institutional structure is the Board of Trustees headed by a Chairman. The board is responsible for all policy-making, strategic planning, and resource management.

This includes the management of Philippine projects as well as strategic planning for partnerships and projects in other countries. The Management Committee, headed by an executive director, coordinates all operations oversight and is responsible for setting the objectives, goals, strategies, and measures (OSGM) for the year. Subsequently, the Area Coordinating Team (ACT), headed by an area coordinator and a team of four to six full-time workers and volunteers, is charged with the task of implementing the OGSM. This obviously varies from country to country and, depending on the stages of the project, may be purely indigenous, led by Filipino advisors, or directly connected to the Management Committee in the case of ACTs in the Philippines.

The Provincial Management Team, led by a GK Head, is tasked with implementing the OGSM in each province and city within an area. This, again, varies from country to country. However, at the grassroots level, both the Community Caretaker Team, headed by a Project Director, and the Kapitbahayan community of residents, headed by a KB President, are integral parts of the GK model and are present in some form, although under different names, in every GK village project. Both serve as important ways for empowering local residents within their own communities and engaging them democratically in their own strategic planning.

Depending on the country, communication across this institutional order can be rather localized. GK teams internationally have faced several linguistic barriers during their initial explorations outside of the Philippines but have quickly partnered with both the local peoples and various agencies to meet the needs of these non-Philippine villages. In these villages, caretaker teams are not majority Filipino, nor is the labor and financing. As Meloto describes it, GK was born in the Philippines, but it is not Filipino; rather, it is a global model for answering the cry of the poor everywhere (see Meloto 2009: ch. 2). This is not to say that communication and links to the Board of Trustees is not maintained on some level across the movement. The board is well aware of what is going on with GK around the world and is actively planning with its partners but is not always in direct and constant communication with them depending on the stages of the various projects and the nature of the partnership. Beyond this, however, GK listserves, blogs, newsletters, and websites link workers and partners to the movement and update them on what is happening around the world. If you were to visit the official GK1world website, for example, an interactive map allows you to click on any location in the world where GK has a presence and read updates, personal stories of volunteers and residents, contact coordinators in the region, or give money to a specific project (for more on Filipino American volunteering see Cherry 2013). Annual international summits also serve the same function but in more dramatic fashion with the benefit of face-to-face interactions with GK members from around the world. At each of these summits successes are celebrated and global benchmarks are touted.

Today, as the movement spreads transnationally and globally, it has become less homogeneous in both its culture and structure. GK is no longer purely a Filipino movement and does not depend on the Filipino diaspora to carry it forward. Clearly, the Filipino diaspora and the Philippines itself are central to the movement. However, in other countries, these forces often now serve only as a model and example of how people can address poverty in their own nations from their own cultural understandings and needs. GK Indonesia or Gerakan Kepudlian in Bahasa (the national language of Indonesia), for example, has now built three villages. Indonesia has made the GK model their own, and while GK in the Philippines remains a major supporter and advisor, GK Indonesia is run by Indonesians for Indonesians. Today, GK Indonesia runs eight GK villages serving well over 300 families. Programs in these villages, ranging from youth development through scholarships to subsistence farming and clean water management, are all locally run and financed. In 2011, for example, the Keppel Group, a real estate conglomerate in Jakarta, raised over $360,000 for GK villages and is now one of the major sponsors of programs in the region.

In places such as Papua New Guinea, GK likewise continues to grow. Having built three villages in some of the most notorious crime-ridden areas of the nation, it is now predominately an indigenous movement. GK Cambodia also continues to expand as a more indigenous movement and GK India just began to build its first village, Hope Town, in India in 2012. Beyond this, both South Africa and Kenya have completed their studies of the GK model, as noted earlier, and look to move forward on building villages in their respective countries over the next several years. Although nations such as Colombia and East Timor have only just begun their study of the GK model, it is clear that the movement has gained momentum and is spreading as a locally adaptable model for indigenous sustainable development.

As the GK movement continues to spread, it will continue to be faced with a host of challenges. How it continues to adapt to local cultures and political systems remains to be seen. Likewise, it remains to be seen what the future relationship of Filipinos in diaspora will be to GK projects around the world. In the Philippines, the movement is still very closely tied to its evangelical and charismatic Catholic roots despite the CFC split. While Filipinos who continue to spread the movement to places such as Papua New Guinea and Cambodia tend to be members of CFC and equally religious, it is not clear if the same can be said of the residents in these other national contexts. GK Philippines remains the center of a burgeoning global movement as does Catholicism, but for how long? GK continues to inspire many around the world, especially Filipinos in diaspora, who not only give money and labor to the movement but who also continue to draw on its successes as evidence of their faith in action. As one Filipino in Houston describes it:

> For those who do not believe in miracles, I suggest that they go to the Philippines and visit one of the project sites of Gawad Kalinga … Yes, miracles happen and a miracle is now in progress in more than 500 sites all over the Philippines. I have witnessed the miracle in progress. However, I don't think I can truly express what I saw and felt when I visited several Gawad Kalinga villages. (Interview 2006)

How the rest of the world sees these successes remains to be seen. Likewise, how successful GK is in other nations and how people will then interpret these successes from their own cultural lenses also remains to be seen.

References

2010. "Documents on the CFC Crisis." Retrieved June 3, 2013 (http://www.cfcffl. org/documents/documents.htm).

Agunias, Dovelyn R., ed. 2009. *Closing the Distance: How Governments Strengthen Ties with Their Diasporas*. Washington DC: Migration Policy Institute.

Alayon, John. 2009. "Migration, Remittance, and Development: The Filipino New Zealand Experience." Unpublished Master's thesis, Institute of Public Policy, AUT University, Auckland, New Zealand.

ANCOP. 2006. Unpublished report. Couples for Christ: Foundation for Family and Life.

Cherry, Stephen M. 2014. *Faith, Family, and Filipino American Community Life*. New Brunswick, NJ: Rutgers University Press.

Cherry, Stephen M. "Catholicism and Filipino American Community Volunteerism and Participation." *Sociological Spectrum* 33(1) 2013: 36-56.

Gawad Kalinga. n.d. Retrieved June 4, 2013 (www.gawadkalinga.org; also see http://www.gk1world.com/).

Gawad Kalinga. (www.gawadkalinga.info/). Gawad Kalinga: Building Communities to End Poverty. 2012. Retrieved June 3, 2013 (http://www.gk1world.com/)

Meloto, Antonio. 2009. *Builder of Dreams*. Mandaluyong City, Philippines: Gawad Kalinga Development Foundation.

Newland, Kathleen. 2009. "Forward." Pp. v-xii in *Closing the Distance: How Governments Strengthen Ties with Their Diasporas,* edited by Dovelyn R. Agunias. Washington DC: Migration Policy Institute.

Newland, Kathleen, Aaron Terrazas, and Roberto Munster. 2010. *Diaspora Philanthropy: Private Giving and Public Policy*. Washington DC: Migration Policy Institute.

Orozco, Manuel and Rebecca Rouse. 2007. "Migrant Hometown Association and Opportunities for Development: A Global Perspective." *Migration Information Source* (February). Retrieved February 8, 2010 (http://www. migrationinformation.org/Feature/display.cfm?ID=579).

Philippine Daily Inquirer. January 28, 2007. "Meloto not the Founder of Gawad Kalinga," (http://services.inquirer.net/print/print.php?article_id=20070206-47677).

Somerville, Will, Jamie Durana, and Aaron Terrazas. 2008. *Hometown Associations: An Untapped Resource for Immigrant Integration*. Washington DC: Migration Policy Institute.

Terrazas, Aaron. 2010. *Connected Through Service: Diaspora Volunteers and Global Development*. Washington DC: Migration Policy Institute and U.S. Agency for International Development.

Chapter 7
Aga Khan Development Network: Shia Ismaili Islam

Karim H. Karim

The stated objective of the Aga Khan Development Network (AKDN) is to raise the quality of life of the transnational Shia Ismaili Muslim community (*jamat*) and "those amongst whom it lives" (Aga Khan IV 2003). The impetus behind this aim is to "realise the social conscience of Islam through institutional action" (AKDN 2007a). In presenting the philosophical basis of its operations in such ethical terms, the organizational network sets a high standard for the performance of its work. Ismaili history has produced a rich literature on ethics. Codes of conduct were also produced in the past to guide those responsible for governance and administration (Klemm and Walker 2011; Muscati and Moulvi 1966), but a contemporary version of such a code has yet to appear.

Aga Khan IV, the founder of AKDN, is the 49th hereditary Imam of the Shia Nizari Ismaili Muslims. He claims descent from the Prophet Muhammad through his daughter, Fatima, and son-in-law, Ali ibn Abi Talib, the first Shia Imam. The honorific title of Aga Khan is of relatively recent origin in the 1,400 year history of the Imamat; a nineteenth-century Qajar ruler of Iran bestowed it on the 46th Imam who was the governor of a province (Daftary 2007: 464). Adverse political developments forced Aga Khan I to move from Iran to India, which was then under the British Raj. India and African territories under European rule, where significant numbers of Indian Ismailis settled, turned out to have generally favorable socio-political conditions for setting up communal institutions. Aga Khan III established himself in Europe in the early twentieth century and used the continent's international communication links to expand contacts with his transnational community. The present Nizari Ismaili leader, Aga Khan IV, became Imam in 1957 and resides in France.

A transnational Ismaili following under a common leadership has come about from the presence of long-standing communities in various regions and migration to other parts of the world. The group's global spread has occurred despite its relatively small population, which is estimated to be a few million worldwide. Nizari Ismaili communities in the Middle East, Central Asia, and South Asia arose from conversion activities of earlier times. However, the community has not engaged in proselytization at least since the eighteenth century and does not preach its religious precepts outside the fold in contemporary times.

Whereas historical precedents for AKDN's work are traced to the tenth through the twelfth centuries Fatimid Ismaili Empire in the Middle East, its organizational roots are in nineteenth-century India. The Aga Khans established community associations in the sub-continent both to meet their religious followers' needs and to consolidate their authority as hereditary Imams. Parallel sets of institutions were built in Africa. These self-governing bodies sought to serve community members from cradle to grave and also offered services to others. The model of the communal (*jamati*) institutional structure progressively spread to other places where significant numbers of the Imam's followers live—the Middle East, Central Asia, East and South-East Asia, Europe, North America, and Australasia. *Jamati* organizations are distinct from AKDN which is described as, "a group of private, international, non-denominational agencies" (AKDN 2007b: 4) and is not directed solely at Ismailis. Apart from promoting social and economic advancement, the network is also involved in disaster relief, major infrastructure building, industry (including telecommunications, media, and air transport), tourism, cultural development, heritage conservation, university education, and research. It has become one of the world's largest international non-governmental organizations. AKDN's partners include United Nations agencies, governments in developed and developing countries, private sector organizations, and civil society associations.

The network's global reach is supported by the transnational presence of the Ismaili community. Its operations in various continents enable members of the relatively small but ethnically diverse and geographically scattered religious group to interact with each other (Karim 2011a; Steinberg 2010). Such relationships serve to integrate those parts of the community which live in isolated regions of the world under the Imamat's authority and organizational structure. They also facilitate the transfer of resources from prosperous parts of the transnational community to disadvantaged ones. Such global flows of human expertise, finance, and materials have required diplomatic engagement with a variety of governments (Karim 2011b). Whereas certain groups suspect harmful motives in the transnational activities of Ismailis (Devji 2009; Kaiser 1996; Ramachandran 2005), many states see AKDN as a key partner in providing vital services and development opportunities to disadvantaged populations (Kaiser 1996; Najam 2006; Steinberg 2010). Apart from the funds donated by Ismailis, substantial amounts are raised from aid agencies, foundations, and other non-Ismaili sources. The Aga Khan Foundation, a linchpin in the network and the Imamat organization with the highest public profile, has been particularly successful in mobilizing volunteer and financial support from community and external sources. AKDN employs large numbers of non-Ismailis, "the fulcrum of the Network's activities, however, remains the Ismaili Community—its traditions of volunteer service, self-reliance, generosity and the leadership of the hereditary Imam" (AKDN 2007b: 5).

There is in this, a nuanced relationship between faith and worldly engagement. Several of the network's agencies are headed by non-Ismailis. Many beneficiaries of AKDN's programs are Ismailis, but many others are not. Whereas AKDN's founder is the leader of a religious community and its philosophical bases are shaped by Islamic ethics, its operations are secular. The Islamic humanism underlying the network's orientation does not take the shape of proselytization; Aga Khan IV (2003) states that the objective of AKDN is the betterment of the quality of life regardless of the religious adherence of its services' recipients.

The Aga Khan views his establishment and personal oversight of AKDN as an integral feature of the office of Imamat:

> This engagement has been grounded in my responsibilities as Imam of the Shia Ismaili community and in Islam's message of the fundamental unity of *din* and *dunia*—spirit and life. Throughout its long history, the Ismaili Imamat has emphasized the importance of activities that reflect the social conscience of Islam, that contribute to the well-being of Allah's greatest creation, humankind, and that reflect the responsibility Islam places on the fortunate and the strong to assist the less fortunate. (Aga Khan IV 2008: 15-16)

He sees his involvement with community and international development as a fundamental obligation for him as Imam. The engagement with the material world is carried out in the context of the "social conscience of Islam." This behoves those charged with their governance, administration, and service delivery in the Imam's institutions to maintain high ethical standards.

Islamic Ethics and Humanism

A humanism inspired by Islamic teachings is viewed as shaping the work of Ismaili institutions (Aga Khan IV 2008; Institute of Ismaili Studies 2000; Kassam 2003). Respect for the dignity of the human being, called "the crown of creation" (*al-ashraf ul-makhluqat*) in Islamic discourse, underlies AKDN's philosophical orientation towards the betterment of the human condition. Aga Khan III viewed life as "a lofty and exalted destiny" (Aga Khan III 1954: v). Caring for people's health has been a constant refrain in the Imams' discourses. AKDN's multi-level engagement in education appears to reflect Qu'ranic exhortations to value the intellect and knowledge. Compassion (*rahmaniyyah*), an attribute of God that is evoked at the beginning of the Qu'ran's chapters and at the initiation of Islamic prayers, seems to shape the development network's work. Voluntary giving (*sadaqah*) is seen as sharing not only material wealth but also one's time and knowledge. This provides support for those in need, but at the same time self-help remains a key principle guiding the path towards development. Islam's support for social justice is represented in the Imamat's promotion of meritocracy as a response to nepotism and cronyism, and pluralism and as a way to ensure a diversity of voices in the workings of society.

The ethical framework for the AKDN's endeavour to improve the quality of life is all-encompassing, according to Aga Khan IV (2003):

> To the Imamat the meaning of "quality of life" extends to the entire ethical and social context in which people live, and not only to their material well-being measured over generation after generation. Consequently, the Imamat's is a holistic vision of development, as is prescribed by the faith of Islam. It is about investing in people, in their pluralism, in their intellectual pursuit, and search for new and useful knowledge, just as much as in material resources. But it is also about investing with a social conscience inspired by the ethics of Islam. It is work that benefits all, regardless of gender, ethnicity, religion, nationality or background. Does the Holy Quran not say in one of the most inspiring references to mankind, that Allah has created all mankind from one soul?

In consonance with the Qu'ran, humanity is viewed as the locus for the services of the development network. This ideal is given shape by focusing firstly on the areas where the Imam's followers live, secondarily on other Muslim societies, and then on other regions which provide for strategic engagement towards the fulfilment of AKDN's objectives. The network is heavily involved in places where Ismaili populations contend with harsh terrain and climate, such as the northern areas of Pakistan and Tajikistan's Pamir region. However, Aga Khan schools, hospitals, and clinics established to meet the needs of the community, are generally open to its neighbors. AKDN agencies have been working for decades in the Ivory Coast in West Africa, which does not have a significant Ismaili settlement. Various projects of the network serve mainly non-Muslim populations. Apart from conducting a broad range of what are viewed as traditional development activities in education and health, AKDN has designed initiatives in the cultural sector that seek to improve the lot of disadvantaged communities in a more comprehensive manner. The Aga Khan Trust for Culture's programs address quality of life issues through social, economic, and cultural development primarily in Muslim societies. Its programs include the restoration and rehabilitation of historic structures and public spaces; the sustenance, development and transmission of musical traditions; endowed centres of excellence in the history, theory, and practice of Islamic architecture at Harvard University and the Massachusetts Institute of Technology; the development of an international online community for architects, planners, urban designers, landscape architects, conservationists, and scholars; and the world's largest prize for architecture to recognize innovative solutions to problems of social development.

The Aga Khan supports the notion of democracy in which the participation in civil society is vital for ensuring good governance (Aga Khan IV 2008). As president of the Paris-based Académie Diplomatique Internationale, he promotes the engagement of corporations, advocacy groups, and others involved in shaping regional and international dynamics. The Imamat has also established the Global Centre for Pluralism in Ottawa in partnership with the Canadian government. Such civic engagement is meant to dovetail with other AKDN initiatives in promoting global well-being by providing intellectual support for informed policy making.

AKDN's mission to "realise the social conscience of Islam through institutional action" (AKDN 2007a) has shaped its activities in ways that encompass a broader ambit than that of most similar institutions. It is much more than a development organization. The network has sought to promote collaboration between its various agencies and external partners to carry out "multi-input area development programs" (AKDN 2009) whose benefits would be greater than the sum of the individual organizations' discrete inputs. AKDN's search for solutions to the problems of human marginalization has led it to devise new ways of dealing with endemic problems. Its focus on early childhood development and the provision of an international standard of schooling through the Aga Khan Academies seeks to strengthen the human capacity available to support the advancement of developing countries. The network's long-term commitment is demonstrated by remaining active for decades in particular areas, including those laden with high risk; this contrasts with the limited timescales of most development organizations. Behind all this is the personal oversight of the Imam himself. Quite distinct from philanthropists operating at arm's length, he mobilizes his followers and provides active leadership to his institutions.

The codes of conduct for the administrators of the Ismaili Fatimid empire (Klemm and Walker 2011; Muscati and Moulvi 1966) were in the medieval Muslim literary genre of the "mirror of princes." A superior standard of personal integrity, ethics and morality was expected; leaders of institutions were viewed as holding a responsibility that was worldly as well as spiritual. According to an eleventh-century Fatimid Ismaili intellectual, Ahmad bin Ibrahim al-Naysaburi:

> When God questions the imam about things connected to the affairs of his community and his safeguarding and caring for them, the imam will ask him (the *da'i*), for the imam made that his responsibility. He is the one answerable for it, and it was up to him to arrange matters in that regard. (Klemm and Walker 2011: 72; also see Muscati and Moulvi 1966: 131-35)

Whereas the recent Imams have frequently referred to ethical matters in their communal and public discourses, formal codes of conduct for the governance of contemporary Ismaili institutions do not appear to have been produced. The 1925 Ismaili rule book published in Zanzibar did encourage appointed leaders to be exemplary in their upholding of the regulations (Hirji 2011: 152), but the current Ismaili constitution (Aga Khan IV 1998) does not include such exhortations. Neither the Institute of Ismaili Studies' "Aga Khan Development Network (AKDN): An Ethical Framework" (2000), its book on "emerging vistas" of *Muslim Ethics* (Sajoo 2004), nor the Aga Khan University's *Development Models in Muslim Contexts* (Springborg 2009) discusses formal ethical guidelines for institutional administrators.

Metamorphosis

More than a century of gradual communal development preceded the establishment of AKDN as a network of agencies in the 1980s. Apart from a few privileged families, most Ismailis in the nineteenth century were small-scale farmers, shopkeepers, and laborers. They were often socially marginalized in the countries where they lived and were frequently persecuted for their religious beliefs. Aga Khan III was a visionary who strived to modernize his community and raise its standing in the world. He sought to emulate his Fatimid forebears who had fostered a progressive society that was at the leading edge of human civilization in its time (Aga Khan III 1955). The Al Azhar University, built a thousand years ago in Cairo by a Fatimid Imam, has remained a primary seat of Islamic learning into the present. Yet, formal higher education was rare among Ismailis in the nineteenth century. The travails of history that featured bouts of severe repression and massacres had shattered most of the community's social structures. Consequently, Ismaili leaders and their followers practiced concealment (*taqiyya*) of their religious identities (Daftary 2007). With the public re-emergence of the Ismaili Imamat in Iran in the late eighteenth century, there began a gradual process of social and economic development. However, it was the move of the Imamat's seat to British India that led to the community's transformation into one of the most progressive Muslim groups in contemporary times.

Aga Khan III is particularly credited with this change. He brought about the "metamorphosis of a moribund society from the depths of degradation to its proud position in modern civilization during the course of only about half a century" (Thawerbhoy 1977: 19). His Imamat was the longest in Ismaili history. Inheriting the community's leadership from his father at the young age of eight in 1885, he was the Imam for 72 years until his death in 1957. Living in a period that saw the end of the Muslim Caliphate, two world wars, and independence of the Asian and African colonies where his followers lived, he was an international figure who was elected the first president of the All India Muslim League, honored by governments of European and majority-Muslim countries and served as president of the League of Nations.

The Imam adopted a step-by-step process of raising his socio-economically disadvantaged followers through various stages of development over several decades. He recognized that wealth-creation would be vital for acquiring the personal and communal means for advancement. Hence, advice for the successful establishment and operation of businesses was an important theme in his guidance. He also advised his followers to share resources, information, and ideas. Conceptualizing the community's progress in generational terms, the Imam stressed the proper care and education of young children. Among the earliest institutions to be established were clinics that provided pre- and post-natal care as well as schools catering to the youngest in the community. Priority was also given to women's education and their social standing as early as the 1920s:

> In paving the way for Ismaili women to go to school, to receive both the
> quality and length of education that would make it possible for them to enter
> the professions and to strive for financial self-sufficiency, Aga Khan III laid
> the groundwork for moving the community away from its inherited cultural

patriarchal mores and attitudes towards a partnership model where women worked alongside men to meet the challenges the community would face in the 20th century. (Kassam 2011: 259)

He also promoted these values in the larger Indian society and among Muslims worldwide.

Institutions including hospitals, kindergartens, primary schools, secondary schools, libraries, hostels, housing societies, and sports facilities were built in South Asia and Africa. The Imam established *jamati* committees to administer them. A key association that he founded was the Ismaili Volunteer Corps, whose members provided service for the running of religious and social gatherings, and which became a model for volunteerism in the community. Aga Khan III's limited access to other places where his followers lived, such as Syria, Iran, Afghanistan, and Tajikistan, severely restricted the community's institutional development in these countries. The Ismaili Imam contributed significantly to Muslim causes, such as the establishment of Aligarh University in India, and also supported the building of Hindu universities (Aziz 1998). He was a founding member of the East African Muslim Welfare Society, which constructed schools and mosques for indigenous Muslims in the region.

Self-help and Self-governance

The practice of concealing religious identity to avoid persecution resulted in a number of Ismailis assimilating into other Shia, Sunni, and Hindu communities over time. Several challenges were launched against the Imam's authority. After the Imamat moved to India, the Aga Khans faced a series of court cases from dissident groups. A major ruling in 1908 by the Bombay High Court affirmed the distinct identity of Nizari Ismailis in India and the legitimacy of Aga Khan III's Imamat (Daftary 2007). This became an important source for the Imam to assert the legal status of his authority and leadership over the Nizari Ismailis in India and around the world.

Among the key points of contention in the litigation was the Imam's sole right to receive religious offerings, to own communal property, and to make appointments to positions in communal associations (Daftary 2007). Adherents give a tithe (*dasond*) based on the Islamic *zakat* and *khums,* calculated as 12.5 percent of earnings (Steinberg 2010). Various other offerings are also made (Morris 1968). Major fundraising campaigns take place during the jubilee anniversaries of Imam's accession to leadership. "Aga Khan III increasingly utilized the offerings submitted to him, including the tithes and the funds collected at jubilee celebrations, for the implementation of socio-economic policies and projects that would benefit his followers" (Daftary 2007: 488). In a specific case where the 48th Imam was encouraging the building of a school in every Ismaili village in the Khurasan region of Iran, he "permitted his followers to set aside

80 percent of their tithes for this purpose and only the remaining 20 percent was to be sent to the imam" (Daftary 2007: 488).

Under the current Imam, fundraising for major institutions has been highly systematized. Tax receipts are issued for monies collected by the Aga Khan Foundation (AKF) in the countries where it has charitable status. A distinction is maintained between the religious offerings and the funds collected specifically for development activities. Information about religious offerings is kept private, but records of AKF's finances (discussed below) are published in annual reports.

In the course of the twentieth century, Aga Khan III and Aga Khan IV established a series of regulations specifying community institutions and their governance. Drawing from the work of Michel Boivin, Jonah Steinberg (2010: 50) notes, "The constitution of 1926 also authorizes the creation of provincial councils and several district *Panjebhai* committees to care for the poor, the infirm, and widows; to provide the poor with funerals, education, and expenses for daily life; and to facilitate employment." The genesis of the rule books and constitutions occurred in the context of the Imamat's interactions with Ismailis in India and Africa; later documents reflect the growing contact with other parts of the transnational community. Promulgated or appearing in 1905, 1925/1926, 1937, 1946, 1954, 1962, and 1986, they articulated the Imam's authority and nature of the institutional bodies. This provided for the structure of internal organization as well as the modality for interactions with governments and other communities (Hirji 2011). The contemporary organizational and bureaucratic forms characterizing Ismaili institutional structures have also facilitated effective engagement with states and international bodies.

The current Ismaili constitution, promulgated in 1986, identifies a "Leaders International Forum" (LIF) in addition to national, regional and local councils (Aga Khan IV 1998). LIF is a transnational consultative body for the Imamat and its membership comprises current presidents of the national councils and some other members. It is one of the several means through which sections of the global Ismaili community interact laterally across borders. The Imamat's secretariat is located on an estate north of Paris (Aiglemont), from where Aga Khan IV oversees both the transnational *jamat*'s institutions and AKDN agencies. The Imam's institutions have been able to ensure increasing levels of interaction with isolated members of the transnational community, like those in Tajikistan who, during the Soviet period, had been largely cut off from their religious brethren. This manifests a unique adjustment of a transnational community to the features of globalization that have swept the planet over the last few decades (Karim 2011a; Steinberg 2010).

The 1986 constitution lists 14 national councils in Asia, Africa, Europe, and North America, and another 44 countries are identified as "Territories without a National Council," which have lower levels of administrative organization (Aga Khan IV 1998). Ismaili self-governing bodies bridge transnational space translocally (also see Hirji 2011; Mandaville 2001). National councils in various countries replicate the same administrative structure, which has boards for religious affairs; (secular) education; health; social welfare; youth and sports; economic planning; grants and review; and conciliation and arbitration. Regional and local councils, appointed under national councils, reproduce this structure vertically within countries.

Among the various aims and objectives specified in Article 5 of the Constitution, the *jamati* councils are expected to:

> (a) endeavour to secure continuing improvement in the quality of life of the jamat, through appropriate policies and programmes in the areas of education, health, social welfare, housing, economic welfare, cultural and women's activities, youth and sports development; (b) analyze fundamental problems confronting the jamat and their relationship to underlying trends in the national and international development process, and set short range and long range goals for the jamat; (c) preserve and foster the tradition of voluntary service and identify, motivate and develop leadership talent; (d) serve the needs of the jamat to enable it to make an effective contribution to the development of the societies in which it lives; (e) make available to the jamat and the public at large, information relating to the role and contribution of the institutions of the Imamat and the jamat towards development in various regions of the world; (f) strengthen the jamat and its institutions; and work in close collaboration with other Councils in different regions of the world and with the Apex institutions. (Aga Khan IV 1998: 14)

The *jamati* councils are expected to meet the community members' needs, foster voluntary service, engage with the larger society, and cooperate translocally with other *jamati* organizations and AKDN ("Apex") institutions. Key appointments such as the president and vice-president, as well as the chairs of the boards, are made by the Imam, generally for three-year terms. Members mainly serve on a voluntary basis supported by a paid administrative staff. Extensive corps of additional volunteers assist in implementing the boards' programs. The existence of the same institutional model translocally reinforces the community's global integration and the standardization of operations under the Imamat's leadership and authority.

Holistic Vision

Aga Khan IV has significantly expanded the Ismaili institutional infrastructure given shape by his predecessor in the early twentieth century. AKDN's organizational chart (see Figure 7.1 below) identifies the agencies working in the areas of social, culture, and economic development. (However, the chart is not a comprehensive representation of all of the Imamat's endeavours; for instance, it does not list the *jamati* organizational structure or bodies such as the Institute of Ismaili Studies and the Global Centre for Pluralism.) AKDN operates in over

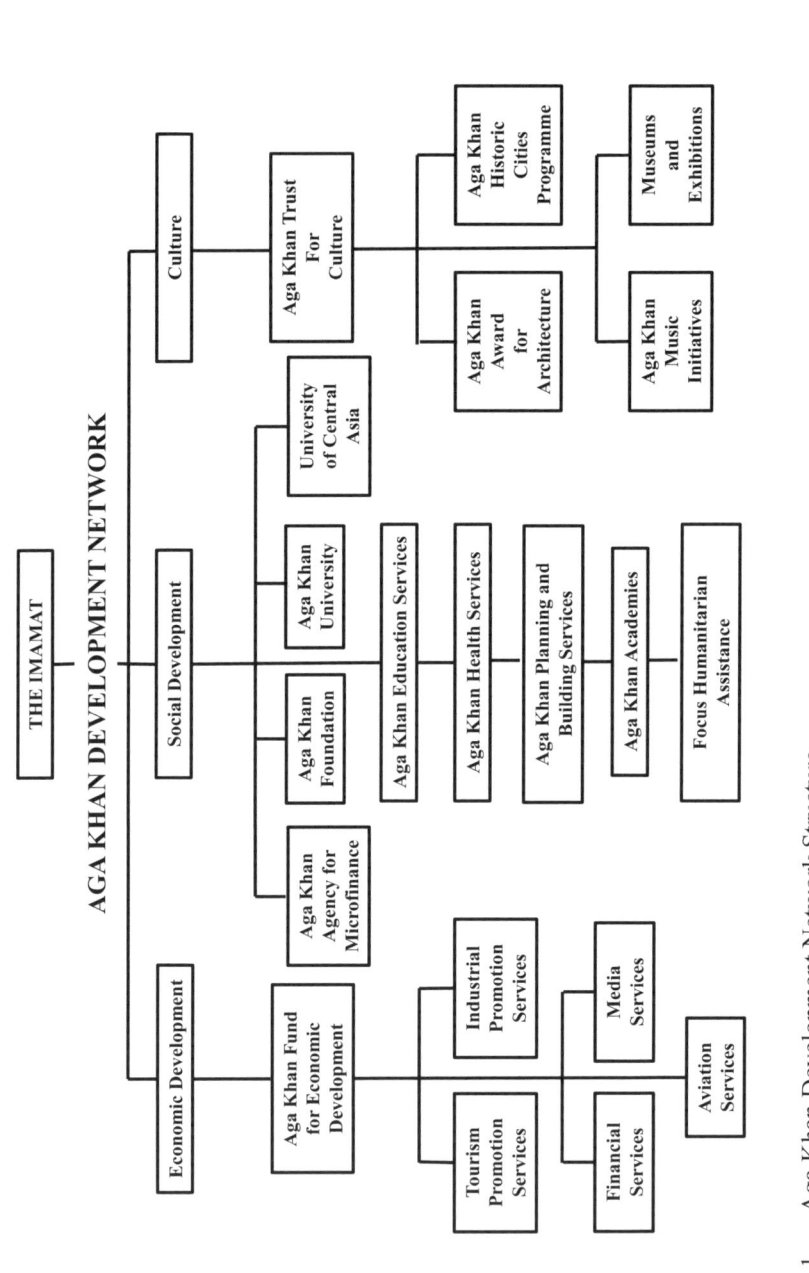

Figure 7.1   Aga Khan Development Network Structure

Source: AKDN (2007a), "About Us" (http://www.akdn.org/about_akdn.asp).

30 countries grouped under eight regions: Eastern Africa; Central and Western Africa; South Asia; the Middle East; Central Asia; the Far East and Southeast Asia; Europe; and North America. It employs some 80,000 people, the majority of whom are based in developing countries.

AKDN's annual budget for non-profit development activities is approximately $625 million in United States currency (AKDN 2007a). The Aga Khan Foundation (AKF), established in Geneva in 1967, is a key institution in the network. It has branch offices in 11 developing countries and affiliates in Canada, Portugal, UK, and the United States; the latter countries have substantial Ismaili communities. The 2006 combined revenues of AKF (head office, branches, and affiliates) were $230.2 million and total assets were $1,015.3 million (AKF 2006); more recent (2010) figures for its American affiliate were in excess of $29.3 million and $173.6 million respectively (AKF USA 2011). AKF's goal is to "seek sustainable solutions to long-term problems of poverty, hunger, illiteracy and ill health, with special emphasis on the needs of rural communities in mountainous, coastal and other resource-poor areas" (AKDN 2007b: 23). One of AKF's best-known and often copied initiatives is the Aga Khan Rural Support Program (AKRSP) which began work in Pakistan's northern areas in the 1980s. It is "regarded by many development agencies, including the World Bank, as one of the world's most effective aid programmes" (Ruthven 2011: 201). Early AKRSP activities were carried out in Ismaili villages, and then were expanded to other Shia and Sunni locales. The program's integrated approach involves participation of village organizations to build institutions, physical infrastructure, and business enterprises. Women's advancement and effective natural resource management are key aims of AKRSP, which has also pioneered micro financing (Wood, Malik, and Sagheer 2006).

AKDN's "holistic vision of development" (Aga Khan IV 2003) is expressed in an integrated set of programs and activities run by the Aga Khan Trust for Culture. Construction of the 30 hectare Al-Azhar urban park in Cairo was carried out in tandem with the conservation of historical buildings and rehabilitation of the adjoining socially and physically depressed Darb al-Ahmar neighborhood (AKTC 2007). Residents were provided with new opportunities including training, employment, and micro credit for small enterprises; programs for women, health, housing, and the environment were also instituted. Similar multi-input area development has also been carried out in Mali, Afghanistan, Tajikistan, Syria, Pakistan, and India (AKTC 2007).

One of Aga Khan IV's earliest business ventures was the founding of the Nation group of newspapers in Kenya. It was established to give room to indigenous voices as the country entered independence in the early 1960s (Loughran 2010). The group has expanded to neighboring countries and has become the largest media organization in East Africa. Other major institutions with the aim of promoting economic development are Industrial Promotion Services and Tourism Promotion Services. Banking and insurance companies founded by Aga Khan III for the Ismaili community's benefit were made into public corporations by his successor.

They have been grouped under the Aga Khan Fund for Economic Development (AKFED) which "operates more than 90 separate project companies, employs over 18,000 people and controls assets in excess of United States \$1.5 billion" (AKDN 2007b: 13). Several of the Fund's projects are run on the basis of public-private partnership. AKFED is the only part of the network that operates on a for-profit basis, with proceeds being "entirely reinvested in future development initiatives" (Aga Khan IV 2003).

Aga Khan institutions work in several countries where conducting business is a risky and perilous exercise, such as Afghanistan, where there is a significant Ismaili community. The Fund is the majority owner of Roshan, the largest telecommunications provider in the country whose infrastructure was largely destroyed by decades of war. Tourism Promotion Services operates a five-star hotel in Kabul, providing an up-scale and heavily secured location for potential investors visiting Afghanistan. AKFED is also the largest share-holder in Seacom, which has built a vital fibre-optic cable linking several African countries with Europe and Asia. "The objective of Seacom's Corporate Social Investment strategy is to achieve universal ICT access for all Africans" (Seacom 2012). AKFED is also involved in the aviation industry in Burkina, Mali, and Uganda, where transportation networks are frail. In the Fund's form of social capitalism, "Investment decisions are based more on the prospects for better lives for the constituencies of people that will be impacted by the investments and their results rather than on bottom line profitability" (Aga Khan IV 2003).

The reputation that AKDN has built over many decades in successfully improving conditions in developing countries has encouraged governments and other NGOs to collaborate extensively with it (AKDN 2007b). Aid agencies of wealthy countries and charitable foundations have provided substantial funding for the network's programs. Its projects have received mostly favorable media coverage in developed and developing countries. The presence of the community in Western countries has served as a bridge to secure resources and partnerships. Ismaili volunteers in various locations regularly organize much publicized fundraising drives.

Discussion: Ethical Obligation and Ethical Conduct

Various religious traditions encourage adherents to assist others in a spirit of fellowship. This service is conducted within respective communities of believers but is also frequently extended outwards. Religious humanism is at the basis of the international development endeavours of many faith groups. Individuals may feel the obligation to contribute to the betterment of humanity because this is an expectation in their religious community; there will also be benefits of a social nature to be derived, including the respect of fellow believers and rewards such as symbolic honors and promotion in the hierarchies of associations. Such benefits bring to attention the grey area between ethical obligation and personal motivation. An individual may contribute to an endeavour out of a sense of duty, but his conduct in performing the obligation may not correspond ethically to the underlying principles of the cause if he does not subscribe to or fully understand them. The likelihood of the latter would increase if the motivation is self-interest.

Even though the operational mode of AKDN is secular and worldly, many Ismailis personally tend to see their involvement with the network's agencies as part of their personal adherence to their Imam's vision. Their involvement with AKDN generally tends to be indistinguishable from the service offered to the institutions specifically addressing the needs of the *jamat*. Affection, loyalty, and dedication to the Imamat are reflected in the distinctive Ismaili bearing towards the communal and AKDN organizations. Service (*khidmat*) and giving (*sadaqah*), as acts of faith (Nanji 2000), underlie the voluntary contributions of time, effort, and material support that they offer the Imamat's institutions. Followers' service to the Imam is acknowledged through his periodic bestowing of titles of honor (*Huzur Mukhi, Alijah, Rai, Aitmadi, Diwan*, and *Vazir*) on them (Aga Khan IV 1998). However, Ismaili discourses are critical of adherents who perform service with the expectation that this will automatically result in the receipt of a title or elevation in the communal governance structure (Hassanally 1970).

In addition to the core forms of prayer and worship, specific modes of symbolic service are incorporated into the community's religious practices. Shia traditions of service to the faith, traced back to the time of Prophet Muhammad and Imam Ali, underlie the ethos of Ismaili "devotional associations" (Morris 1968: 83). Historical memory is frequently invoked of the exemplary contributions of adherents who served the family of the Prophet (embodied in the person of the current Imam). The pledging of oneself for a number of years or the dedication of one's entire life is symbolically expressed through membership in respective devotional associations. It is very likely that this religious attitude influences an adherent's personal approach when serving in the Imamat's secular institutions.

At the Golden Jubilee of Aga Khan IV in 2007, a practice involving the gift of time and knowledge (*Time and Knowledge Nazrana* or "TKN") by community members to the Imamat was established. It enables individual adherents to be placed for service in communal or AKDN organizations for voluntary, unpaid service for specific periods. This has contributed to the enthusiasm among a significant number of adherents to offer their energy and professional skills to the Imam's institutions (Lalani 2011). It has mobilized the talents of Ismailis to work in socio-economically depressed locations and is adding to the increasing number of transnational contacts among community members. However, such interactions, which have preceded the establishment of TKN, are also causing some stress stemming from the varying world-views of parts of the community that had developed for centuries in isolation from each other (Devji 2009; Steinberg 2010). Additionally, the simultaneous co-existence of AKDN institutions that serve non-Ismailis and the persistence of poverty among some community members have also led to questions about the distribution of benefits flowing from the Imamat's institutions (Kaiser 1996).

As indicated by the Fatimid writers Noaman (Muscati and Moulvi 1966) and Naysaburi (Klemm and Walker 2011), the Imam puts the responsibility for appropriate management on his appointed administrators. In squarely placing the work of his institutions within an ethical context, Aga Khan IV has put a high premium on the proper conduct of leaders, staff, and volunteers engaged in the operations of the organizations. The ethically charged obligation to improve the human condition requires that the work towards fulfilment of this obligation be carried out in an ethical manner. The governance of historical Ismaili states was conducted by the administrative structure of the *da'wa* ("the call"), which was also referred to as *al-da'wat al-haqq* ("the call to truth") (Klemm and Walker 2011: 1). According to Naysaburi, "the *da'wa* is built on knowledge [*ilm*], God fearing piety [*taqwa*] and good management [*siyasa*]" (Klemm and Walker 2011: 76). However, if these characteristics are missing then "Security, decency, piety, life, honour and chivalry cease" in society (Klemm and Walker 2011: 75). Naysaburi indicates that there was significant corruption in his time and that the current Imam [Al-Hakim] was disenchanted with his administrators (Klemm and Walker 2011).

The extensive and widely-dispersed contemporary Ismaili communal bodies and AKDN agencies, as well as the continuing expansion of the institutional network, pose enormous challenges for ensuring integrity and propriety across the board. As would be expected in similar enterprises in other communities, disaffected individuals have tended to express disagreements with certain operational methods of the administrative leadership of Ismaili institutions (Hassanally 1970; H.H. The Aga Khan Shia Imami Ismailia Association 1976). The availability of Internet-based media has facilitated the mass distribution of such communications. It is inevitable that ethical lapses, such as personal aggrandisement, expressions of cultural superiority, and nepotism and cronyism in administrators' behavior will occur. On the other hand, factors such as the self-perception of a moral community, the personal ethics of individuals and modes of self correction (Muscati and Moulvi 1966) that reorient one to "the straight path" (Qu'ran: *al-sirat al-mustaqim*) would ideally serve to prevent severe damage to the institutional system. However, more than these factors, it is loyalty to the Imamat and reluctance to appear as if criticism is being directed at the Imam himself that keeps most adherents from complaining openly and vigorously against administrators.

The Imam's lofty vision, expressed frequently in his communal and public discourses, is the primary source of institutional innovation and ethical guidance. Aga Khan IV's dynamic leadership and personal engagement has hitherto produced a remarkable network of organizations; he has succeeded in the last half-century in bringing together people of diverse backgrounds to make a viable contribution to the human condition. "How will this charisma and authority, deservedly earned by the Aga Khan in his own right, be transferred to a much younger and relatively unknown successor in the future?" (Devji 2009). Ismaili history has seen several crises of succession, and for the community, the successful continuation of the Imamat over 1,400 years is demonstrative of its resilience. The current Imam has also invested considerably in establishing long-term institutions.

Whereas the intent of building robust structures is to ensure the continuity of the Imamat's goal of improving human life, Ismaili history also points to the finite nature of worldly institutions. Like all empires, the Fatimid state eventually fell. A Canadian Ismaili magazine, conducting a rare contemporary critique of the community's current administrative leadership in an institutional publication, referred to a crisis in the Fatimid period stemming from the personal corruption of the Ismaili state's "prime minister" (*vazir*) who had interfered in an Imam's succession (H.H. The Agakhan Shia Imami Ismailia Association 1976: 5). The magazine's "Letter from the Publisher" declared that it was the unwavering integrity of the Imam's loyal adherents (particularly Hassan-i Sabbah) in the face of the institutional head's corruptibility that served to ensure the continuity of the (Nizari) Ismaili Imamat (H.H. The Agakhan Shia Imami Ismailia Association 1976). Such moral steadfastness at the risk of personal peril is the stuff of narratives that serve to inspire dedication and service among the Imam's contemporary followers.

AKDN's website states that the network is "a contemporary endeavour of the Ismaili Imamat to realise the social conscience of Islam through institutional action" (see AKDN 2007a). Varying forms of Ismaili organizations have been established in successive periods of history. However, building a specific type of institution in a particular time serves only as a means towards achieving a constant, permanent aim "to realise the social conscience of Islam" (AKDN 2007a). However, as often happens in worldly affairs, such essential long-term goals of institutions can be overshadowed by the pressing demands of the work at hand. The means tend to become an end in themselves, and the higher purposes may be compromised in order to fulfil the organization's current requirements. Even though there are historical Ismaili precedents for codes of conduct to guide the work of administrators, neither a formal code nor regimes for corrective measures for serious ethical lapses exist at the present. One would expect that integrity and ethical conduct would be prioritized over expediency, given that social conscience is named as the foundational basis of Ismaili institutions. The greater goal would necessarily be to remain ethical at all times, regardless of the situation. Naysaburi warns that, if administrators lose integrity, then "chaos will reign" in the Imam's community (Klemm and Walker 2011: 75).

References

Aga Khan III. 1954. *The Memoirs of Aga Khan*. London: Cassell.

Aga Khan III. 1955. *Mowlana Hazir Imam's Talika and Messages*. Mombasa, Kenya: Shia Imami Ismailia Associations for Africa.

Aga Khan IV. Circa 1998. *The Constitution of the Shia Imami Ismaili Muslims*.

Aga Khan IV. 2003. "Speech by His Highness the Aga Khan at the Opening of Alltex EPZ Limited at Athi River (Kenya)." Aga Khan Development Network, December 19. Retrieved March 31, 2012 (http://www.akdn.org/Content/596).

Aga Khan IV. 2008. *Where Hope Takes Root: Democracy and Pluralism in an Interdependent World.* Vancouver, Canada: Douglas and McIntyre.

AKDN (Aga Khan Development Network). 2007a. "About Us." Retrieved March 30, 2012 (http://www.akdn.org/about_akdn.asp).

AKDN (Aga Khan Development Network). 2007b. "AKDN: Aga Khan Development Network." Retrieved June 4, 2013 (http://www.akdn.org/).

AKDN (Aga Khan Development Network). 2009. "Multi-Input Area Development." AKDN Development Blog, April 29, 2009. Retrieved May 7, 2012 (http://www.akdn.org/Content/737).

AKF (Aga Khan Foundation). 2006. *Aga Khan Foundation: Annual Report 2005.* Geneva, Switzerland: Aka Khan Foundation.

AKF USA (Aga Khan Foundation U.S.A.). 2011. *Aga Khan Foundation U.S.A.: Annual Report 2010.* Retrieved April 6, 2012 (http://www.akdn.org/publications/2010_akf_usa_annual_report.pdf).

AKTC (Aga Khan Trust for Culture). 2007. *Aga Khan Trust for Culture: The Cultural Agency of the Aga Khan Development Network.* (Geneva: Author).

Aziz, Khursheed Kamal, ed. 1998. *Aga Khan III: Selected Speeches and Writing of Sir Sultan Muhammad Shah.* Vol. I. London: Kegan Paul.

Daftary, Farhad. 2007. *The Ismailis: Their History and Doctrines.* Cambridge, UK: Cambridge University Press.

Devji, Faisal. 2009. "Preface." Pp. ix-xvi in Marc van Grondelle, *The Ismailis in the Colonial Era: Modernity Empire and Islam, 1839-1969.* London: Hurst & Co.

H.H. The Agakhan Shia Imami Ismailia Association. 1976. "Letter from the Publisher." *Hikmat* 1(1): 5.

Hassanally, (Vazir) Abdul Hamid. 1970. "Dedication Needed, Pure and Intense." *Africa Ismaili* 3:10, 26.

Hirji, Zulfikar. 2011. "The Socio-Legal Formation of the Nizari Ismailis in East Africa, 1800-1950." Pp. 129-59 in *A Modern History of the Ismailis: Continuity and Change in a Muslim Community*, edited by Farhad Daftary. London: I.B. Tauris.

The Institute of Ismaili Studies. 2000. "Aga Khan Development Network (AKDN): An Ethical Framework." Retrieved April 2, 2012 (http://www.iis.ac.uk/view_article.asp?ContentID=101094).

Kaiser, Paul J. 1996. *Culture, Transnationalism and Civil Society: Aga Khan Social Service Initiatives in Tanzania.* Westport, CT: Praeger.

Karim, Karim H. 2011a. "At the Interstices of Tradition, Modernity and Postmodernity: Ismaili Engagements with Contemporary Canadian Society." Pp. 265-94 in *A Modern History of the Ismailis: Continuity and Change in a Muslim Community*, edited by Farhad Daftary. London: I.B. Tauris.

Karim, Karim H. 2011b. "Muslim Migration, Institutional Development and Geographic Imagination: The Aga Khan Development Network's Transnationalism." Pp. 205-21 in *Transnational Europe: Promise, Paradox, Limits*, edited by Joan DeBardeleben and Achim Hurrelmann. London: Palgrave Macmillan.

Kassam, Tazim R. 2003. "The Aga Khan Development Network: An Ethic of Sustainable Development and Social Conscience." Pp. 477-96 in *Islam and Ecology*, edited by Richard C. Foltz, Frederick M. Denny, and Azizan Baharuddin. Cambridge, MA: Centre for the Study of World Religions, Harvard Divinity School.

Kassam, Zayn R. 2011. "Gender Policies of Aga Khan III and Aga Khan IV." Pp. 247-64 in *A Modern History of the Ismailis*: *Continuity and Change in a Muslim Community*, edited by Farhad Daftary. London: I.B. Tauris.

Klemm, Verena and Paul E. Walker. 2011. *A Code of Conduct: A Treatise on the Etiquette of the Fatimid Mission*. London: I.B. Tauris.

Lalani, Farah. 2011. "US TKN Volunteers and International Assignments." *The Ismaili: United States of America* (December 13): 14-16.

Loughran, Gerry. 2010. *Birth of a Nation: The Story of a Newspaper in Kenya*. London: I.B. Tauris.

Mandaville, Peter. 2001. *Transnational Muslim Politics: Reimagining the Umma*. London: Routledge.

Morris, Harold S. 1968. *The Indians in Uganda: Caste and Sect in a Plural Society*. London: Weidenfield and Nichloson.

Muscati, Jawad and A.M. Moulvi. 1966. *Selections from Qazi Noaman's Kitab-ul-Himma fi Adabi Ataba-el-a'emma or Code of Conduct of the Followers of Imam*. Mombasa, Kenya: Ismailia Association for Africa.

Najam, Adil. 2006. "Working with Government: Close but Never Too Close." Pp. 426-53 in *Valleys in Transition: Twenty Years of AKRSP's Experience in Pakistan*, edited by Geoffrey Wood, Abdul Malik, and Sumaira Sagheer . Karachi, Pakistan: Oxford University Press.

Nanji, Azim. 2000. "Charitable Giving in Islamic Contexts." P. xx in *Philanthropy in Pakistan: A Report of The Initiative on Indigenous Philanthropy*, edited by David Bonbright. London: Aga Khan Development Network.

Ramachandran, Sudha. 2005. "Ismailis in Deadly Education Spat." *Asia Times Online*, March 11. Retrieved April 6, 2012 (http://www.atimes.com/atimes/South_Asia/GC11Df06.html).

Ruthven, Malise. 2011. "The Aga Khan Development Network and Institutions." Pp. 189-220 in *A Modern History of the Ismailis: Continuity and Change in a Muslim Community*, edited by Farhad Daftary. London: I.B. Tauris.

Sajoo, Amyn B. 2004. *Muslim Ethics: Emerging Vistas*. London: I.B. Tauris.

Seacom. 2012. "Corporate Social Investment." Retrieved April 2, 2012 (http://www.seacom.mu/csi).

Springborg, Robert, ed. 2009. *Development Models in Muslim Contexts: Chinese, 'Islamic' and Neo-Liberal Alternatives*. Edinburgh, UK: Edinburgh University Press.

Steinberg, Jonah. 2010. *Ismaili Modern: Globalization and Identity in a Muslim Community*. Chapel Hill, NC: University of North Carolina Press.

Thawerbhoy, Esmail. 1977. "The Imam of the Socio-Economic Revolution." *Ilm* 3(2): 18-26.

Wood, Geoffrey, Abdul Malik, and Sumaira Sagheer, eds. 2006. *Valleys in Transition: Twenty Years of AKRSP's Experience in Pakistan*. Karachi, Pakistan: Oxford University Press.

Chapter 8
Bahá'í International Community: Bahá'í Faith

Mike McMullen

This chapter will examine how the Bahá'í Faith, one of the newest independent world religions, translates its ethic of "unity in diversity" and the "oneness of religion and humanity" into a network of global service projects coordinated through its growing Bahá'í Administrative Order. Through a combination of grassroots empowerment and top-down coordination from the Bahá'í World headquarters in Haifa, Israel, Bahá'ís are engaged in two main service activities: (1) consciousness-raising, or trying to infuse debates about interfaith dialog, women's rights, spiritual education, religious freedom, and sustainable development with Bahá'í values; and (2) actual grassroots social and economic development projects that not only impact the material fortunes of individuals and communities, but also attempt to elevate the spiritual health of society. After a brief discussion about the history of this little-known global movement, as well as its beliefs and organizational structure, this chapter will outline the three main types of service activities in which Bahá'ís engage as part of their effort to "think globally, but act locally."

Bahá'í History and Growth

The Bahá'í Faith was historically preceded by the Bábí religion, which began in 1844 when a Persian merchant named Siyyid 'Alí-Muhammad revealed himself to be the Qá'im,"He Who Ariseth," the title of the Promised One in Shi'ite Islam, also known as the Twelfth, Hidden Imam (Hatcher and Martin 1985). He took the title of the Báb, "the Gate" in Arabic, and began to reveal new religious teachings. The thrust of his message was to herald the coming of "One Whom God Will Make Manifest," a prophet of greater importance who would lead humankind into a new era of peace. Thus, many Bahá'ís compare the function of the Báb to that of John the Baptist, who heralded the coming of Christ. The Báb attracted a substantial following from Shi'ite Muslims, arousing the suspicions and distrust of Islamic authorities, especially the Islamic clergy (*ulama*). In an effort to crush the religious movement and its followers, Babis, the government of Persia executed the Báb in 1850 which almost destroyed the new religious movement. The Báb had not revealed when the "One Whom God Shall Make Manifest" would come, but had indicated the time would be soon (Esslemont 1970).

The narrative then shifts to Mírzá Husayn-'Alí, a Persian whose family was part of the governing class of the country. Upon hearing of the religion of the Báb, he converted and began teaching its message. His growing leadership role within the Bábí movement revitalized and invigorated the new religion. His social position protected him at first from the persecutions of the Persian authorities, but as fervor increased, he too was imprisoned. While he was in prison in Tehran in 1852-53, Bahá'ís believe, God revealed to Mírzá Husayn-'Alí that he was the "One Whom God Will Make Manifest" prophesied by the Báb, whose teachings would usher in the long-awaited Kingdom of God. Persian authorities banished Mírzá Husayn-'Alí, his family, and fellow-Bábís, to Baghdad, thus beginning a lifetime of exile. While in Baghdad, he took the title Bahá'u'lláh ("The Glory of God" in Arabic) and announced that he was the one promised by the Báb, whereupon the vast majority of Bábís pledged allegiance to Bahá'u'lláh and his authority as a new religious leader (Hatcher and Martin 1985).

In 1863, the group of Bahá'ís, the new name given to the new followers of Bahá'u'lláh, were banished from Baghdad and sent to Constantinople (now Istanbul) and then to Adrianople (now Edirne) in Turkey. Finally, in 1868, the group was exiled permanently to 'Akká, Palestine, the prison-city of the Ottoman Empire ('Akká is near present-day Haifa, Israel, the location of the Bahá'í World Center). Here, as in the other cities of his banishment, Bahá'u'lláh carried on his ministry, wrote nearly one hundred volumes that partially comprise Bahá'í scripture, and met with pilgrims who traveled to 'Akká to see the man whose message was spreading throughout Persia and the Middle East (Hatcher and Martin 1985).

When Bahá'u'lláh died in 1892, he left behind a growing movement and a will and testament that named his eldest son, 'Abdu'l-Bahá ("Servant of the Glory" in Arabic), his successor and the authoritative interpreter of Bahá'í writings. After the Young Turk revolution in 1908, all political and religious prisoners of the Ottoman Empire were released, thus freeing 'Abdu'l-Bahá to begin establishing his father's Covenant: the institutionalization of the Bahá'í Administrative Order as communicated through Bahá'u'lláh's writings (Hatcher and Martin 1985).

'Abdu'l-Bahá helped define two major institutions: the Guardianship and the Universal House of Justice (UHJ). The Guardianship imparted sole authority of the religion to 'Abdu'l-Bahá's eldest grandson, Shoghi Effendi Rabbani, who would continue the establishment of the religion's Administrative Order. Upon 'Abdu'l-Bahá's death in 1921, Shoghi Effendi led the Bahá'í Faith as its "Guardian" until his death in 1957. From 1957 until the first election of the UHJ in 1963, the "Hands of the Cause of God," a temporary administrative institution of charismatic, faithful Bahá'ís (inaugurated by Bahá'u'lláh), governed the Bahá'í Faith. Since 1963, the UHJ is the recognized global authority of the world's approximately six million Bahá'ís.

The growth of the Bahá'í Faith, and its rise as a truly global social service movement, continues today through the institutionalization of a network of structures at the local, national, and international levels of social life. This expansion to every corner of the globe has taken place through methodical, rational blueprints called "Teaching Plans," first developed by Shoghi Effendi in 1937 and now coordinated by the Universal House of Justice (UHJ) in consultation with National Spiritual Assemblies (NSAs). Systematic plans for growth have followed a pattern that seeks to first establish local communities through missionary activity and then to utilize indigenous resources to expand both horizontally in a local area and vertically to link with the global headquarters.

Administrative Structure and Growth

Bahá'ís consider their ecclesiastical organization to be unique in the world, in part because it was designed, they claim, not only to be the model of world unity, but also because Bahá'u'lláh was the first prophet-founder of a world religion to deliberately design the organization. Bahá'í sources say this about the Bahá'ís' perceived unique organizational system:

> Not until the advent of the Bahá'í Dispensation did a Manifestation of God include administrative principles among His spiritual teachings. This is an entirely new dimension which Bahá'u'lláh has introduced; He has placed the spiritual and administrative principles on a par with each other. A violation of an administrative principle … is as grave a betrayal of the Cause of Bahá'u'lláh as breaking a spiritual law. (Taherzadeh 1992: 156)

The Bahá'í Administrative Order consists of two pillars or functional branches. This is significant for Bahá'ís, considering that Bahá'u'lláh strictly forbade the formation of clergy in the Bahá'í Faith (Bahá'u'lláh 1992; Esslemont 1970). Bahá'ís believe that humanity has developed beyond the need for a special class which monopolizes religious knowledge and they claim that the lack of clergy protects their faith from being corrupted by the power which accrues to any one individual. No one Bahá'í, theoretically, has any authority over anyone else. Instead, all religious authority lies in elected councils or "assemblies" which operate at all levels of society. The Administrative Order consists of two branches (or pillars): elected assemblies (the "Rulers") and appointed boards (the "Learned") operating at the local, national, and international levels of society.

The Rulers

The first, and more important, of the two branches of Bahá'í organization is a series of democratically elected "spiritual assemblies" at the local, national, and international levels of social life—referred to as the "institution of the Rulers" since they are that branch of the Administrative Order that governs or has authority over the Bahá'í community. These assemblies constitute the core of the Bahá'í

World Order. Each year, wherever there are at least nine adult Bahá'ís, age 21 and older, within a recognized municipal boundary, an election is held to form a Local Spiritual Assembly (LSA) of nine members, which constitutes the foundation authority of local Bahá'í community life. Every community member votes for nine individuals, and the nine receiving the most votes become LSA members—this is true of Bahá'í elections at all three levels of the structure. If there is a tie for the ninth spot, Bahá'í administrative law dictates that the position goes to the individual who is a "minority" in the community—a form of electoral "affirmative action." Local elections take place the first day of the 12-day Festival of Ridván held April 21 through May 2 each year. Ridvan ("Paradise" in Arabic) is the Bahá'í holy period commemorating Baha'u'llah's first public declaration of his message for humanity. None of the individuals who are elected to the assemblies have any authority—only the decisions arrived at through consultation by the institution are authoritative. Bahá'ís are not allowed to "run" for office since Bahá'u'lláh strictly forbade campaigning in his writings. Instead, Bahá'ís are instructed to vote for any Bahá'í who is eligible, based on their spiritual character.

Usually the first weekend in October, Bahá'ís in the United States attend their District Convention, an administrative meeting where a National Delegate is elected. These two elections—the April Ridván festival and the October District Convention—are the two democratic rituals in which all Bahá'ís have a chance to participate; indeed, they are viewed as spiritual obligations for members. The elected National Delegates then go in May to the National Convention, held in Wilmette, Illinois—site of the Bahá'í National Center—to elect the National Spiritual Assembly (NSA); again, a nine-member body that oversees Bahá'í activity within a nation or region. Finally, once every five years, the members of all the NSAs in the world gather at the Bahá'í World Center in Haifa, Israel, to elect the nine-member Universal House of Justice (UHJ), the highest authority in the Bahá'í world. Unlike the LSAs and NSAs, the UHJ is limited by Bahá'u'lláh's writings to males only. The first UHJ was elected in 1963, a few years after the death of Shoghi Effendi.

Bahá'u'lláh promised Bahá'ís that decisions made by the UHJ are divinely guided and infallible. Although the UHJ cannot change any law revealed by Bahá'u'lláh, it is empowered to legislate on all other matters. This administrative flexibility, Bahá'ís say, prevents the religious laws and organization of their Faith from becoming obsolete, which often results in sectarian divisions. Subsequently, Bahá'ís believe that, through the collective decisions of the institution of the UHJ (again, not in theory based on any charismatic authority or individual revelation), the Bahá'í world, and eventually the global civilization which will supposedly be generated from Bahá'í institutions and laws, is assured of divine guidance until the appearance of the next prophet.

The Learned

The second pillar of the Administrative Order, in addition to the elected assemblies, is what is known as the "Learned" branch, or the "protectors" and "propagators" of the Bahá'í Faith. This function of protection and propagation falls to the members of an institution called the Continental Board of Counselors, appointed by the UHJ for five-year terms, and below them the various Auxiliary Board members who are appointed for one-year terms by the Continental Counselors but approved by the UHJ. Under the Auxiliary Board members are their Assistants, who are also appointed for one year terms and work directly with Local Spiritual Assemblies. None of the Counselors or Auxiliary Board members and their assistants have any individual authority over the decisions of a Local or National Assembly or the UHJ, which is where administrative authority and decision-making legitimately lie; they also have no formal authority over any individual Bahá'í. Instead, they are individuals who are knowledgeable about Bahá'í law and administrative principles, hence the expression "institution of the Learned." They function to offer assistance to newly formed assemblies just learning the principles of Bahá'í administration, to offer aid to teaching projects undertaken by LSAs, and also to assist local or national communities in handling the expulsion of deviant members from the religion. In effect, they are Bahá'í "consultants" representing the UHJ in its work with the elected assemblies.

In addition to these major components of the Administrative Order, the UHJ oversees a Research Department, an Archives division, a Center for the Study of Holy Texts, an Office of Social and Economic Development, and the Bahá'í International Community (BIC). The latter is the name of the non-governmental organization (NGO) registered with the United Nations, first chartered in March 1948. BIC was granted consultative status with the UN Economic and Social Council in May 1970, with UNICEF in 1976, and in 1989 it developed a working relationship with the World Health Organization. BIC's goal is to promote "world peace by creating the conditions in which unity emerges as the natural state of human existence" (McMullen 2000: 39). BIC is the main arm of Bahá'í service projects throughout the world and will be discussed at length below.

Since Bahá'u'lláh declared his mission over 150 years ago, the Bahá'í Faith has seen rapid development. According to the 1992 *Encyclopedia Britannica Book of the Year*, the Bahá'í Faith has established "significant communities" in more countries and territories than any other independent religion with the exception of Christianity. Its fastest growth has been in the developing world. The *World Christian Encyclopedia* (Barrett 1982) indicated that from 1970-82, the Bahá'í Faith grew at an average rate of 3.63 percent, compared with 2.74 percent for Islam, 2.3 percent for Hinduism, 1.67 percent for Buddhism, 1.64 percent for Christianity, and 1.09 percent for Judaism.

The period of most intensive growth came at the beginning of the 1950s, coinciding with the worldwide increase in transnational institutions (Waters 1995). For example, in 1953, there were 9 NSAs and 611 LSAs. By 1964, at the end of the Ten-Year World Crusade, the first globally encompassing teaching plan inaugurated by Shoghi Effendi, there were 56 NSAs and 4,566 LSAs (from Smith 1987). In 1954, the first year of the Ten-Year Plan, 94 percent of the world's Bahá'ís lived in Iran, the land of its birth. By 1988, only 6 percent lived there (Smith and Momen 1989). It is estimated that in 1963, at the end of the Ten-Year Plan, there were approximately 400,000 Bahá'ís world-wide, that number expanding to 3.5 million in 1985, and to 5 million six years later (a 43 percent increase since 1985; for further data on the rate of growth of the Bahá'í Faith globally, see Smith 1987; Smith and Momen 1989). It is only in the last 40 to 50 years that the Bahá'ís have become a truly "global" movement—expanding beyond a bi-polar concentration, in the "Islamic heartland"—primarily Iran but also Iraq; and "the West"—primarily the United States and Canada.

The organizational structure and the method of expansion of the Administrative Order facilitates the development of a Bahá'í identity as "situated universalists" (McMullen 2000: 12). Built from the ground up by universal participatory democracy, the Administrative Order links Bahá'ís in a local jurisdiction to a global central authority believed to be infallible. The UHJ as the highest Bahá'í authority reflexively acts back upon a Bahá'í's situated local community through the development of regular, rational teaching plans, which act as a blueprint and guide for local activity. The teaching plans help coordinate an individual's and local community's vision as participants in universal salvation, building what Bahá'ís believe to be the Kingdom of God.

Progressive Revelation and Universal Ideology

In order to understand the universalizing goal of Bahá'í ideology and its promotion of global order and solidarity, one must understand the central ideological concept for Bahá'ís: Progressive Revelation. Bahá'ís' vision of global unity includes the ideological claim that all of the world's major religions are only evolutionary stages in God's plan to educate and unify the whole planet—in effect, there is only one religion, but it is revealed by God in distinct historical periods by "Manifestations of God," which include founders such as Buddha, Abraham, Zoroaster, Moses, Jesus, Mohammad, and most recently, Baha'u'llah. Bahá'ís claim that the spiritual truths of all religions are the same; religions superficially appear to be in conflict due to the social laws that differ because of the need throughout history for new moral and social codes by which larger segments of humanity are unified.

Bahá'ís do admit, however, that there are differences in the content (but not the function) of the message brought by the "Manifestations of God." For Bahá'ís, there is a two-fold function of religion: the spiritual education of individuals and the social solidarity of humanity through various laws and institutions. Thus, Bahá'ís consider that God's revelation to humanity has been evolutionary, teleological, functional, and progressive. Bahá'ís believe that the solution to the problems of the modern age is global unity based on the recognition of one common faith which fulfills the prophesies of all the world's functionally equivalent, yet historically specific, religions. Bahá'ís do not think that theirs is the last stage of religious evolution for humanity, but cite Bahá'u'lláh's statement that a full one thousand years will pass before the next Manifestation will appear.

Who Are the Baha'is?

Because of the focus on education, the independent investigation of the truth and the expectation that Bahá'ís will study the many volumes of texts that comprise Bahá'í scripture, Bahá'ís—at least in the developed world—tend to be at the higher end of the socio-economic and educational spectrum. Most Bahá'ís who converted were either "pushed" out of their religion of birth because of dissatisfaction or were "pulled" into the Bahá'í Faith because of attraction to its spiritual or social teachings (McMullen 2000). What Bahá'í ideology resolves for these people who are "pushed" away from "traditional" religion is what Berger (1969) called the "problem of plausibility" in a pluralistic, globalized world.

These two issues—Bahá'ís being "pushed" out of their religion of birth due to disillusionment, together with the "pull" of the attractiveness of the social and spiritual principles of the Bahá'í Faith—help define Bahá'ís as "seekers." Both when seeking a universal ethic in a globalized world and after formally enrolling in the Bahá'í Faith and continuing to seek spiritual deepening, Bahá'ís adopt a "seeker" identity. In general, Bahá'ís are disillusioned with organized religion or are searching for a "logical" or "rational" religious faith that makes sense and provides meaning in a globalized world and are attracted by either the religious ideology of progressive revelation or by the corresponding community life of the unity in diversity in local communities of the Bahá'í Faith. Both are crucial aspects of a Bahá'í identity, and both reflect the global world-view of this religion. Research by Garlington (1977) and Warburg (1986) suggests that Bahá'í ideology appeals also to lower-class individuals in the developing world, probably due to its empowerment at the local level.

The Bahá'í Faith as a Global Service Movement

The Bahá'í perspective on global service focuses on two areas of human development. The first is education, focusing on consciousness-raising activities about the Bahá'í Faith itself and its global values, and also on issues of importance to Bahá'ís, such as racial unity, the equality of women and men, and human rights and sustainable development. The other thrust of Bahá'í global service emphasizes direct social services, such as programs for literacy, agricultural improvement, or medical clinics. Both are reflected below in the following review of the three institutionalized approaches Bahá'ís take as a global social movement.

The Bahá'í Faith pursues its goals of social service on a global scale, reflecting its identity as a global religious movement and its goal to influence the eventual establishment of a global civilization. Their efforts as a global service movement rooted in their religious beliefs are manifested in both in top-down projects, governed by direction and principles from the Universal House of Justice, and in initiatives at the grassroots level cultivated by Bahá'ís as individuals or in local communities to live out the Bahá'í belief that, "work done in the spirit of service is the highest form of worship" (Abdu'l-Baha [1918] in Universal House of Justice 1976: 59). There are three major initiatives for global service for Bahá'ís, two of which require coordination by all levels of the Bahá'í Administrative Order: (1) The Bahá'í International Community (BIC), the NGO affiliated with the United Nations; (2) efforts at recruiting "pioneers" for international service that has the parallel goal of fostering Bahá'í converts; and (3) more localized efforts, coordinated by the National Spiritual Assemblies, to foster what Bahá'ís call "capacity building" or developing individual Bahá'ís human resources, which culminates in local service projects all over the world. Each will be discussed below.

Consciousness-Raising and Social/Economic Development in the Bahá'í International Community

The Bahá'í International Community (BIC) was established on April 18, 1948 when nine National Spiritual Assemblies of the Bahá'í's of the world were recognized collectively as an International NGO under the title Bahá'í International Community for the purpose of fostering and maintaining a relationship with the United Nations. However, efforts of the Bahá'ís to have international influence extend back even further, with efforts to reduce the persecution of the movement in its native land and around the Middle East. For example, Bahá'í representatives were sent by Shoghi Effendi to be present at the founding of the United Nations in 1945, and before that, Bahá'ís petitioned the League of Nations in 1928 to regain access to the house in which Baha'u'llah lived while in exile in Baghdad, which has since been destroyed by Muslim clerics (BIC 2010a).

The Bahá'í International Community is an international non-governmental organization with affiliates in over 180 countries and territories, which together represent the 6 million members of the Bahá'í Faith at the United Nations. BIC is ultimately under the direction and authority of the Universal House of Justice. The BIC defines its mission "to promote and apply principles—derived from the teachings of the Bahá'í Faith—which contribute to the resolution of current day challenges facing humanity and the development of a united, peaceful, just and sustainable civilization" (BIC 2005). Bahá'í representatives are active in numerous coalitions of NGOs, focusing particularly on human rights, the advancement of the equality of women and men, and social and economic development (SEC).

BIC has offices at the United Nations in New York, Geneva, and most recently in 2007, an office was established in Brussels, Belgium, to represent the Bahá'í Faith to the European Union. It also has representatives at United Nations Regional Commissions based in Addis Ababa, Bangkok, Nairobi, Rome, Santiago, and Vienna. An Office of Public Information based at the Bahá'í World Centre in Haifa, Israel, disseminates information about the Bahá'í Faith around the world and publishes a quarterly newsletter, *One Country*. BIC's United Nations Office has consultative status with the United Nations Economic and Social Council and

UNICEF and working relations with several other United Nations agencies and NGOs. In its quadrennial report on 2006-2009, BIC reported:

> The Bahá'í International Community seeks to contribute to the processes of advancing human civilization by bringing the principles of the Bahá'í Faith and the insight and experience of its worldwide membership to bear on the issues under consideration by the United Nations. Among the principles shaping our contributions and working methods at the United Nations are: the oneness of humanity; the elimination of all forms of prejudice; the equality of men and women; the nobility of the human being; the elimination of the extremes of wealth and poverty; universal education; freedom of conscience; an ethic of sustainability; harmony of science and religion; unity in diversity; and consultation—processes of collective deliberation and decision-making. (BIC 2013)

BIC focuses on three activities: human rights generally, and the persecution of Bahá'ís specifically; women's rights; and social and economic development.

Human Rights

The focus on human rights most often takes specific form in BIC advocacy of the rights of the Bahá'í minority in Iran. Babis and Bahá'ís have suffered persecutions since its inception in the 1840s in what was then Persia. Over 20,000 were executed by the Shah between 1844 and 1853 (Hatcher and Martin 1985), and persecution intensified in Iran following the 1979 Islamic Revolution. Many Bahá'ís fled right before or in the immediate aftermath of the return of Ayyatohlah Khomeni. Since 1979, Bahá'ís have been systematically denied access to higher education and employment, and have been subjected to summary arrests, detentions, and executions. They have never been able to openly practice their religion. The United States Congress has repeatedly passed resolutions calling for the end to Bahá'í persecutions and even named the treatment of Bahá'ís "genocide" (Nash 1982). The Bahá'ís have been focusing on human rights violations on religious grounds for over eight decades, since the League of Nations recognized Bahá'í efforts to end persecution of Bahá'ís in Iraq and Iran. The situation of Bahá'ís is difficult in most Muslim-majority countries, especially Iran, but also Egypt.

Bahá'ís are the largest minority religion in predominantly Shi'ite Iran, numbering over 300,000 (followed by Zoroastrians and Christians). As of 2010, there were 35 Bahá'ís in prison in Iran and over 300 arrests since 2005. A campaign of arrests, interrogations, and intimidation has been waged against Bahá'ís of all ages—even kindergarten children have been humiliated in class and expelled from local schools. Across the country, Bahá'í cemeteries have been desecrated and, in some instances, razed (BIC 2008f)). The most notorious case is that of seven Iranian Bahá'í leaders incarcerated in Evin prison for refusing to recant their faith, with no space to lie down, no furniture, no bedding, and no natural light or fresh air (BIC 2010e). These seven each received a sentence of 20 years' imprisonment (later reduced to 10 years) on charges of apostasy. The persecution of Bahá'ís takes various forms:

> Arson and other violent attacks against Bahá'ís have increased in parallel with widespread incitement to hatred. Bahá'í children are intimidated and harassed by teachers and school officials, and Bahá'í students denied access to university. The government applies many restrictions on employment, including a list of 25 trades from which Bahá'ís are banned, and denies their right to pensions and inheritance. (BIC 2010e)

The pattern of this latest repression follows the Iranian government's guidelines set down in two confidential government documents, both endorsed by the Supreme Leader, Ayatollah Khomeini:

- The 1991 memorandum that established a detailed policy on how the Bahá'ís should be treated, given no religious freedom and limited to a minimum livelihood; and
- the letter sent by the Command Headquarters of the Armed Forces, at the end of 2005, to all of Iran's intelligence and enforcement agencies, instructing them to identify Bahá'ís throughout the country—presumably to ensure that the 1991 memorandum could now be thoroughly implemented (BIC 2010c).

The government of Iran has called the Bahá'í Faith a "cult" or an "illegal Zionist" organization, and BIC has come to their defense by stating:

> These latest developments are especially disturbing when viewed in the light of an established pattern whereby the authorities make or purvey false statements about the Bahá'ís, then deliberately repeat and widely disseminate these falsehoods and misrepresentations to give them credence. The intention, of course, is to foment hatred and mistrust of the Bahá'ís so that there exists within the general population an atmosphere wherein egregious violations of the Bahá'ís' human rights are either condoned or not questioned. (BIC 2008f)

Even internationally-known Iranian lawyer, Shirin Ebadi, founder of the Defenders of Human Rights Center in Iran and 2003 recipient of the Nobel Peace Prize, has defended the religious freedom of Bahá'ís in her native Iran. Most damaging for young Bahá'ís is the policy of refusing Bahá'í youth access to higher education (BIC 2008f). Bahá'ís in the United States have responded by forming the Bahá'í Institute for Higher Education (BIHE), a free online accredited university accessible to Iranian Bahá'í youth.

Women's Rights and Equality

For 60 years, the Bahá'í International Community's United Nations Office has worked for women's advancement and gender equality through its participation in and contributions to the session of the Commission on the Status of Women. Along with national affiliates, BIC has been involved in each of the United Nations world conferences on women and children and led the NGO Committee on the Status of Women during the 4th World Conference on Women (Beijing).

In its quadrennial report on 2006-2009, BIC reported that since 2006, their representatives have played a leadership role in the United Nations Gender Equality Architecture Reform Group. BIC representatives have served as chair or past chair of the Committee on the Status of Women. BIC submitted statements to the 50th, 51st, 52nd and 53rd Sessions of the Commission. Since 2006, BIC has co-organized over 50 side events with various agencies including the United Nations Development Fund for Women (UNIFEM), United Nations Fund for Children (UNICEF), United Nations Development Programme (UNDP), and with member states. BIC representatives are members of seven NGO Committees working on gender equality (BIC 2010b).

BIC statements at the United Nations in support of women's rights flow from their religious teachings about the need for gender equality in order to achieve world peace. A statement by BIC to the United Nations World Conference for International Women's Year in Mexico City in 1975 stated:

> In the Bahá'íworld community the education of women has high priority. Although universal compulsory education applies to both sexes, the education of women, because mothers are the first teachers of the child, is considered more important than that of men. Therefore, if parents, who have the primary responsibility for the education of their children, are not able to fulfill their duty to educate both boy and girl in a family, preference is given to the girl. In no way does this choice suggest that women are to be limited to the rearing of children and to household duties; for it is vital that women develop all their talents and skills, so that they may achieve through their constructive activities recognition of complete equality. (BIC 2010d)

More recently, BIC has submitted a statement to the eighth session of the UN Human Rights Council in Geneva in 2008, saying:

> The challenge is how to create conditions for women and girls to develop their full potential and for all of society to support the changes required. This means not only changing legal, political and economic structures, but also transforming individuals—men and women, boys and girls—whose morals or values consciously or inadvertently sustain exploitative behavior. (BIC 2008c)

While policy changes at all levels of society are needed, according to Bahá'ís, BIC concludes that the state has ultimate responsibility to protect individual rights. As will be seen below, these policy positions inform the kinds of global service projects sponsored by Bahá'í institutions.

Bahá'í United Nations policy positions also reflect the connection between women's education and women's reproductive health. While Bahá'í theology states that God creates a soul at the moment of conception, the UHJ has stated that issues of family planning, contraception use, abortion, and so on, are currently left to the decision of the women in consultation with her family and doctor. In 2011, BIC made a presentation to the 44th Session of the UN Commission on Population and Development, stating the oft-repeated Bahá'í perspective that true development can only take place when women and men are equally shouldering their social responsibilities and benefiting from equal rights:

> We aim to address the need to transition to a more comprehensive approach to addressing women's reproductive health and human rights. We do so guided by the understanding that the ultimate aim is not only to enable women to participate fully in the affairs of society within the present social order. Rather, women must be enabled to work shoulder to shoulder with men to construct a new social order characterized by justice, peace and collective prosperity. (BIC 2011)

Social and Economic Development

BIC attempts to influence leaders of thought through the elucidation of Bahá'í principles among global leaders at the United Nations and its affiliated NGOs. For Bahá'ís, influenced by its theology of the oneness of humanity, helping to change discourse in various social arenas at local, national, and global levels is part of their *raison d'être* as a global service movement. However, that is only half the equation. The other half is to encourage Bahá'ís to translate this consciousness-raising into acts of service toward humanity. This is motivated in part by the Office of Social and Economic Development at BIC, under the direction of the Universal House of Justice, which helps coordinate and collect data on the myriad of Bahá'í-inspired social and economic development (SED) projects around the world.

The philosophy of Bahá'í SED projects flows from their specifically religious worldview. As described above, all levels of the Bahá'í Administrative Order are involved in SED, and the impetus for SED activities are to be of service to humanity to promote the unity of humanity, one of the highest Bahá'í values. It seeks to balance individual initiatives and collective needs. BIC says, "This collective hierarchy devolves decision making to the lowest level practical—providing thereby a unique vehicle for grassroots action—while at the same time conferring a level of coordination and authority that makes possible cooperation on a global scale" (*Betterment* 2008).

Bahá'ís see themselves as building a global civilization built on spiritual principles that elevates the capacity of individuals, communities, and institutions to meet the spiritual and material needs of humanity (*Betterment* 2008). As such, Bahá'í development attempts to balance spiritual and scientific knowledge, teaching not only moral conduct and global citizenship, but also skills and sciences to "carry forth an ever advancing civilization" (Baha'u'llah 1976: 215). BIC says:

> At the heart of all Bahá'í development undertaking is the recognition of a deep and inseparable connection between the practical and spiritual aspects of daily life. Creating a desire for social change and instilling confidence that it can be achieved must ultimately come from an awakening of the human spirit. While pragmatic approaches to problem solving play a key role in development initiatives, tapping the spiritual roots of human motivation provides the essential impulse that ensures genuine social advancement. (BIC 2008d)

Material advancement for Bahá'ís is not an end in itself, but a vehicle for moral, spiritual, and social progress, with the goal being a unified global civilization that realizes the value of the unity of humanity. This goal necessitates a process of what Bahá'ís call "consultation," or collective decision-making, whereby decisions are made at the grassroots level if possible with all stake-holders around the table.

These global service activities are not only meant to serve humanity, but also infuse in people's consciousness a sense of what the Bahá'í Faith is about and to spread Bahá'í values. However, Bahá'í documents on SED emphasize that:

> As a demonstration of its integrity, Bahá'í social and economic projects are not used as an inducement to conversion … Bahá'í development activities draw their inspiration and direction from a spiritually centered values system, but these activities are not used as a vehicle for religious propagation. (BIC 2008e)

Since the benefits of Bahá'í development initiatives are designed to benefit all members of a community and not just Bahá'ís, funds from private, national, or international agencies are sometimes accepted for such projects. However, Bahá'ís refuse to accept funds from non-Bahá'ís for purely religious reasons or Bahá'í institution-building.

How Do Baha'is Raise Money?

Bahá'ís are, as in all religious organizations, encouraged to contribute money to their faith. There are various funds that enable Bahá'ís to carry out their various activities: local, regional, national, continental, and a special fund called "Huquq'u'llah" ("The Right of God" in Arabic). Non-Bahá'ís are not allowed to give any money to Bahá'í projects nor are Bahá'ís who have lost their administrative or voting rights. It is considered a spiritual bounty as well as a duty to give money to Bahá'í Funds. Bahá'ís consider their projects—whether a health clinic in the developing world or the House of Worship in Illinois—to be "gifts to the world" from the Bahá'í Faith.

Huquq'u'llah is a specifically mentioned tax found in the *Kitab-i-Aqdas*, the book of laws revealed by Baha'u'llah. It is to be paid by Bahá'ís on a voluntary basis, normally yearly, directly to the Universal House of Justice or their representative in a specific area. It amounts to 19 percent of an individual Bahá'í's yearly increase in their wealth, after living expenses are deducted from their income. Payment of Huquq is completely up to the conscience of the individual Bahá'í—no appeals are made by the UHJ for payment, nor are reminders sent out. This fund is the primary vehicle through which global social and economic development projects are funded in the Bahá'í world.

Three Levels of Global Social and Economic Development

Bahá'í efforts at social and economic development (SED) tend to take the form of relatively simple grassroots initiatives carried out by individuals or small groups in a local community. Sometimes they grow to require more permanent administrative structures under the aegis of the Bahá'í Administrative Order, or qualify for funding from government agencies or NGOs. Bahá'ís divide their development projects into one of three categories: activities of fixed duration; sustained projects; and organizations with capacity to undertake complex action. Each is explained below in detail.

Activities of Fixed Duration

Activities of a fixed duration include tree-planting and clean-up projects, health camps, or seminars/workshops on racial unity and the advancement of women. It is estimated by BIC that there are thousands of such projects throughout the Bahá'í world. Most are funded by Local Bahá'í Funds. Examples of this most grassroots model of development and service include: Bahá'ís in Michigan participated in an Earth Clean Sweep event in which 300 tons of unwanted electronic equipment was collected and recycled. More than 60 small-scale income-generating projects were initiated at the grassroots level by local Assemblies and believers in Kenya, covering activities such as beekeeping, fruit-drying, brick-molding, crafts, literacy, and textiles. In the Democratic Republic of Congo, 188 community health agents were trained; 24 literacy centers were established; and 72 agricultural facilitators were trained. The Bahá'í community of St. Lucia, working with the Ministry of Education, used the Bahá'í Kenya Mothering Program to train mothers in child care. In Taiwan, believers started moral education projects such as the Keelung Culture Centre, the Songs School in Chungshing New Village, and seminars in the city of T'ai-chung. The seminars were supported by the Board of Education in T'ai-chung. In Hawaii, the third Bahá'ís in Recovery conference was held, and the Local Spiritual Assembly of Hana sponsored a Co-Dependents Anonymous support group. The Rose Garden kindergarten was launched in Suva, Fiji, with financial assistance from the United Nations. Kindergartens also operated in Lomaivuna and Moce. Free dental camps, organized by the European Bahá'í Association for Oral Health in Korçë, Albania, were so successful that a permanent social and economic project was started in that region. Additionally, Health for Humanity, a Bahá'í-inspired development organization based in the United States, sponsored the Improvement of Eye Services in Albania project.

Sustained Projects

BIC estimated that in 2008 there were 550 of these longer-term global service projects throughout the world; this number was 224 in 1997 (*Betterment* 2008). The vast majority are full academic schools, while others focus on areas such as basic literacy, basic health care, immunization, substance abuse, child care, agriculture, the environment, or microenterprise. These are still mostly grassroots movements, but may have received funding from Bahá'í National Funds or a confederation of Bahá'í Local Funds. Examples of these more institutionalized Bahá'í projects include: The Uganda Program of Literacy for Transformation (UPLIFT) works with illiterate adult women, which stresses not only learning to read, but also the issue of the equality of men and women. Part of the curriculum introduces community decision making, virtues, and better health practices, including the prevention of HIV/AIDS and malaria. The Olinga Foundation in Ghana promotes literacy and moral education in rural areas; some 260 teachers in elementary and middle school have assisted 16,000 students in learning to read and write in their native language. The Santitham Vidhayakhom School in Thailand, begun by Bahá'ís, provides government-accredited nursery, kindergarten, and primary education to over 700 children in rural areas. In Haiti, Centre d'Apprentissage et de Formation pour la Transformation developed teacher-training and curriculum in collaboration with UNICEF, serving 170 schools and over 1,000 teachers. In Zambia, over 1,600 individuals have been trained on health education courses by Bahá'í volunteers. The Community Health Educators participate in government immunization campaigns, discuss women's health concerns, and provide nutrition and HIV/AIDS education, as well as education on the dangers of alcohol and drugs. In the United States, the Tahirih Justice Center in Washington, D.C. provides pro bono legal services to refugee women seeking protection from gender-based human rights abuses. The Education, Curriculum and Training Associates (ECTA), a Bahá'í-inspired NGO in Nepal, has developed a program where between 10 and 30 individuals form and manage community banks for the purpose of engaging in microbanking and microfinance.

The "Hope for the Heart" project in Cambodia seeks to improve reading and writing skills in young people, but also trains them in values that promote a nonviolent culture. They also teach about spiritual values and the empowerment of women. Very little foreign aid is needed for this project which, instead, relies upon Cambodian volunteers. Most front-line workers are Cambodian high school students. The lessons in moral values and nonviolence come in the form of stories and parables, pitched at appropriate levels of reading and writing. The project is managed by the Cambodian Organization for Research, Development and Education, established in 1994 by the Bahá'í community of Cambodia to promote development.

The Menu Bahá'í Institute in Kenya is a project to promote vaccinations and to train rural health workers, most of them women. In addition to immunizations, health workers teach about basic hygiene, breast-feeding, and stopping infantile diarrhea. This Bahá'í project was established in part to support the national Kenya Expanded Program on Immunization begun in 1986. Another benefit to the project has been the interfaith cooperation engendered by these health projects. Similar projects have subsequently been started in Burkina Faso, Chad, Uganda, and Zambia.

A microenterprise foundation called FUNDAEC (Spanish acronym for The Foundation for the Application and Teaching of the Sciences) has been set up in Colombia by Bahá'ís who not only train rural women in business practices, but also emphasize cooperation with other villagers to build community solidarity. Like the Grameen Bank, FUNCAEC organizes potential borrowers into "solidarity groups" of three to five people who collectively pledge to repay loans. The unique feature of FUNCAEC is the application of Bahá'í principles such as conflict resolution, unity, responsibility, and honesty (BIC 2008b).

Organizations with Capacity for Complex Action

BIC estimated that in 2008 there were at least 50 such projects in the Bahá'í world, though only 31 in 1997 (*Betterment* 2008). These are projects with relatively complex programs and significant spheres of influence. They not only provide services but also train human resources across multiple disciplines. Institutions in this category include large schools, and also NGOs with significant reach and multiple projects (discussed below). According to data from BIC, by far the most active area of the world with Bahá'í SED projects is in the Americas (mostly South America), followed by Asia, and then Africa (BIC 2008a). Most of these types of projects are funded by the Huquq'u'llah funds directed through the Universal House of Justice.

One example of these more mature institutional service projects is *The Rabbani Charitable Trust* established in 1991 by Dr. Mahmoud and Mrs. Eshraghieh Rabbani. Dr. Rabbani, a pharmacist by profession, and his wife, a businesswoman, were both born in Iran and were third-generation Bahá'ís. Both served on Bahá'í spiritual assemblies in Europe and North America. After "pioneering" as missionaries for their faith, upon retiring to central Florida, they incorporated the Rabbani Charitable Trust, a registered 501 (c) 3. Their goal is to raise and disburse funds for charitable, religious, literary and educational purposes to promote the spiritual and social well-being of the whole of humanity. While the Rabbani Charitable Trust is still in a relatively early development stage, it has become best known for its initiatives in the field of Bahá'í-related social and economic development. The Trust provided key support to Mottahedeh Development Services, the social and economic development arm of the National Spiritual Assembly of the Bahá'ís of the United States and to the Magdalene Carney Bahá'í Institute, a Regional Training Institute in Florida. In addition, since 1993, it has sponsored, organized, and conducted the well-known and acclaimed Bahá'í Conference on Social and Economic Development (SED) in Orlando, Florida, each December. In early 2012, this Conference underwent a name change, to the Rabbani Trust Bahá'í Conference in Orlando. According to the terms of the Trust Agreement, which became effective January 25, 1991, the approved purposes for Trust distributions are: homes for the aged and needy; archives of Bahá'í books, documents and other materials; schools; Bahá'í conferences; medical clinics; dental clinics; mental health clinics; medical research centers; housing for low or moderate income families; hospitals for the relief or benefit of the disabled or unemployed persons residing in the United States or anywhere in the world.

Another example, *The William Mmutle Masetlha Foundation*, was established in 1995 in Zambia under the direction of the NSA of Zambia to deepen individuals' knowledge of spiritual principles and to provide training in health, literacy, and trades. The Bahá'í Literacy Campaign is an example of a program initiated by the Masetlha Foundation. It began in the early 1990s to train tutors in literacy for rural students, subsequently growing into a national movement with additional resources coming from the Office of Social and Economic Development at the Bahá'í World Center. Likewise, the Bah'ai Primary Health Care Project began in 1993 to identify and train over 100 community health-care workers to work in local communities. After starting locally, the Health Care Project began training other development agencies to spread the knowledge. Finally, the Banani International Secondary School was opened in the mid-1990s to teach students not only English as a second language but also mathematics, geography, history, agriculture, biology, world religions, character development, and community service. As can been seen from this example, the Masethlha Foundation has multiple projects, all of which began as grassroots initiatives but, with systematic learning at the local level, were able to expand to a wider reach. It also is able to be interdisciplinary, in that, as a Bahá'í development vehicle, it addresses issues of health, education, and character building.

A third example is *The Djalal Eghrari Institute*, one of the components of the Association for the Coherent Development of the Amazon (ADCAM). ADCAM, a non-profit organization based on Bahá'í principles and dedicated to the education and development of the population of the rural regions of the Amazonas state, was initiated following the call of the Universal House of Justice in 1983 for greater involvement of Bahá'í communities in social and economic development. This non-profit focuses on three aspects of development in the Amazon in Brazil: education, health care, and the rural economy. The first major initiative of ADCAM was the establishment of the Eghrari Institute in 1984 to fulfill two distinct purposes: to assist with Bahá'í activities and to provide practical and academic education for the local youth. In order to expand its capacity to serve the needs of the region, the school is presently shifting from a four-year state-sponsored curriculum to address the following five lines of action:

1. formal education, through modifying the existing school to follow the System of Tutorial Apprenticeship (SAT), an integrated rural education program pioneered by FUNDAEC in Colombia;
2. community development, focusing on the creation of community structures based on the Bahá'í teachings to maintain basic health, education, production, and organization;
3. preparation of sufficient educational materials for the execution of short training courses and for the application of SAT;
4. training of human resources, which includes creating opportunities for the staff of the institute to develop their administrative abilities, as members of a non-governmental organization, in rural education and development and in the SAT program; and
5. the establishment of an efficient administrative model for the institute capable of executing its diverse programs.

The second major program of ADCAM, the Nucleus or Center for Social Welfare, located in Manaus, Amazonas, emerged from the Lar Linda Tanure orphanage. Here, in 1985, the Bahá'ís were asked by a group of businessmen and the government to establish and administer a home for abandoned children.

Fourthly, *The New Era Development Institute* (NEDI) in India provides rural students with vocational skills that can be used to earn a living. Practical skills include house wiring; tree-planting and environmental conservation; small-scale income-generating projects such as crafts; diesel mechanics; motorcycle repair; data processing; dressmaking; air-conditioning and refrigeration repair; animal husbandry; and teacher training. Like many Bahá'í SED projects, NEDI has had a 70 percent success rate in placing successful trainees in jobs after their education. All training programs have a "core curriculum" that teaches respect for universal spiritual values and how to apply them in one's everyday life (*Betterment* 2008).

Pioneering and Teaching the Faith

Another way in which Bahá'ís engage in global service activity is in the way they combine service with "teaching the Faith." Teaching is indeed the primary focus of all Bahá'í institutional and personal labors. As Bahá'ís realize, if their values and institutions are to have any impact on the development of a global civilization, they must communicate their message to the world. Bahá'ís engage in such communication on the basis of rational, systematic plans for growth and development—"Teaching Plans." Shoghi Effendi crafted the first of these plans in 1937. Following Effendi's example, the UHJ has continued to promulgate plans that set goals for later stages in the spread of the Bahá'í Faith. "Teaching the Faith" is socially constructed as a sacred duty for all Bahá'ís.

The most venerated type of teaching that a Bahá'í can engage in is called "pioneering"—the Bahá'í term for missionary activity. Shoghi Effendi designated those Bahá'ís who went to another country to teach the Bahá'í Faith as "pioneers," and those who moved to another city within their home country as "homefront pioneers." Thus, Bahá'í pioneers consider themselves part of a larger, divinely ordained project of global institution-building, institutions which they believe constitute the Kingdom of God. However, not only are Bahá'ís educating others about their faith, but they are also engaging in acts of global service by applying their skills and knowledge to benefit the indigenous population.

The goal of the pioneer was not just to teach their faith so that a viable, functioning LSA was formed from members of the indigenous population. Pioneering, according to Bahá'ís, is also a way to bear witness to the unity of humankind, in that a person would move from their native country to Brazil, or Nigeria, or Thailand, settle down, and manifest the characteristics of a "world citizen." Pioneers may receive an initial stipend from a local or national institution for the plane ticket to their new location but are then expected to find a job and become self-sufficient; it is preferable, especially for foreign pioneers, to secure a job prior to entering the country. Some Bahá'ís plan their education or engage in a profession with an eye towards using those skills as a pioneer.

In 2011, the Bahá'ís of the world were completing the second in a series of four five-year plans. Part of the numerical goals of the five-year plan included the United States sending out 1,300 international pioneers. The progress in reaching this goal was tracked in the magazine *The American Bahá'í* (TAB), which is published six times a year by the American NSA and serves as its official organ of communication. In the March/April 2011 edition, Bahá'ís were informed through colorful graphics that 1,118 pioneers were registered as of February 11, and a plea went out to American Bahá'ís for an additional 182 that were needed to meet the goals of the five-year plan (*The American Bahá'í* 2011c).

International pioneers are expected to work while in their overseas post and cannot assume they will be supported by national or local Bahá'í funds. Thus, most pioneers combine their "teaching" work, spreading the message of Baha'u'llah, with providing service to the local population through some occupation. TAB has stories in every issue about the types of global service work that pioneers are doing. The following are examples of how Bahá'ís are engaged in global service while at the same time "pioneering" to spread the message of Baha'u'llah:

- One California women went from homefront pioneering in Arizona to teaching English as a second language as an international pioneer at a school in rural Laos (*The American Bahá'í* 2012a).
- A Bahá'í couple both applied to teach at the El Alba Bilingual School in the village of Siguatepeque, Honduras, a Bahá'í-inspired institution serving poor children in the region, and also taught Bahá'í children's classes

(*The American Bahá'í* 2012b).
- A Bahá'í youth spent a "year of service" between high school and college by teaching English to K-4th graders at a school in Santa Tecla, El Salvador, and then teaching "virtues classes" after school and English to community members (*The American Bahá'í* 2011b).
- A Bahá'í couple who were both physicians moved to Addis Ababa, Ethiopia to work in a medical clinic where the husband also continued his work with an immunization program with the World Health Organization (*The American Bahá'í* 2011a).

Individual Initiatives through Core Activities

Finally, another aspect of global service that is encouraged by the Bahá'í Faith is at the very local community and individual level. In 1998, the Bahá'í Publishing Trust in the United States began publishing a series of workbooks called "Institute Courses" that were intended to help Bahá'ís understand the central tenets of their Faith, as well as its rather complicated history. These courses are referred to as "Ruhi courses" after the system designed in Colombia to help new Bahá'í converts better understand their faith. Since its inception in Colombia in 1980, this essentially oral knowledge-system has been published by the American National Spiritual Assembly and Bahá'ís across the United States have been encouraged to come together in "study circles" of 5-10 members to work their way through the series of workshops. Each Ruhi course culminates in a required service project before a Bahá'í gets "certified" as completing one of the seven courses.

These service projects are voted on by the members of the study circle which tries to put into practice the knowledge gained through the course. *The American Bahá'í* also runs stories about how many people have completed the Institute process in each area of the country and what kind of service projects result. These service projects could be as simple as going out door-to-door to tell people about the Bahá'í Faith; or perhaps an environmental clean-up on a beach or along a stretch of highway; or helping immigrant neighbors settle into their new home. But, as Bahá'ís all over the world are engaged in Ruhi courses since the UHJ began promoting them, these very local service projects are having a global impact.

Conclusion

As can be seen from the above analysis, Bahá'ís translate their global values and world-view into a global service movement by promoting service to humanity at all levels of their Administrative Order. BIC, as an arm of the Universal House of Justice, interacts with global NGOs and national representatives to influence global discourse, as well as coordinating social and economic development projects. The pioneering efforts promoted by all Bahá'í National Spiritual Assemblies move people around the world to not only "teach the Faith," but also to engage in local service. Finally, the "Institute process" has thousands of Bahá'ís worldwide engaged in local service to others.

References

The American Bahá'í. 2011a. "Falling in Love with an Adopted Homeland." September/October, vol. 42, no. 5, p. 18.

The American Bahá'í. 2011b. "International Service Opens New Vistas." January/February, vol. 42, no. 1, p. 18.

The American Bahá'í. 2011c. "Status Toward Reaching the Goals of This Plan." March/April, vol. 42, no. 2, p. 17.

The American Bahá'í. 2012a. "A Boost for Youth in Laos." May/June, vol. 43, no. 3, p. 21.

The American Bahá'í. 2012b. "Teachers Leap at Service Opportunity." March/April, vol. 43, no. 2, p. 21.

Bahá'í International Community. 1991. "Toward the 21st Century and Peace." New York: Bahá'í International Community. Retrieved August 15, 2012 (http://www.bic.org/statements/toward-21st-century-and-peace).

Bahá'í International Community. 2005. "Quadrennial Report to the United Nations Economic and Social Council." New York: Bahá'í International Community. Retrieved June 6, 2013 (http://www.bic.org/statements/quadrennial-report-united-nations-economic-and-social-council).

Bahá'í International Community. 2008a. "Bahá'í Development Projects: A Global Process of Learning." New York: Bahá'í International Community. Retrieved May 21, 2012 (http://info.bahai.org/print/article-1-8-1-1.html).

Bahá'í International Community. 2008b. "In the Field: Some Examples." New York: Bahá'í International Community. Retrieved May 21, 2012 (http://info.bahai.org/print/article-1-8-1-3.html).

Bahá'í International Community. 2008c. "Oral Statement of the Bahá'í International Community to the Seventh Session of the Human Rights Council." New York: Bahá'í International Community. Retrieved June 10, 2013 (http://www.bic.org/statements/eradication-violence-against-women-and-girls).

Bahá'í International Community. 2008d. "Social and Economic Development." New York: Bahá'í International Community. Retrieved May 21, 2012 (http://info.bahai.org/print/article-1-8-0-1.html).

Bahá'í International Community. 2008e. "The Integrity of the Development Process." New York: Bahá'í International Community. Retrieved May 21, 2012 (http://info.bahai.org/print/article-1-8-1-4.html).

Bahá'í International Community. 2008f. "Iran Intensifies Disinformation and Attacks on Bahá'ís." New York: Bahá'í International Community. Retrieved June 19, 2013 (http://www.bahainews.ca/en/080812BIC).

Bahá'í International Community. 2010a. "Bahá'í International Community: United Nations Office Timeline." New York: Bahá'í International Community. Retrieved August 10, 2012 (http://www.bic.org/timeline).

Bahá'í International Community. 2010b. "Bahá'í International Community's Quadrennial Report (2006-2009)." New York: Bahá'í International Community. Retrieved August 10, 2012 (http://www.bic.org/statements/bahai-international-community%E2%80%99s-quadrennial-report-2006-2009).

Bahá'í International Community. 2010c. "Current Situation of the Bahá'ís in the Islamic Republic of Iran." New York: Bahá'í International Community. Retrieved August 10, 2012 (http://www.bic.org/statements/current-situation-bahais-islamic-republic-iran).

Bahá'í International Community. 2010d. "International Women's Year: Statement to the United Nations World Conference for International Women's Year." New York: Bahá'í International Community. Retrieved August 10, 2012 (http://www.bic.org/statements/international-womens-year).

Bahá'í International Community. 2010e. "Situation of the Bahá'ís in Iran—item 4." New York: Bahá'í International Community. Retrieved August 10, 2012 (http://www.bic.org/statements/situation-bahais-iran-%E2%80%93-item-4).

Bahá'í International Community. 2011. "Women's Health and Human Rights: The Case for Comprehensive and Sustainable Development." New York: Bahá'í International Community. Retrieved August 15, 2012 (http://www.bic.org/statements/women%E2%80%99s-health-and-human-rights-case-comprehensive-and-sustainable-development).

Bahá'í International Community. 2012. "Over 30 Years of Systematic Persecution of the Bahá'ís in Iran." New York: Bahá'í International Community. Retrieved August 15, 2012 (http://www.bic.org/statements/over-thirty-years-systematic-persecution-bahais-iran).

Bahá'í International Community. 2013. "What is the Bahá'í International Community?" New York: Bahá'í International Community. Retrieved August 15, 2012 (http://www.bic.org/who-we-are/what-bahai-international-community).

Bahá'u'lláh. 1976. *Gleanings from the Writings of Bahá'u'lláh*. Translated by Shoghi Effendi. Wilmette, IL: Bahá'í Publishing Trust.

Bahá'u'lláh. 1992. *The Kitab-i-Aqdas*. Translated by Universal House of Justice. Haifa, Israel: Bahá'í World Center.

Barrett, David B., ed. 1982. *World Christian Encyclopedia*. Oxford: Oxford University Press.

Berger, Peter L. 1969. *The Sacred Canopy: Elements of a Sociological Theory of Religion*. New York: Doubleday Anchor.

For the Betterment of the World: The Worldwide Bahá'í Community's Approach to Social and Economic Development. 2008. New York: Office of Social and Economic Development, Bahá'í International Community.

Esslemont, John. E. 1970. *Bahá'u'lláh and the New Era*. Wilmette, IL: Bahá'í Publishing Trust.

Garlington, W.1977. "The Bahá'í Faith in Malwa." Pp. 161-92 in *Religion in South Asia*, edited by Geoffrey A. Oddie. London: Curzon Press.

Hatcher, William S. and J. Douglas Martin. 1985. *The Bahá'í Faith: The Emerging Global Religion*. San Francisco: Harper and Row.

McMullen, Mike. 2000. *The Bahá'ís: The Religious Construction of a Global Community*. Piscataway: Rutgers University Press.

Nash, Geoffrey. 1982. *Iran's Secret Pogrom: The Conspiracy to Wipe Out the Bahá'ís*. Suffolk, VA: Neville Spearman.

Smith, Peter. 1987. *The Babi and Bahá'í Religions: From Messianic Shi'ism to a World Religion*. Cambridge: Cambridge University Press.

Smith, Peter and Moojan Momen.1989. "The Bahá'í Faith 1957-1988: A Survey of Contemporary Developments," *Religion* 19: 63-91.

Taherzadeh, Adib. 1992. *The Covenant of Bahá'u'lláh*. Oxford: George Ronald Publisher.

Universal House of Justice. 1976. *A Compilation on Bahá'í Education*. Compiled by the Research Department of the Universal House of Justice. Haifa: Bahá'í World Center.

Warburg, Margit. 1986. "Conversion: Consideration Before a Field-work in a Bahá'í Village in Kerala." In *South Asian Religion and Society*, ed. Aska Parpola and Bent Smidt Hansen. London: Curzon Press.

Waters, Malcolm. 1995. *Globalization*. London: Routledge.

Chapter 9

Studying Global Transnational Religious Service Movements

Stephen M. Cherry

Looking across the movements presented in this volume, from Swaminarayan (BAPS) to Soka Gakkai International and Redeemed Christian Church God (RCCG) or from the Bahá'í International Community and Gawad Kalinga to the Gulen Movement and the Aga Khan Development Network (ADKN), we have demonstrated that religion has clearly not died out in the wake of an increasingly globalized world. As mass communication and technological innovation have increased and accelerated flows of goods, services, and people across borders, religion has facilitated these processes both influencing globalization and transnationalism as well as being shaped by them. Although many scholars have written about the global spread of religious traditions and likewise studied transnational immigrant religious communities around the world (Bowen 2004; Csordas 2009; Ebaugh and Chafetz 2002; Levitt 2004, 2007; Marquardt 2005; Yang 2002), this volume is one of the first studies to attempt to describe the service movements that these immigrants and religious adherents have established through their faith traditions to aid people across political and geographic boundaries. Even though many of these service movements are among the largest philanthropic organizations in the world, the fact that little scholarship has focused on them can be attributed to a host of issues, as we have seen (see discussion in Chapter 1), but may also have something to do with the difficulties inherent in describing or defining these groups and movements.

We began this study with the arduous task of trying to situate and define what many might rightly suggest is indescribable within the logic and terms of a single body of academic literature (McDonald 2006; Tarrow 1983). At first glance, the phrase "global transnational service movements rooted in religious traditions" seems to be somewhat redundant or a hodge-podge of terms that reveals the earnest struggles of a group of scholars trying to describe what is increasingly observable around the world, but clearly difficult to contain within the singular catch-all category of "global social movements" (McDonald 2006). We do not claim that we have found the final solution to this definitional problem by using these terms. We simply use the phrase "global religious movements across borders" as a way to categorize and describe an emergent phenomenon that is sorely under-theorized but central to our understanding of the influence religion can have on global movements working to challenge or transform some aspect of an increasingly transnational and global civil society.

The movements in this volume, as we have seen, originate from multiple global locales but are not necessarily uniform across them and hence, can be both global and transnational. Regardless of their geographic contexts and boundaries, each of these movements is collectively organized through networks of both formal and informal interactions between pluralities of individuals, groups, and/ or organizations (see Diani 1992: 13). Mobilizing on a host of aims and causes, these movements are raising both non-institutional and institutional challenges to authorities, powerholders, and cultural beliefs across borders (McDonald 2006; Melucci 1996). As such, they not only meet the most rudimentary criteria for what many scholars define as social movements or "new social movements," but they also meet the criteria to be considered global or transnational movements (Diani 1992; Goodwin and Jasper 2009; McDonald 2006; Melucci 1996). Acknowledging this, however, we understand that what constitutes a global or transnational social service movement is subject to a host of theoretical debates.

We also recognize, as outlined in Chapter 1, the introduction to this volume, that we are catching the movements in this study at various points in their evolution and history without the luxury of looking at them in hindsight regardless of whether they have succeeded or failed. In some cases, as we have seen with Gawad Kalinga, the people involved in these groups consider themselves to be a part of a movement and many scholars would agree. In other cases, scholars might define these groups as movements despite the fact that some members, such as those in the Gulen Movement, do not consider themselves to be a movement (see Cetin 2009). Conversely, scholars might question whether some of these movements, such as the AKDN or the Bahá'í International Community, have ceased to be movements by working with the state or becoming non-governmental organizations themselves. Rather than forcing any particular categorization, we have attempted to situate these groups within a host of literatures to best help us explore not only what they are but also to understand where and how they are engaging religious migrants and diaspora peoples across borders on service projects that have spread around the globe.

In Chapter 1 we brought together a host of literatures to meet this end. From the general religion and globalization/transnational literatures to the social movement and development literatures, to name a few, we culled from these specified areas a group of wide-ranging topics, debates, and issues and then situated them along ten central themes that would allow us to analyze these movements comparatively across the themes. As you may recall, these themes include the following:

1. origins and history of the respective movement within a specific country and religious tradition;
2. goals of the service movement and the religious roots of these aims within specific traditions and denominations;
3. specific types of civic engagement and social outreach;

4. organizational structure of the movement;
5. financial structure of the movement;
6. spread of the movement across borders highlighting the carriers of the movement, who it attracts and why, as well as the scope of its transnational service;
7. adaptation of the movement to local cultures and political systems;
8. systems and degrees of communication among members transnationally or globally;
9. response of the media to the movement as well as the response of the group itself to the media; and
10. change in the movement over time highlighting its growth and/or decline in terms of membership or relative scope, its aims and goals, and the impact of its transnational or global service.

For the most part, we developed lines of exploration that allowed us to situate these movements both within the literatures we specified and in comparison with each other. However, as we noted in Chapter 1, we were also forced to chart new areas of study. Although each of our contributing authors did not necessarily think about this larger comparative perspective and, instead, largely focused their attention on their own specific movements of interest, by asking them to explore the same set of themes, the comparisons arose naturally from chapter to chapter. Elaborating on these comparisons, in the following sections we revisit the various literatures we outlined in the Introduction as a means to situate these movements and further define what they are and how they are similar or different. We then compare and contrast the various ways in which they draw on religious roots to carry out transnational and global service projects by engaging the issues and debates we believe are critical to the future study of global transnational service movements rooted in religious traditions.

Globalization and Movement Origins and Opportunity

Why movements form, how they form, and under what circumstances are typically at the forefront of questions scholars often ask about social movements (Goodwin and Jasper 2009). However, when the scope of these movements is truly global, this approach can become quite complicated. The groups we present in this volume bridge local and global divides to impact transnational civil society through new and emerging forms of communication, networks, and experiences (see McDonald 2006; Melucci 1996). They are truly global social movements, but they are also distinctly faith-based. Some of the movements we present may still be struggling to gain momentum or, as with the BAPS community, entering a new phase of their development. Others may have partially failed to meet their aims or in other contexts, become co-opted by mainstream institutions or become an NGO or RNGO that works directly with the state. Gawad Kalinga, for example, while spreading transnationally and seemingly very successful at serving communities around the world, did not meet its GK 777 goal in the Philippines and was forced to set a new goal, the GK 2024 vision, which is tied to a host of partnering NGOs and the Philippine government itself. Other movements, such as the Gulen Movement and the AKDN, like Gawad Kalinga, may be at the point of their history and development that they are working both with the state and outside of it. Wherever we have taken the snapshots of these movements, ultimately, if the people involved in these groups believe them to be a movement and describe them as such, we must assume to some degree they still are (Nash 2000; also see the case of the women's peace movement: Mayo 2005; Roseneil 1997). This is the case for most movements in this volume. The members of Gawad Kalinga, for example, see their movement as an exemplar of what God can do for the world, while the members of the RCCG see their church as a movement held together by a divine covenant. This is also the circumstance for members of the AKDN who see their movement as part of their imam's vision for society. The one exception is the Gulen Movement. Although its members often reject the notion of being a movement, given their collective actions in civil society, it meets the scholarly conditions for being a movement. In all cases, even for the Gulen Movement, the groups in this volume take on many of the characteristics of social movements regardless of the extent to which the people in these groups wrestle to describe or define themselves.

Since the 1960s, social movement scholars have attempted to explain the rise and origins of social movements from a host of theoretical positions. From Collective Behavior (Turner and Killian [1957] 1987; Smelser 1963) and Resource Mobilization (Buechler 1995; McCarthy and Zald 1977) to Political Process or Political Opportunity (McAdam 1982; Meyer 2004; Tilly 2004;) and the more cultural turn in Framing (Benford and Snow 2000; Snow and Benford 1988), there has been no shortage of attempts to capture the emergence and proliferation of social movements. Although some scholars, such as Diani (1992), have attempted to synthesize these seemingly disparate views in their call for a more comprehensive definition of new social movements, and with relative success, less analytical attention has been devoted to the place and relevance of these theories in the more globalized context of contemporary social movements (Nash 2000). Complicating matters, the theorizing that has emerged has been subject to intense debate and often with relatively little agreement (Ruggiero 2005; Ruggiero and Montagna 2008).

At one point in time, it was assumed that the emergence of global and transnational social movements would be similar to and behave like more so-called traditional or old movements within the nation-state, but this has not necessarily been the case (della Porta and Tarrow 2005). Global and transnational movements, as their name implies, are much more diffuse in their influence and spread geographically. They are also organized supranationally to engage social problems and forces beyond the local (Appadurai 2006; della Porta and Tarrow 2005; Montagna 2008; Ruggiero and Montagna 2008). Given the reality that the independent state is increasingly fading, hence weaker or at least more open to change and challenge in a globalized world, we might rightly argue that globalization has created the opportunity and context for the rise of transnational or global movements (McAdam 1996; Tilly 1978). The sovereign state has been displaced by globalization, and with this change, a more global civil society has emerged and given birth to a host of supranational political institutions, multinational non-profit corporations, and transnational organizations. Global social movements are an important part of these emerging patterns, but scholars have historically "grossly undervalued" the global political arena and thus to some extent ignored global social movements (Appadurai 2006; McAdam 1996; Nash 2000). This is particularly true of the variety of global service movements we present in this volume.

Today we have no choice but to focus on globalization and its relationship to the state and beyond (Rudolph and Piscatori 1997; McAdam 1996). The challenge of NGOs to the state in transnational space, for example, is no longer a brief occurrence but the norm, and religion, as we have seen, is a prime mover in this arena. Religious communities are helping to shape world politics, but this is not to say that the nation-state cannot still play a central role in these ongoing relations (Castells 1996; Held and McGrew 2000; McAdam 1998; Nicholson 1998; Skrentny 2006). The state still matters. As we have seen in the chapters presented in this book, the nation-state can and does work with religious groups and movements, particularly religiously committed diasporic peoples and migrants who work fluidly across traditional national divides and borders to solve or ameliorate global problems. Gawad Kalinga, the AKDN, and the Gulen Movement, for example, all have declared global poverty or its causes to be a moral outrage. This has helped to push other large-scale cross-national entities such as the United Nations to proclaim that the fight against poverty is a moral imperative that must bind all nations of all creeds if a solution is to be found (Marshall 2001; Marshall and Van Saanen 2007). Likewise, movements such as the RCCG, Soka Gakkai International, and BAPS have also raised international concern over global issues such as women's rights, AIDS, and universal education, and in doing so, not only rallied individual people to their cause but also accumulated international support and partners from nation states and like-minded organizations in the process.

None of this would be possible without increases in global flows of people, goods, and services and the technological advancements in communication and transportation that animate these processes. Understanding this, we must conclude that globalization has provided the context for these types of service movements to arise (della Porta, Kriesi, and Rucht 1999). This should not be all that surprising. It is fairly indicative of what we would expect from so-called new social movements but on a global and transnational scale. New social movements are often seen as non-instrumental and driven by protest or collective actions in the name of moral authority rather than the direct interest of any particular social group (Calhoun 1995; Crook, Pakulski, and Waters 1992; Scott 1990). They are more oriented toward civil society or, as is the case with movements described in this book, transnational civil society, rather than focusing on any one state (Calhoun 1995; Crook et al. 1992). They are often suspicious of centralized bureaucratic structures and likewise often organized in loose or flexible ways with fluid hierarchies or loose authority structures (Calhoun 1995; Crook et al. 1992; Scott 1990). Although they can and do share qualities with so-called old or traditional movements, contemporary movements often operate as signs (Melucci 1989; Nash 2000). They translate their actions into symbolic challenges to the dominate codes of their society (Melucci 1989). From the Bahá'í Faith International's aim to change the global condition of women and minority peoples around the world to the AKDN, the Gulen Movement, and Soka Gakkai International that seek to challenge traditional views of sustainable development and education, to highlight but a few, this appears to characterize the service movements we present.

While the emergence of a more global civil society and an ease of transnational communication and transportation has provided the arena and technology by which the movements in this volume have found their voice and staked out their challenges to globally oriented social and economic problems, it is the impact of globalization on mass migration that is the most central cause of their formation and spread. From the Filipino diaspora spurred on by a dwindling Philippine economy or the entrepreneurial spread of the Turkish diaspora to the mass migration of highly educated young professionals out of the Indian diaspora (Gujarati and Ismaili) or evangelical missions emerging from Nigeria and the African Diaspora, the cases we present, in some way or another, are a product of global migration. Whether these migrations were forced by economic collapse, natural disaster, political instability, or are a matter of opportunity and mobility, diasporas appear to be the central vehicle of their origins.

The only possible exceptions to this may be the cases of the Bahá'í International Community and perhaps Soka Gakkai International. Like the RCCG, global evangelization was one of the key reasons people in these groups migrated around the world and brought the movement with them. Likewise, at least in the case of Bahá'ís, followers of Bahá'u'lláh were part of the early Iranian diaspora and today remain a persecuted group in Iran. However, Iranian Bahá'ís make up only a relatively small portion of the Bahá'í International Community today. In the case of Soka Gakkai International, SGI missionaries, as we have seen with other groups in this volume, are still a vital part of the globalization of their religion and hence, the service movements they create but today they are less tied to Japan than in their early history (Csordas 2009; McLeod 2004; Wuthnow and Offutt 2008). Across these cases, technological advances in communication and transportation have eased migration or, at the least, heightened the impact of these flows to unprecedented levels over the last several decades (Rudolph and Piscatori 1997). Acknowledging this, however, we understand that it is not simply the global migration of people that has given birth to these movements but the global migration of religious adherents. Given that religion has always been global and transnational on some level, the movements in this study are not simply shaped by the forces of globalization but are active shapers of globalization themselves.

Drawing on religious roots and shared understandings of history and theology, they reimagine community on a global scale and ask how they can best serve humanity by capturing or challenging civil society for some higher power or purpose.

Power of Transnational and Global Religion

The movements presented in this volume are not religious traditions or sects, for the most part, but are social movements with religious roots. They are rooted in their respective religious traditions but do not claim to represent all traditions or views within their particular faiths or to be sects of them (see Lofland 1996; McAdam, McCarthy, and Zald 1988; Robbins 1988). Like the American Civil Rights movement, religious institutions and people of faith have simply acted as these movements' midwives and provided the central resources that facilitate and animate their ongoing collective action (Morris 1986; Smith 1996). Some of these movements, such as the RCCG or the AKDN, are rooted in older, more familiar religious traditions such Christianity and Islam. Others, such as Soka Gakkai International and the Bahá'í International Community, are rooted in religious traditions that can be defined as new religious movements and thus may be less familiar. In either case, whether these roots are from more progressive religious traditions such as Nichiren Buddhism or more conservative and orthodox traditions such as Protestant Pentecostalism, their ability to transcend nation states and borders, or at least bypass them, reminds us of the power and saliency of global and transnational religion.

The transnational and global scope of these religious movements may seem at first to be very localized. This is the case for movements such as Gawad Kalinga that come from the people for the same people they serve and involve some form of popular or indigenous religiosity; a variety of charismatic Catholicism acted as a form of religion from below, shaping and serving the very communities in the Philippines that gave birth to the movement and from which it spread. Other movements leave their national origins and involve a form of religiosity that is distinctly foreign to those they serve. For instance, in the case of the Gulen Movement, a variety of moderate Islam was introduced by Turkish migrants to communities outside of Turkey to aid people beyond their own nation and faith tradition. In general, as people move across the globe for work or in migration to new homes, they bring their religions with them. These religious messages and practices, as we have seen, are portable and transposable, and hence unbound geographically (Csordas 2009). They are initially a source of unity in diaspora and a rallying point of ethnic and cultural identity in the face of uncertainty, confusion, and distress associated with the stressors of migration (Ebaugh and Chafetz 2000; Hagan and Ebaugh 2003; Warner and Wittner 1998; Wuthnow and Offutt 2008) but quickly become the central resources that link their new communities to their homelands (Basch, Schiller, and Blanc 1994; Cherry 2014; Ebaugh and Chafetz 2002; Faist 2000; Levitt 2001, 2007; Mahler 1998; Portes, Guarnizo, and Landolt 1999). However, beyond the importance of these resources to remittances and transnational ties, these transposable religious messages and practices serve as the foundation upon which global service movements are built.

All of the movements we present have moved well beyond their national origins, some more so than others, and have engaged in collective actions, both by themselves and in partnership with others. They seek to fulfill aims and goals that are not only rooted in a wide range of religious traditions but sustained over time by their faith in the power of religion to carry these visions to fruition. From goals to improve global socio-economic development and promote the equality of all peoples which may or may not at first glance appear to be all that religious in nature, to near eschatological and prophetic calls to bring about global healing and an end to poverty and injustice, each of the movements we present professes its mission as somehow blessed by or mandated by a higher power. Like the movements studied by Davis and Robinson (2012), the movements in this volume seek to stake claim or capture civil society for God or some higher entity and purpose. Although each movement does so from varied and unique positions of faith, all of the movements we present are working to saturate civil society with religiously instilled cultures and institutions that they believe will bring about the ultimate success of their goals and aims (Davis and Robinson 2012: 145).

Scholars have widely acknowledged the role religious beliefs, commitments, and networks can play in not only framing and mobilizing collective action but also sustaining it (see, for example, Rudolph and Piscatori 1997; Sherkat and Ellison 1999; Young 2006). However, unlike the cases in Davis and Robinson (2012), the movements we present seek to fulfill goals and missions that are set on a global scale or on a local or national level within a broader transnational vision. While the same can be said of groups such as Salvation Army or Comunione e Liberazione that are included in Davis and Robinson's study, they do not look at the global and transnational reach of these groups. In either set of cases, religion serves both as a rallying point of a collective and shared identity and as a transcendent source of motivation across geographic and political divides.

As a source of motivation, religion has legitimized the collective actions of the members of the movements in this volume by aligning movement aspirations and goals with the divine or a higher power. Moral imperatives such as equality and justice, cited from sacred texts or drawn from powerful religious icons and symbols, have compelled the members of these movements to take social action as an extension of their faith. It is a moral injunction to do what they believe is right for the people of the world (Hart 1992; McAdam 1982; Smith 1996) and it is framed in such a way that it mobilizes others outside of their own faith traditions (see Montagna 2008). These master frames must be both inventive and generic enough to bring multiple groups and organizations together while providing the grammar and structure along which members can be mobilized (Goffman [1974] 1997; Snow and Benford 1992). In some situations, these master frames can bind a host of service projects and aims under one vision to improve the general condition of humanity. This is the case of movements such as BAPS and Soka Gakkai International. In other cases, movements like Gawad Kalinga, the RCCG, or the AKDN may develop singular visions—such as the end of world poverty or AIDS—that are both the master frame and the central focus of their global service. Unlike service movements not rooted in religious traditions that find their sources of motivation in more rights-oriented conceptual frames of justice and equality, the movements in this volume are motivated by conceptual frames of divine justice and spiritual beliefs in the unity of humankind (Berger 2003; Petersen 2010). This is particularly evident with the Bahá'í International Community. While religion often serves as the source of inspiration and legitimation across these frames, it does not necessarily mean that these movements seek to convert people to their faith traditions or seek religious promotion through their aims and goals.

In some cases, the people working to carry out the mission of the movement appear to be solely focused on their stated goals without seeking to make religious converts. Movements such as the Gulen Movement and the AKDN that work to promote secular ends such as sustainable development or the building of schools without proselytizing of any kind are a clear example of this. Other movements such as the RCCG and Soka Gakkai International, however, not only seek somewhat secular ends through their missions to educate and care for others but also seek to spread their faith traditions through gaining converts and adherents. Conversely, there are movements such as the Baha'i Faith International Community and Gawad Kalinga who explicitly state that they seek secular ends through their missions to end poverty and women's inequality but also hope that in accomplishing their good deeds, they can promote their faith and thereby use these works as a model to promote the inherent merit of their religious traditions.

In general, when we compare the movements in this volume to what we know about religious non-governmental organizations (RNGOs) working with the United Nations, the pattern is fairly similar. Roughly 47 percent of RNGOs work solely for secular ends and another 14 percent work purely for religious ends. The majority, however, roughly 39 percent, work for both simultaneously (Petersen 2010). As such, the movements we present, like traditional RNGOs, highlight the importance of shared religious identities as a strategic source for collective action amongst globally dispersed peoples. Likewise, they highlight how religious clergy and spiritual leaders in groups such as the AKDN, BAPS, and the RCCG, can serve these movements as respected sources of organizational authority and, in many cases, become the voice of the movements (also see Morris 1986). By speaking truth to what they perceive as injustice in the world, these leaders can take on the role of prophet or sage, as we have seen, and thus also provide the spiritual and emotional resources that sustain their movements over time and around the world (also see Oberschall and Kim 1996; Zald 1982).

Table 9.1   Defining Characteristics of Global Transnational Religious Service
            Movements

Movement	Religious roots	Country of origin and age	Aims and goals	Transnational spread	
Aga Khan Development Network (AKDN)	Islam (Ismaili)	India Developed through 1800s CE	Global socio-economic development through intellectual and financial partnerships	Afghanistan Canada Egypt Kazakhstan Mali Pakistan Switzerland Tajikistan Uganda USA C'ote d'Ivoire Cambodia Bosnia-Herzegovina	Bangladesh Congo India Kenya Mozambique Portugal Syria Tanzania UK Madagascar Australia
Bahá'í International Community	Bahá'í Faith	Iran Founded 1948 CE	Global socio-economic sustainability for humanity and equality for all women	Cambodia Ghana Thailand Kenya Nepal India Australia Estimated 180+ countries	Uganda Zambia Columbia Chad USA Canada
Swaminaryan (BAPS)	Hinduism	India Founded 1907 CE	Global service and communal care to the poor and those in need	India Kenya Uganda Tanzania USA UK Canada	New Zealand Ethiopia
Gawad Kalinga	Catholicism	Philippines Founded 2000 CE	End to global poverty Elevation of the Philippines to First World nation status by 2024	Indonesia Singapore India Kenya Australia Philippines Austria	Papua New Guinea Cambodia South Africa USA Canada
Gulen Movement	Islam (Moderate)	Turkey Founded early 1980s CE	Combating global ignorance and poverty through education	Azerbaijan Turkmenistan Denmark Australia Germany Turkey Cambodia India Estimated 130+ countries	Kyrgyzstan Belgium UK Spain Ireland USA Kenya

Movement	Religious roots	Country of origin and age	Aims and goals	Transnational spread	
Redeemed Christian Church of God (RCCG)	Pentecostal Protestantism	Nigeria Founded 1952 CE	Divine healing of global sickness Combating HIV/ AIDs and drug use/abuse in Africa and the world	Germany Nigeria Kenya Uganda Cameroon Zambia C'ote D'Ivoire Italy France Switzerland Sweden Haiti Australia Cambodia Estimated 110+ countries	USA Ghana Tanzania Gambia South Africa Malawi Spain Greece Austria Denmark Norway Jamaica India
Soka Gakkai International	Buddhism (Nichiren)	Japan Founded 1930. Expansion overseas 1960s CE.	Global human security and the improvement of the human condition through education and self-empowerment	Australia India Canada Cambodia Taiwan Peru South Africa Venezuela Spain UK Estimated 200+ countries	New Zealand USA Japan Korea Brazil Kenya Singapore Italy Iceland

Looking at Table 9.1, no matter where the movements find their genesis, from India, Iran, Japan, Nigeria, the Philippines, or Turkey, and regardless of the specific religious tradition that animates their religious roots, it is clear that all the movements we present in this volume have moved well beyond their once local origins to spread around the world to an astonishing number of countries. Although it is difficult, due to the lack of a central organization and formal records, to ascertain exactly in how many countries movements such as the Gulen Movement are presently working, other groups, such as RCCG and Soka Gakkai International, that have more exhaustive records are working in well over a hundred countries each. Unlike most international NGOs, the movements in this volume do not have their origins and central organizational headquarters in Western Europe and North America (Petersen 2010). Although this is partly because we deliberately sampled groups from diverse faith traditions, the cases we present do remind us that the field is much more varied geographically than many have studied to this point. Moreover, unlike more traditional non-governmental organizations (NGOs) the majority of which have been established after 1960 (Scholte 1999), the movements in this volume, while fairly young in their genesis, are more akin to religious non-governmental organizations in that they were largely established before the

1960s (Petersen 2010). In fact, as Table 9.1 highlights, movements such as the AKDN and BAPS are over a hundred years old. In other cases, while their global spread may be seen as relatively recent, the religious roots that animate their growth and more contemporary development across borders are often much older in historic age.

Today, many of the movements we present are carrying out projects in the same set of countries. All of the movements, for example, are either presently working in or have plans to work in India and Kenya. Understanding that each of these religiously rooted movements comes to their respective projects from a unique position of faith, questions remain about the extent to which these movements will ultimately compete with each other for resources and adherents to fulfill their aims and goals or will find common ground or a spirit of ecumenism to work collaboratively. Whatever the future holds, it is clear that each of these movements would not be as successful today if it could not effectively organize and mobilize considerable resources to carry out its aims and goals. While many of the movements in this volume are able to do so, drawing solely on their own diasporas and religious adherents, many actively seek out partnerships with others both out of necessity and as a part of their ecumenical missions.

Resource Mobilization, Organization, and Partnership

As recently as forty years ago social movements were thought to be extremely disorganized, chance collective happenings of irrational participants with very little planning and resource mobilization (Goodwin and Jasper 2009). Today, scholars understand that movements not only happen because of political opportunities and specific structural circumstances (McAdam 1982; Meyer 2004; Tilly 2004) but are dependent on their ability to collectively mobilize rational participants through culturally resonating frames and messages (Goffman [1974] 1997; Snow and Benford 1992), in addition to mobilizing critical resources that can sustain their collective actions (Buechler 1995; McCarthy and Zald 1977). Movements require planning, organization, significant resources, and, in some circumstances, partnerships with other groups and organizations if they are to meet their aims and goals. This is especially true at the global and transnational level where mobilizing across political and geographic divides is no chance happening.

As we have seen, religion can play a crucial role in these processes. Although much of the renewed interest in the role of religion in social movements, even at the global and transnational level, is a direct result of the more cultural turn in movement theorization, scholars have come to acknowledge that religion is not just a cultural resource for transcendent motivation and inspiration but also a source of hard or physical resources that can provide the opportunity for the movement to both grow and succeed (Harris 1999; Smith 1996). Congregations, for example, can mobilize what Smith (1996) defines as "enterprising tools" such as computers with Internet access and email, phones, fax machines, photocopying machines, office supplies, office space, trained or voluntary office staff, connections to in-house or networked legal advice, and newsletters and papers/magazines that are needed for collective action. This is particularly true for movements in this volume that depend on global and transnational communication and supply networks to carry out their projects.

Globalization and technological advances have eased these flows of needed resources, but acquiring them and managing them is a different story all together. This requires significant people power. However, as we have seen in this volume, it is not just any people but religious people who make these flows possible. Religious clergy, for example, serve as trained and experienced leaders who can mobilize their congregations by drawing on existing membership rolls and pre-existing networks of communication to carry out their projects. This can lead to quick and decisive grassroots organization despite the fact that these movements are engaging in projects in several nations simultaneously. This is the case for movements such as the AKDN, BAPS, and the RCCG, where imams, gurus, and ministers serve these movements as legitimized and respected sources of authority who have a host of physical resources at their disposal to carry out their respective projects. They are known movers in their communities with access to membership rolls of religious adherents that ease communication and planning. For movements such as the Gulen Movement or Gawad Kalinga, it is the religious fellowship found among peoples in diaspora that facilitates these networks, not clergy per se. In other movements, such as the Baha'i International Community or Soka Gakkai International that have no clergy, both local and international communication among members of the movement is facilitated by newsletters and webpages that support their larger international structures. As we have seen, the religious adherents within these movements are the keys to their success and often the source from which financial resources can be mobilized to their causes (Aho 1990; Barkun 1994; Zald 1992).

One major way that all of the movements described in this book mobilize and motivate commitment of members is the vitality that is created within small groups. Typically, members meet together frequently, often once a week, to discuss religious texts, pray together, learn about service projects that need support and share personal/family issues of concern to those present. Soka Gakkai members meet at least twice a month in one another's homes to study Nichiren Buddhism, tell each other about their own problems, and provide each other with moral support and advice. For the Bahá'ís, attending the local spiritual assemblies is one of the two pillars of the faith and the assemblies consist of groups of Bahá'ís in a locale who come together to share their beliefs, support one another, and to elect nine members to be leaders in the group. Since Bahá'ís have no formal clergy, these leaders call together the local group and keep them focused upon the mission of the group to educate in issues of equality and human rights and also to emphasize direct services. The "heartbeat" of the Gulen Movement, the *sohbets*, are local groups that meet in members' homes to study the Qu'ran and the writings and sermons of Mr. Gulen and to share personal/family issues of concern. It is in these *sohbets* that members learn of service projects that are in need of volunteers, finances, and in-kind services and goods. For Gawad Kalinga, local groups in Houston and elsewhere meet regularly to share camaraderie and food, to pray together, to report on fundraising activities, and to reminisce about life and family in the Philippines. Regardless of how bureaucratic and hierarchically structured a movement becomes over time, the movement relies on local, face-to-face, and intimate interactions among members on a frequent basis to sustain the activities and mission of the group.

In some cases, the mobilization of financial resources within these groups can be seen as a religious obligation. From members of BAPS, who see service and giving in the Hindu terms of *seva* and *dana*, to the AKDN and the Gulen Movement, who see voluntary financial giving from the Islamic perspective of *sadaqah* or as a religious obligation of Muslim *zakat*, giving money to these causes and projects is seen as a spiritual endeavor. The same can be said of members of other movements such as Bahá'í religious understandings of *Haququllah* or the tithing ethics contained within other faith traditions. In fact, for the Bahá'í International Community, although they are partners with a host of agencies and international organization such as the United Nations that receive funds from various sources, Bahá'í-specific projects can only be financed by Bahá'ís. Although this is not the situation with other movements in this volume, in general, the financial support of service projects raised by others outside their faith may be drawn from those that are not in complete philosophical alignment with the teachings of their religious roots. This can lead to problems within the movement. As you may recall, this was the case with Gawad Kalinga in its struggle over the degree to which cooperate sponsors such as Pfizer, whose products were widely seen as a direct contradiction of Catholic teachings, should be allowed to contribute to the GK cause. Money is important to the longevity of these movements and their ability to continue their aims and goals. However, as we have seen, where that money comes from can be as important to those in the movement as receiving it. Likewise, the manner in which finances are managed and organized is of central concern.

Formal organizations play important roles in framing movement aims and goals, organizing and mobilizing movement resources, cultivating collective identities, and directing the collective action of the movement (Smith 2008). This is particularly important for global movements that work across borders. Transnational and global movement organizations, when centralized and structured hierarchically, must be able to demonstrate geographic representation if they are to be effective at mobilizing people across national lines and within a multilateral political arena (Smith 2008: 318). By raising membership and leadership from the various countries in which the movement operates, the movement gains a sense of credibility and allows people within these countries to take ownership of both the movement and its aims and goals. It also allows centrally organized movements that are not headquartered in the countries in which they operate to gain first-hand knowledge of each project in each locale, thus empowering the movement to adapt and change to cultural differences and the unique political context of each situation

(Smith 2008). This is the case with movements such as the Bahá'í International Community and the AKDN. In other movements, such as the Gulen Movement or Gawad Kalinga, it is networks in diaspora that animate their localized projects. This is also somewhat true for Soka Gakkai International, although each of its local chapters is somewhat tied to a larger international headquarters in Japan with a formal president as leader.

Conversely, there are movements in this volume such as BAPS and the RCCG who, while tied to centralized organizations and trusts, are organized more locally through their religious communities and congregations. This is also somewhat true for the AKDN and Soka Gakkai International as well. As a publically defined sacred space, congregations are often the only safe spaces where these movements can meet without fear of state intervention or persecution from oppositional forces (Meyer and Marullo 1992; Smith 1991; Smith 1996). They are also safe havens in diaspora that allow the members of these movements to collectively organize, while not only maintaining their faith practices, but also reproducing their cultural identities in a foreign land (Ebaugh and Chafetz 2000; Warner and Wittner 1998; Wuthnow and Offutt 2008). Like non-religious international NGOs and service movements, there is nothing to indicate that the organizational structure of movements in this volume are unique outside of the fact that they are religious and, in some cases, formally attached to the organizational structure and hierarchy of their specific faith traditions and denominations (Petersen 2010). Likewise, the movements we present, similar to non-religious international NGOs, are organized in a diversity of shapes and forms.

The groups we present do share organizational and structural characteristics of new social movements. As we noted earlier and in Chapter 1, the Introduction to this volume, new social movements are often organized in loose or flexible ways because they are suspicious of centralized bureaucratic structures (Scott 1990; Calhoun 1995; Crook et al. 1992). This is certainly true of many of the movements in this volume. In fact, only three movements—the AKDN, the Bahá'í International Community, and the RCCG—have fairly strict centralized hierarchical organizational structures. The remaining groups rely on less centralized, more network-structured organization.

Looking across Table 9.2 (next page), the cases we present remind us that contemporary global and transnational social movements are not always concerned with visible political conflicts as was the case with traditional social movements. Public action is only part of their collective action and, in many of the movements we have examined, the majority of their collective aims and projects are carried out through a multiplicity of groups that are dispersed, fragmented, and submerged into everyday life (McDonald 2006; Melucci 1996). Through these networks and groups, they work to permeate all facets and arenas of transnational civil society with religious institutions, symbols, and narratives (Davis and Robinson 2012). In doing so, they often bypass the state or, at the least, partner with it as they build vast networks of organizations, associations, agencies, schools, businesses, hospitals and places of worship to carry out their visions of a better society (Davis

Table 9.2   Organization, Finance, and Partnership of Global Transnational Religious Service Movements

Movement	Carriers	Type of organization(s)	Financial support	Partners/ Networks
Aga Khan Development Network (AKDN)	Ismali migration; Muslims	Central/hierarchical; RNGO; Independent indigenous orgs	Ismalis; Local partners	Local agencies/networks by country
Swaminarayan (BAPS)	Guajarati and Indian migration; Hindus	Independent local orgs; International Non-profit trusts; Religious organization	Gujaratis/ Indians; Local partners	Local agencies/networks by country; Nation-states; USA United We Serve Initiative; United Nations
Bahá'í International Community	Iranian migration; Baha'is; Converts and pioneers	Central/hierarchical; RNGO; Religious movement	Bahá'ís	Local agencies/networks by country United Nations
Gawad Kalinga	Filipino diaspora; Local partners	Independent local orgs and partners; NGO	Filipinos; Local partners; Corporate sponsorship	Corporate sponsorship; Local agencies/ networks by country; MIT and Harvard University; Nation-states; United Nations
Gulen Movement	Turkish diaspora	Independent local orgs and partners	Turks	Local agencies/networks by country; Local-states (public school districts)
Redeemed Christian Church of God (RCCG)	RCCG members and converts	Central/hierarchical; RNGO; Religious organization	Nigerians; RCCG members	African Missions of North America; CitiHope International; Local agencies/ networks by country; United Nations
Soka Gakkai International (SGI)	Japanese migration; SGI members and converts	Independent local orgs; Religious organization	SGI members	Local agencies/networks by country

and Robinson 2012). From Gawad Kalinga to the RCCG or even BAPs, the Gulen Movement, and the AKDN that work through a host of partnering institutions and their own diasporic peoples, there is a host of often unseen work and collaboration that animates their efforts. These submerged networks, while visible, but not essentially public and directed toward the state, act as cultural laboratories (see Melucci 1989; 1996) that are bound by anything from informal interaction that is very loose and dispersed (Gerlach and Hine 1970) to tightly clustered groups (della Porta 1988). In all cases, they are held together by shared beliefs and a sense of solidarity. These networks promote the circulation of essential resources for action as well as the elaboration of specific world-views and lifestyles that can be propagated to fulfill certain aims and goals. In the movements we present in this volume, these views are rooted in religious traditions that are linked through vast networks and organizations that can convey these meanings.

There has been a dramatic increase in the number and visibility of faith-based and religious non-governmental organizations (FBOs and RNGOs) in the last decade. The number of funded faith-based or religious non-profits and non-governmental organizations in the United States alone doubled between 2001 and 2005 and is expected to do so again in the next few years (James 2009; Petersen 2010). At the global level, there are roughly 33,500 international NGOs in the world and roughly 10 percent consider themselves to be religious or faith-based (Boli and Brewington 2007; Petersen 2010). Most of the movements in this volume seek to establish, have established, and continue to establish partnerships with multilateral agencies, their home states and other states, global funders, international NGOs, and other local and global forces in an emerging transnational civil society (Appadurai 2006). In some cases, movements such as BAPS, the Bahá'í International Community, Gawad Kalinga, the Gulen Movement, and the RCCG also have formal and informal relationships to the United Nations and engage in a host of activities including consulting on projects and issues, lobbying for certain issues and causes, implementing projects, or monitoring certain issues and situations (Petersen 2010).

The religious roots of some of these movements can complicate the degree to which they work with the United Nations. This is especially true when political or philosophical differences on key issues and collaborative projects cannot be agreed upon or where certain groups may be in conflict with others, including the extreme cases in which these movements may voice critical views of the United Nations itself (Petersen 2010). Under these circumstances, opposition to the United Nations through lobbying may actually open political opportunities for these movements to work with certain nation-states. However, in most of the cases we present, where the movements have a relationship to the United Nations, the United Nations also has a good relation to the states in the countries in which these movements are carrying out their projects. Where these movements are not working with the United Nations, it may not be a question of whether they are in opposition, because they may in fact be seeking a relationship with the United Nations. Additionally, it may be a matter that these movements are focused on specific religiously-related problems that the United Nations or more secular NGOs have ignored or about which they are less concerned (Berger 2003; Petersen 2010). Oddly, whether it is the United Nations or some other NGO or international agency, these partnerships have not been explored much by social scientists despite the fact that they constitute a rather important part of movements' abilities to leverage resources and support networks across borders (see McDonald 2006; Melucci 1996).

With this in mind, we must consider these international organizations and partners as some of the key political opportunity structures that facilitate transnational advocacy and projects (Khagram, Riker, and Sikkink 2002). However, it is important to note that these international opportunity structures do not circumvent or displace more domestic structures but work with them, often in collaboration towards mutually agreed upon and beneficial ends (Keck and Sikkink 1998; Khagram et al. 2002; Risse, Ropp, and Sikkink 1999). This is not to say that domestic structures cannot become closed to these movements under more repressive and authoritarian situations or as a result of conflicting philosophical and religious differences but, at least in the cases we present in this volume, each can support the other for the betterment of those they seek to serve (Khagram et al. 2002). This is important to their longevity and ultimately allows them to adapt and change as they spread across political and geographic borders. In general, there is often little established cooperation between religious NGOs from the same specific faith tradition, but there are several examples where RNGOs from various religious roots have engaged in cooperation and partnerships across faith traditions (Petersen 2010). The extent to which this is true of the movements in this volume is not known and should be a focus of future study.

Adaptation, Change, and Moving Forward

There can be little doubt that as the movements in this volume continue to spread globally and transnationally, a myriad of forces and circumstances will bring about changes to their aims and goals, their membership, the structure of their movement, and, ultimately, the extent to which they see their own successes and failures. To some extent, depending on the circumstances, the movements we present have already changed or, at the least, adapted as their movements have grown. Gawad Kalinga, for example, has gone from a very Philippine movement funded and spread by the Filipino diaspora and charismatic Catholic roots to essentially a secular brand or model of sustainable development that is no longer solely funded by Filipinos and is being widely modified and adapted to meet the specific needs of people from vastly different cultural and political backgrounds.

In places such as Indonesia, Gawad Kalinga has taken the name *Gerakan Kepudlian* in Bahasa, the national language of Indonesia. While still GK by initials, as an homage to its root model, Gerakan Kepudlian is not a Filipino movement, nor is it Catholic, but now fully Indonesian and Muslim. However, in the Philippines Gawad Kalinga remains a very diasporic and Catholic movement. As we have seen, the extent to which the religious advocacy and base of GK shifted through its development and spread brought about a split in the organization and continues to be a point of contention. Similarly, although lacking a history of organizational schisms, movements, such as the Bahá'í International Community, that work with the United Nations, are being consulted for global and transnational projects, more for their model than any specific diasporic project that they have initiated at the local level. In this sense, any changes and adaptations to their aims and goals have been carried out indigenously, although with considerably more ties to a global organizational infrastructure than GK, through the Bahá'í Universal House of Justice. In both cases, as we noted earlier, these projects, while purely indigenous and secular, are still tied to the proselytic aims of their movements.

The majority of the movements we present have gone through a series of adaptations and changes, not so much as a result of shifts in the global management and approach of the movements, but as a direct result of the changes that are associated with migration and diaspora itself. One important factor in the adaptation process is taking into account the majority or minority status of the religion in the home and host countries (Yang and Ebaugh 2001). For religions that are majority religions in the home country but minority religions in their settlement country (for example, Japanese Buddhism or Ismaili or Sunni Islam in America), often "entering mainstream America" or any other national mainstream is an important goal. Likewise, native-born citizens in these nations, especially in the United States, who are seeking a "new religion," sometimes are drawn to non-Christian immigrant religions. BAPS, for example, has experienced this as it has moved into its post-colonial phase of development under the leadership of its spiritual leader, Pramukh Swami Mahaaraj. Although their spiritual leader has shaped the movement's aims and goals, ultimately spurring tremendous growth and spread, the movement has remained a very diasporic movement and has changed to simply fit the context of the new homes to which Indians have migrated, especially in those countries where Hinduism is not a majority religion. BAPS clearly serves those outside of its own diaspora, but the majority of its structural and cultural adaptations have been to meet the circumstances of their own migrants not others.

The RCCG, on the other hand, is a majority religion both in home and host countries and offers little "new" religion to Christians in America. As a result, it has remained essentially an evangelical African religion that appeals to African immigrants. Conversely, Soka Gakkai, a majority religion in Japan, is a minority religion in North America but also appeals to native-born Americans who are attracted to Buddhist teachings. In fact, in recent decades there has been a vast expansion of Buddhism in North and South America, Southwest Asia, Europe, India and Australia-New Zealand, all countries where Buddhism is a minority religion. Over time, native, local members have come to greatly outnumber ethnic Japanese in many of Soka Gakkai's international chapters.

In the case of the Aga Khan Foundation, like BAPS, the Indian diaspora has been the engine of the movement's spread and growth. Although rooted in Islam among Ismailis, both movements adapted and changed to meet the needs of their own migrations. They were also forced to adapt to the change from majority religion status in the regions of India from which they migrated to that of a religious minority in almost all the contexts to which they moved around the world. As minority peoples of faith, they have faced discrimination and certain oppositional forces that inhibited their ability to extend their aims and goals to others outside their own communities. They were also forced to better educate their own community about their faith in the cases where it had been more culturally ingrained as part of their identity or taken for granted without any formal education about their religious roots. To a lesser extent, this is also true for the Gulen Movement. Although in this case, while the movement is supported by the Turkish diaspora, its aim is not toward those who have migrated but toward those in their new countries outside their own Turkish communities whom they feel need to be served through better education. The movement has changed the most in terms of generation. The Gulen Movement has increasingly become supported by second- and third-generation Turks who not only have fewer or weaker ties to Turkey compared to the old supporters, but were born or raised in ethnic enclaves in the very countries they now serve. In this sense the movement has become less about diaspora and increasingly indigenous, which has raised questions about the future use of Turkish *sohbets* in local circles, as well as the extent to which women's increased cultural mobility will challenge the patriarchy of the older movement.

Although other movements we present, such as the RCCG, are also largely changing as a result of their responses to diaspora contexts, they have been successful in rallying forms of bridging capital to build diverse network ties. However, in some cases these networks have been rather short-lived with the majority of the movement's organization remaining rooted in the proselytizing of the Nigerian or broader African diaspora. As a majority faith migrating largely to majority contexts, members of the RCCG may initially find themselves as Christians in better structural circumstances than BAPS or the AKDN and Gulen Movement, but this is not necessarily always the case. As members of an increasing number of formerly colonized people in the global south who are now proselytizing back to the heart of their former empires and proclaiming that their former colonial rulers have lost their way, the members of the Redeemed Christian Church of God may find themselves outside the normative Christianity of the countries to which they have immigrated and now call home. As several scholars have commented, these more "southern" manifestations of Christianity are not only markedly more theologically conservative but are also more likely to incorporate more animistic and folk religious practices, including beliefs in spirits and possession, with which Western Christians may be less familiar or flat out reject (Jenkins 2002). On a larger scale, these trends are compelling several social developments internationally that may impact both the way Christianity is identified or defined by both Christians and non-Christians as well as the way in which global socio-cultural relations are structured (Jenkins 2002). What this means for the future of the RCCG and its ability to carry out its aims and goals remains to be seen.

The exceptions to the diaspora adaptation patterns we have seen in the majority of the movements we present are the Bahá'í International Community and Soka Gakkai International. Although the Bahá'í International Community and Soka Gakkai International are linked to the Iranian and Japanese diaspora respectively in their early histories, both have spread and likewise adapted to new cultural contexts largely through conversion. The early Baha'i and Soka Gakkai International movements coming out of Iran and Japan looked much more like the RCCG in their diasporic adaptation yet were distinctive minority faiths and hence, shared certain challenges parallel to movements such as BAPS and the AKDN. Today, like the RCCG, both the Baha'i International Community and Soka Gakkai International have been remarkably successful at rallying diverse networks to their cause through conversion. However, unlike the Redeemed Christian Church of God, Soka Gakkai International's emphasis on human problems through small group practices has resulted in SGI physically looking representative of the demographics of the communities in which SGI members live and serve while still being connected to a larger global organization. To a certain extent, although through differing mechanisms, this is also true of the Bahá'í International Community.

Despite the fact that the movements in this volume, for the most part, are old enough in their historic development to have adapted and changed depending on their spread and context, it may, in many ways, be far too early to say anything definitively that defines what is unique about these movements across these cases outside of their religious and diasporic roots. As these movements continue to spread, they will continue to be faced with a host of challenges. How they continue to adapt to local cultures and political systems, however, largely remains to be seen. Moving forward, in some ways, we are left with more questions than answers. What is the future relationship of diaspora to these movements and their projects around the world? Will they remain firmly rooted in their religious faith traditions or, as in the case with Gawad Kalinga, become something entirely different or even secular as they spread? How does success or failure in certain local contexts impact the influence of these forces on the movements as they spread? If they succeed, do they spread or do they retreat to their origins if they fail? Is it possible that failure in one context raises success in others? The AKDN, the Bahá'í International Community, the Gulen Movement, and to some extent Soka Gakkai International, have all largely been more successful outside of their countries of origin. Why? How does the rest of the world see the successes of these movements? As these movements spread and ultimately initiate projects in the same countries, how will they interact? Will they compete or will they work ecumenically towards the same aims and goals? Clearly, future research will need to look at specific nations such as India and Kenya to see which is the case or if some other pattern that is perhaps more complicated and operating in both directions has emerged.

Much remains to be seen and studied. However, in charting the cases we present in this volume we believe we have built the foundation for future studies. While we may not have solved definitional problems or fully settled any ongoing debates in a host of literatures and disciplines, we have demonstrated that there is something here that begs our collective analytical attention. We can no longer assume that religion will die out in the wake of increasing globalization. It obviously has not. Religion and religious adherents have shaped globalization and its flows of goods, people, and services as much as globalization has shaped them. In fact, all the movements we present in this volume, spread, at least initially, as a result of global migration. Specifically, they spread and are now largely supported by global religious diasporas. As global migration continues to increase, and at a rapid pace, the likelihood that service movements like those presented here will continue to spread is not only very probable but inevitable. They are an important part of our future understandings of global and transnational migration. Likewise, they are an important part of our future understandings of the power and saliency of transnational and global religion. Looking across the cases we present, it is no longer a matter of whether or not these transnational global service movements rooted in religious traditions should be studied; rather, we contend it is a priority that has yet to be fully realized.

References

Aho, James Alfred. 1990. *The Politics of Righteousness: Idaho Christian Patriotism*. Seattle: University of Washington Press.

Appadurai, Arjun. 2006. *Fear of Small Numbers: An Essay on the Geography of Anger*. Durham, NC: Duke University Press.

Barkun, Michael. 1994. *Religion and the Racist Right*. Chapel Hill: University of North Carolina Press.

Basch, Linda, Nina Glick-Schiller, and Cristina Szanton Blanc. 1994. *Nations Unbound: Transnational Projects, Postcolonial Predicaments, and Deterritorialized Nation-States*. Basel, Switzerland: Gordon and Breach.

Benford, Robert and David Snow. 2000. "Framing Processes and Social Movements: An Overview and Assessment." *Annual Review of Sociology* 26: 611-39.

Berger, Juila. 2003. "Religious Non-Governmental Organizations: An Exploratory Analysis." *International Society for Third-Sector Research* 14: 1-23.

Boli, John and David Brewington. 2007. "Religious International Nongovermental Organizations." Paper presented at the annual meeting of the American Sociological Association, August 11, 2007, New York City, New York.

Bowen, John R. 2004. "Beyond Migration: Islam as a Transnational Public Space." *Journal of Ethnic Migration Studies* 30: 870-94.

Buechler, Steven M. 1995. "Social Movement Theories." *Sociological Quarterly* 35: 441-64.

Calhoun, Craig. 1995. "New Social Movements of the Early Twentieth Century." Pp. 173-216 in *Repertoires and Cycles of Collective Action*, edited by Mark Traugott. Durham, NC: Duke University Press.

Castells, Manuel. 1996. *The Information Age*. Vol. 1, *The Rise of the Network Society*. Cambridge, MA: Blackwell Publishing.

Cetin, Muhammed. 2009. *The Gulen Movement: Civic Service without Borders*. Clifton, NJ: Blue Dome Press.

Cherry, Stephen M. 2014. *Faith, Family, and Filipino American Community Life*. New Brunswick, NJ: Rutgers University Press.

Crook, Stephen, Jan Pakulski, and Malcolm Waters. 1992. *Postmodernization: Change in Advanced Society*. London: Sage.

Csordas, Thomas J. 2009. *Transnational Transcendence: Essays on Religion and Globalization*. Berkeley: University of California Press.

Davis, Nancy J. and Robert V. Robinson. 2012. *Claiming Society for God: Religious Movements and Social Welfare*. Bloomington: Indiana University Press.

della Porta, Donatello. 1988. "Recruitment Processes in Clandestine Political Organizations: Italian Left-wing Terrorism." Pp. 155-72 in *International Social Movement Research*. Vol. 1, *From Structure to Action*, edited by Bert Klandermans, Hans Peter Kriesi, and Sidney Tarrow, Greenwich, CT: JAI Press.

della Porta, Donatello, Hans Peter Kriesi and Deiter Rucht, eds. 1999. *Social Movements in a Globalizing World*. London: MacMillan.

della Porta, Donatello and Sidney Tarrow. 2005. *Transnational Protest and Global Activism*. Lanham, MD: Rowan and Littlefield.

Diani, Mario. 1992. "The Concept of Social Movement." *Sociological Review* 40(1): 1-25.

Ebaugh, Helen Rose and Janet Saltzman Chafetz. 2000. *Religion and the New Immigrants: Continuities and Adaptations in Immigrant Congregations*. Walnut Creek, CA: AltaMira Press.

Ebaugh, Helen Rose and Janet Saltzman Chafetz. 2002. *Religion across Borders: Transnational Immigrant Networks*. Walnut Creek, CA: AltaMira Press.

Faist, Thomas. 2000. *The Volume and Dynamics of International Migration and Transnational Social Spaces*. Oxford: Oxford University Press.

Gerlach, Luther and Virginia Hine. 1970. *People, Power, and Change*. Indianapolis, IN: Bobs-Merrill Company.

Goffman, Erving. [1947] 1997. *Frame Analysis*. New York: Harper & Row.

Goodwin, Jeff and James Jasper, eds. 2009. *The Social Movement Reader: Cases and Concepts*. Oxford: Wiley-Blackwell.

Hagan, Jacqueline and Helen Rose Ebaugh. 2003. "Calling Upon the Sacred: Migrants' Use of Religion in the Migration Process." *International Migration Review* 37(4): 1145-62.

Harris, Fredrick. 1999. *Something Within: Religion in African American Political Activism*. New York: The Free Press.

Hart, Stephen. 1992. *What Does the Lord Require?* New York: Oxford University Press.

Held, David and Anthony McGrew, eds. 2000. *The Global Transformations Reader: An Introduction to the Globalization Debate*. Cambridge, UK: Polity.

James, Rick. 2009. "What is Distinctive about FBOs?" *INTRAC Praxis Paper* no. 22: 5.

Jenkins, Philip. 2002. *The Next Christiandom: The Coming of Global Christiantiy*. New York: Oxford University Press.

Keck, Margaret and Kathryn Sikkink. 1998. *Activist across Borders*. Ithaca, NY: Cornell University Press.

Khagram, Sanjeev, James V. Riker, and Kathryn Sikkink. 2002. *Social Movements, Protest and Contention*. Vol. 14, *Restructuring World Politics: Transnational Social Movements, Networks, and Norms*. Minneapolis and London: University of Minnesota Press.

Levitt, Peggy. 2001. *Transnational Villagers*. Berkeley: University of California Press.

Levitt, Peggy. 2004. "Redefining the Boundaries of Belonging: The Institutional Character of Transnational Religious Life." *Sociology of Religion* 65(1): 1-18.

Levitt, Peggy. 2007. *God Needs No Passport: Immigrants and the Changing American Religious Landscape*. New York: The New Press.

Lofland, John. 1996. *Social Movement Organizations*. New York: Aldine de Gruyter.

McAdam, Doug. 1982. *Political Process and the Development of Black Insurgency*. Chicago, IL: University of Chicago Press.

McAdam, Doug. 1996. "Conceptual Origins, Current Problems, Future Directions." Pp. 23-40 in *Comparative Perspectives on Social Movements: Political Opportunities, Mobilizing Structures, and Cultural Framings*, edited by Doug McAdam, John McCarthy, and Mayer Zald. Cambridge, UK: Cambridge University Press.

McAdam, Doug 1998, "The Future of Social Movements," Pp. 229-45 in *From Contention to Democracy*, edited by Marco Giugni, Doug McAdam, and Charles Tilly. Lanham, MD: Rowman and Littlefield.

McAdam, Doug, John McCarthy, and Mayer Zald, 1988, "Social Movements." Pp. 695-737 in *Handbook of Sociology*, edited by Neil Smelser. Beverly Hills, CA: Sage.

McCarthy, John and Mayer Zald. 1977. "Resource Mobilization and Social Movements: A Partial Theory." *American Journal of Sociology* 8(6): 1212-31.

McDonald, Kevin. 2006. *Global Movements*. Oxford: Blackwell.

McLeod, Alex. 2004. "A New Reformation Is Happening in Global Christianity." *Presbyterian Record* 128: 44-45.

Mahler, Sarah .J. 1998. "Theoretical and Empirical Contributions toward a Research Agenda for Transnationalism. Pp. 64-102 in *Transnationalism from Below*, edited by Michael P. Smith and Luis E. Guarnizo. New Brunswick, NJ: Transaction Books.

Marquardt, Marie Friedmann. 2005. "From Shame to Confidence: Gender, Religious Conversion and Civic Engagement of Mexicans in the U.S. South." *Latin American Perspective* 32(1): 27-56.

Marshall, Katherine. 2001. "Religion and Development: A Different Lens on Development Debates." *Peabody Journal of Education* 76(3 & 4): 339-75.

Marshall, Katherine and Marisa Van Saanen. 2007. *Development and Faith: Where Mind, Heart, and Soul Work Together*. Washington DC: The World Bank.

Mayo, Marjorie. 2005. *Global Citizens: Social Movements and the Challenge of Globalization*. New York: Zed Books.

Melucci, Alberto. 1989. *Nomads of the Present: Social Movements and Individual Needs in Contemporary Society*, edited by John Keane and Paul Mier. Philadelphia, PA: Temple University Press.

Melucci, Alberto. 1996. *Challenging Codes: Collective Action in the Information Age*. Cambridge, MA: University of Cambridge Press.

Meyer, David S. 2004. "Protest and Political Opportunities." *Annual Review of Sociology*, 30: 125-45. Retrieved May 17, 2013 (https://campus.fsu.edu/bbcswebdav/institution/academic/social_sciences/sociology/Reading%20Lists/Stratification%20(Politics%20and%20Social%20Movements)%20Copies%20of%20Articles%20from%202009/Meyer-AnnualReview-2004.pdf) doi: 10.1146/annurev.soc.30.012703.110545.

Meyer, David S. and Sam Marullo. 1992. "Grassroots Mobilization and International Politics: Peace and the End of the Cold War." *Research in Social Movements, Conflict, and Change* 14: 99-140.

Montagna, Nicola. 2008. "Social Movements and Global Mobilization." Pp. 349-56 in *Social Movements: A Reader*, edited by Vincenzo Ruggiero and Nicola Montagna. New York: Routledge.

Morris, Aldon. 1984. *The Origins of the Civil Rights Movement: Black Communities Organized for Change*. New York: The Free Press.

Morris, Aldon. 1986. *Origins of the Civil Rights Movement*. New York: Free Press.

Nash, Kate. 2000. *Contemporary Political Sociology: Globalization, Politics, and Power*. Malden, MA: Blackwell Publishing.

Nicholson, Michael. 1998. *International Relations: A Concise Introduction*. New York: New York University Press.

Oberschall, Anthony and Hyojoung Kim. 1996. "Identity and Action." *Mobilization* 1: 63-86.

Petersen, Marie Juul. 2010. "International Religious NGOs at the United Nations: A Study of a Group of Religious Organizations." *The Journal of Humanitarian Assistance* (November 17). Retrieved May 2012 (http://sites.tufts.edu/jha/archives/847).

Portes, Alejandro, Luis Guarnizo, and Patricia Landolt. 1999. "Introduction: Pitfalls and Promise of an Emergent Field." *Ethnic and Racial Studies* 22(2): 217-38.

Risse, Thomas, Stephen C. Ropp, and Kathryn Sikkink. 1999. *The Power of Human Rights: International Norms and Domestic Change*. Cambridge, UK: University of Cambridge Press.

Robbins, Thomas. 1988. *Cults, Converts, and Charisma: The Sociology of New Social Movements*. Newbury Park, CA: Sage.

Roseneil, Sasha. 1997. "The Global Common: The Global, Local, and Personal; Dynamics of the Women's Peace Movement in the 1980s." Pp. 55-74 in *The Limits of Globalization: Cases and Arguments*, edited by Alan Scott. London: Routledge.

Rudolph, Susanne Hoeber and James Piscatori. 1997. *Transnational Religion.* Boulder, CO: Westview Press.

Ruggiero, Vincenzo. 2005. "Dichotomies and Contemporary Social Movements," *City* 9(3): 297-306.

Ruggiero, Vincenzo and Nicola Montagna. 2008. *Social Movements: A Reader.* New York: Routledge.

Scholte, Jan Aart. 1999. "The WTO and Civil Society." *Journal of World Trade* 33(1): 107-24.

Scott, Alan. 1990. *Ideology and New Social Movements.* London, UK: Unwin University Books.

Sherkat, Darren E. and Christopher Ellison. 1999. "Recent Developments and Current Controversies in the Sociology of Religion." *Annual Review of Sociology* 25: 363-94.

Skrentny, John. 2006. "Policy-Elite Perceptions and Social Movement Success: Understanding Variations in Group Inclusion in Affirmative Action." *American Journal of Sociology* 11(6): 1762-815.

Smelser, Neil. 1963. *Theory of Collective Behavior.* New York: Free Press.

Smith, Christian. 1991. *The Emergence of Liberation Theology: Radical Religion and Social Movement Theory.* Chicago, IL: University of Chicago Press.

Smith, Christian. 1996. *Disruptive Religion: The Force of Faith in Social Movement Activism.* New York: Routledge.

Smith, Jackie. 2008. "Global Resistance: The Battle for Seattle and the Future of Social Movements." Pp. 316-26 in *Social Movements: A Reader*, edited by Vincenzo Ruggiero and Nicola Montagna. New York: Routledge.

Snow, David A. and Robert D. Benford. 1988. "Ideology, Frame Resonance, and Participant Mobilization." *International Social Movement Research* 1: 197-217.

Snow, David A. and Robert D. Benford. 1992. "Master Frames and Cycles of Protest." Pp. 133-55 in *Frontiers in Social Movement Theory*, edited by Aldon D. Morris and Carol McClurg Mueller. New Haven, CT: Yale University Press.

Tarrow, Sidney. 1983. "Struggling to Reform: Social Movements and Policy Change during Cycles of Protest." *Western Society Paper 15*. Ithaca, NY: Cornell University.

Tilly, Charles. 1978. *From Mobilization to Revolution.* Reading, MA: Addison-Wesley.

Tilly, Charles. 2004. *Social Movements, 1768-2004.* Boulder, CO: Paradigm.

Turner, Ralph and Lewis Killian. [1957] 1987. *Collective Behaviour.* Englewood Cliffs, NJ: Prentice Hall.

Warner, R. Stephen and Judith G. Wittner. 1998. *Gatherings in Diaspora: Religious Communities and the New Immigration.* Philadelphia, PA: Temple University Press.

Wuthnow, Robert and Stephen Offutt. 2008. "Transnational Religious Connections." *Sociology of Religion* 68(2): 209-32.

Yang, Fenggang. 2002. "Chinese Christian Transnationalism: Diverse Networks of a Houston Church." Pp. 175-204 in *Religion Across Borders*, edited by Helen Rose Ebaugh and Janet Saltzman Chafetz. Walnut Creek, CA: AltaMira Press.

Yang, Fenggang and Helen Rose Ebaugh. 2001. "Transformations in New Immigrant Religions and Their Global Implications." *American Sociological Review* 66: 269-88.

Young, Michael P. 2006. *Bearing Witness Against Sin: The Evangelical Birth of the American Social Movement*. Chicago, IL: University of Chicago Press.

Zald, Mayer. 1982. "Theological Crucibles: Social Movements in and of Religion." *Review Religious Research* 23: 317-36.

Zald, Mayer. 1992. "Looking Backwards to Look Forward: Reflection on the Past and Future of the Resource Mobilization Research Program." Pp. 326-48 in *Frontiers in Social Movement Theory*, edited by Aldon Morris and Carol McClurg Mueller. New Haven, CT: Yale University Press.

Index